Crime, Punishment and the Drinking Offender

Judith Rumgay
Department of Social Policy and Administration
London School of Economics and Political Science

Foreword by Ronald V. Clarke

Consultant Editor: Jo Campling

First published in Great Britain 1998 by
MACMILLAN PRESS LTD
Houndmills, Basingstoke, Hampshire RG21 6XS and London
Companies and representatives throughout the world

A catalogue record for this book is available from the British Library.

ISBN 0–333–67659–9

First published in the United States of America 1998 by
ST. MARTIN'S PRESS, INC.,
Scholarly and Reference Division,
175 Fifth Avenue, New York, N.Y. 10010

ISBN 0–312–21679–3

Library of Congress Cataloging-in-Publication Data
Rumgay, Judith, 1952–
Crime, punishment and the drinking offender / Judith Rumgay ;
consultant editor Jo Campling.
    p.   cm.
Includes bibliographical references and index.
ISBN 0–312–21679–3 (cloth)
1. Criminal liability—Great Britain.   2. Drunkenness (Criminal
law)—Great Britain.   3. Extenuating circumstances—Great Britain.
4. Alcoholism and crime.   I. Campling, Jo.   II. Title.
KD7897.5.R86   1998
345.41'0273—dc21   98–7076
                                                                        CIP

This book is printed on paper suitable for recycling and made from fully managed and
sustained forest sources.

10   9   8   7   6   5   4   3   2   1
07   06   05   04   03   02   01   00   99   98

Printed and bound in Great Britain by
Antony Rowe Ltd, Chippenham, Wiltshire

Contents

To Joan and Bruce

Foreword

All too often, social researchers seek to address a broad topic from a narrow theoretical perspective, which generally results in confusion and disappointment. Judith Rumgay has avoided this trap. In the best traditions of applied research, she reports instead a wide-ranging enquiry into a narrowly defined topic. This topic is defined in her remarkably clear style in the opening sentence: 'How might we account for the perennial and pervasive popularity of an appeal to intoxication for our moral failings?'

This may seem at first not merely a narrow but a peripheral topic of criminology. However, in seeking to provide an answer, Dr Rumgay had to go to the heart of the discipline and undertake a careful analysis of the full range of criminological theories and the links they make between offending and alcohol. Most of these theories are 'dispositional' in character and see crime as the result of psychological or social disadvantage. These were of limited value in answering her question. More helpful to her were theories that treat crime as the outcome of a decision made by the offender in a tightly prescribed situational context. Some versions of these theories, such as the routine activities approach, confine themselves to the objective characteristics of the situation. Other versions, such as the rational choice perspective, concern themselves also with offenders' feelings, perceptions and judgements. It is assumed that offenders reflect on their criminal actions, that they may justify them in advance or subsequently, and that these justifications play an important part in their decision-making. The technical concepts employed in these theories include rationalisation and neutralisation, crime 'scripts' and offender 'accounts'.

Dr Rumgay puts these concepts to good use in her empirical study of the intoxication excuse offered by a large sample of defendants brought before a city magistrates' court. She listens to the statements made by defendants or on their behalf by lawyers. She talks to the probation officers concerned and examines the social enquiry reports they have filed. Finally, she interviews the magistrates to discover what they think about drunkenness as a mitigating factor.

One of her fascinating conclusions is that the intoxication excuse is so frequently used because of its versatility: 'Intoxication, like mental illness, offers a ready explanation for a range of extraordinary behaviours, accessible through the common store of knowledge.' Alcohol is assumed to make people euphoric and it can make them surly. It can make them aggressive and it can make them affectionate. It can give them confidence, but it can impair their judgement. As for its relationship to crime, this is as varied as crime itself. Thus it can induce aggression in a disappointed lover. It can result in vandalism by late-night revellers. It might also lead to drunk driving through impairing the judgement of normally law-abiding citizens.

The fact that many of these 'commonsense' ideas about alcohol and crime have little support in research seems almost irrelevant. More important is that the intoxication excuses offered by Dr Rumgay's group of offenders were readily understood in the pressured atmosphere of the courtroom, which gave little opportunity for the critical analysis of motives. Offenders themselves, who are no more immune to commonsense theorising about crime than anyone else, no doubt often believed that their actions were affected by alcohol. Probation officers and magistrates often seemed disposed to agree since they too were looking for mitigating circumstances that would prevent the imposition of a custodial sentence. This was not just because they thought prison was harmful, but also because they had been made aware of the need to avoid putting further burdens on an already overloaded system.

Dr Rumgay therefore provides a persuasive and satisfying answer to the question raised at the beginning of her study: the popularity of the appeal to intoxication as a mitigating factor is explained by its versatility and, at least in the apparently liberal court she studied, also by its effectiveness! In the process of reaching this conclusion she accomplishes much else. She undertakes a critical review of the alcohol–crime relationship in which she exposes weaknesses in the evidence and ambiguities of interpretation; she develops a case for the explanatory value of criminal decision-making theory that has relevance beyond the immediate topic of her enquiry; she examines the relationship between commonsense notions of crime and more formal criminological explanation, with unsettling implications for the latter; and she reports a detailed study of sentencing in a magistrates' court that stands in its own right as a valuable contribution to the socio-legal literature. For all these reasons, I believe her book will find a wide and appreciative audience.

RONALD V. CLARKE
School of Criminal Justice, Rutgers University
Newark, New Jersey

Acknowledgements

While undertaking the research for, and writing this book, I received help, advice and support from many quarters.

I am very grateful to David Downes and Derek Cornish at LSE for their support, guidance and comments. Richard Wright, University of Missouri-St Louis, helpfully commented on parts of the text, and subsequently nagged until I was shamed into completion. To the late Bill McWilliams I also owe thanks for early consideration of a draft chapter, followed by continuing interest in my progress.

My thanks are due to the Clerk to the Justices at City Magistrates' Court and the Chief Probation Officer at City Probation Service for their agreement to participate in the study. I owe an incalculable debt to the magistrates, court clerks, administrative staff, ushers, caretakers – all staff in fact – at City Magistrates' Court. If there was anyone there who did not help me at some stage, it is only because I did not meet that person. I am deeply indebted to the probation officers and senior probation officers of City team, and to their support staff, for all their assistance, interest in and enthusiasm for the project. And to the solicitors, police officers and defendants at City court, who were not formally recruited to the project, but who cheerfully helped me anyway, I owe many thanks.

I am grateful to the Social Research Division at LSE, and the Probation Educational and Research Trust for financial assistance. And I am indebted to the staff of the Radzinowicz Library at the Institute of Criminology, Cambridge University, for their patient helpfulness during my almost continuous presence among their shelves.

On a more personal level, special thanks are due to Alan, for patience and calm when I lacked both, and Joan and Bruce for tireless interest. Thanks also to Ian, Steen, Sue, Todd, Ray and Libby for the support of friendship.

Each of these people supported the project in their different ways. But to all of them I extend my greatest thanks for simply believing that I would succeed.

List of Abbreviations

ABH   Assault occasioning actual bodily harm
CPS   Crown prosecution solicitor
Def   Defendant
DS   Defence solicitor
GBH   Assault occasioning grievous bodily harm
M   Magistrate
PO   Probation officer
SER   Social Enquiry Report

1 The Intoxication Excuse: a Challenge to Reason?

How might we account for the perennial and pervasive popularity of an appeal to intoxication for our moral failings? We invoke the excuse of intoxication for many acts of social and sexual impropriety, when we seek the exoneration, understanding, forgiveness or leniency of family, friends, colleagues, strangers and law enforcers, in informal situations, starting in the home, and formal ones, including courts of law. In this latter context, criminal offenders and their legal representatives persist in proffering the intoxication excuse even though the law officially rejects it.

The attempt to answer this question begins with an examination of the legal dilemma over the intoxication excuse. It will be argued that the persistent legal debate is founded on unquestioned, but questionable, commonsense assumptions about the effects of alcohol on the human mind and will. A theoretical and empirical framework will then be described for exploring what is, arguably, the most common motive for invoking the intoxication excuse: to achieve mitigation of punishment for a deviant act.

THE LEGAL DILEMMA

The legal attribution of criminal responsibility serves a vital social function in securing and maintaining order (Schafer 1968). The law sets standards of behaviour to which most citizens manage to conform for most of the time because they are minimum, and not maximum, standards (Shiner 1990). Punishment of those whose conduct falls short of the minimum standards is justified by the assumption of free will, which attributes human action, or failure to act, to the exercise of conscious, rational deliberation. Thus, while there may be limits to the freedom of the will, the law requires that such freedom as an individual has in any situation will be exercised in accordance with its standards (Schafer 1968).

The law is concerned primarily with the regulation of external behaviour, and not of internal states of moral integrity (Shaver

1

1985). Nor does the law seek to punish those who break the law involuntarily.

> If order requires that conduct be regulated, justice requires that sanctions be applied only to those who truly deserve them. (Shaver 1985, p. 68)

The just application of sanctions, therefore, requires that deliberate law breakers are distinguished from those whose offences are caused by some interference with the freedom of will. To achieve this, however, the law must address itself to internal states after all, and consider individual intentions and capacities for exercising free will. This is the basic legal issue of *mens rea*: the intention to commit a prohibited act, or recklessness as to the likelihood of a prohibited outcome of an act (Smith and Hogan 1982; Williams 1983).

> The fundamental substantive question that the criminal law properly faces here is whether, in a particular case, the defendant's capacity to act rationally in regard to the criminal significance of the act has been so impaired as to have rendered him nonresponsible at the time of the act. (Fingarette and Hasse 1979, p. 193)

To compound an already problematic issue, it is important to note that there are two aspects to the judgement of criminal responsibility: the legal and the moral. The legal aspect concerns whether the individual can be said to have acted with sufficient rationality and intentionality that he may justifiably be held responsible for his offence. The moral aspect concerns the quality of the response to that offence. Judgements of legal responsibility are intrinsically connected to consequential, practical decisions about punishment, recompense and rehabilitation. But these consequential decisions rest on considerations, not of legal, but of moral responsibility. Moral judgements about the offender mediate the response to the legal attribution of responsibility, by implying censure and retribution if the offence is seen to be committed with malicious intent, but leniency or treatment if the decision to offend is seen to spring from circumstances beyond the person's control (Freidson 1966).

The intoxication excuse affects both legal and moral judgement. Firstly, it requires judges to be satisfied that the capacity for rational and intentional behaviour has not been destroyed by intoxication. Secondly, it requires a decision about the appropriate response to the crime. Should the moral degeneracy of the intoxicated state attract greater punishment? Should the impairment to powers of moral reasoning wrought by intoxication mitigate punishment? Should rehabilitative treatment be provided, to inculcate greater responsibility in the use of intoxicants?

The criminal law has primarily been preoccupied with the first issue: the legal grounds for holding individuals responsible for their intoxicated crimes. The extent of its preoccupation with this question is surprising, given that it is a basic rule of criminal law that intoxication does not excuse criminal behaviour (Mosher 1981). The reason for this rule is essentially pragmatic: it is feared that acceptance of the claims of defendants to have been incapable of intentional action through intoxication would bring about wholesale acquittals on these grounds because of the difficulty of disproving such assertions. Such an outcome would conflict with the public's need for the protection of the law against the depredations of intoxicated law breakers (Mitchell 1988; Mosher 1981; Shiner 1990). In the public interest, therefore, the intoxication excuse is prohibited. Thus, the judgement of legal responsibility for intoxicated crime is itself shaped by anticipation of the disastrous consequences of allowing defendants unrestricted access to the intoxication excuse.

> The reason why the courts have been fearful of giving the [intoxication] defence too wide a scope is the possibility that those who inflict serious injury to the person or damage to property, or who bring about dangerous situations, would escape the sanctions of the criminal law by relying on a defence of intoxication. (Criminal Law Revision Committee 1980, p. 111)

Nevertheless, courts have, in fact, repeatedly given serious consideration to defendants' claims to have been prevented, through intoxication, from rational and intentional action at the time of their offence. Academic legal argument and judicial decisions have accepted that intoxication can cause automatism (Mitchell 1988), insanity (Howard and Clark 1985; Mitchell 1988) and violence (Mackay 1990; Mitchell 1988), and can negate murderous intention (Kittrie 1971). Contrary to the expectation of the basic rule asserting the invalidity of the intoxication excuse,

> [c]ourt decisions and review articles assert the legal relevance of intoxication with little critical comment and even less hard evidence. (Mitchell 1990, p. 79)

The cause of this sometimes blatant disregard of the basic rule lies in the apparent injustice of denying defendants' rights to have their state of mind at the time of the offence taken into account.

> [T]he present law requires an intoxicated person to be convicted of an offence which as it is defined by statute he has not been proved to have committed, because there was no proof that he had the necessary mental element. (Criminal Law Revision Committee 1980, p. 111)

Shiner (1990) observes that the continuing tension between the public interest and defendants' rights has produced no less than seven different legal strategies for dealing with the problem. It is unnecessary here to examine these different solutions in detail, but only to remark on the lengths to which the law has gone in the attempt to resolve the dilemma. However, it is ironic that all of the strategies, save one, involve further rationalisations for the denial of defendants' rights in order to pursue the public interest (Shiner 1990). Two examples show how this is achieved.

Firstly, the Butler Committee on Mentally Abnormal Offenders (Home Office, Department of Health and Social Security 1975) recommended the creation of a new offence, proposing that a defendant achieving an acquittal on a main charge through the intoxication excuse would automatically be convicted of 'dangerous intoxication'. The Committee reasoned:

> There would be no injustice to the defendant in providing for the possibility of conviction of dangerous intoxication as an alternative charge, because the evidence of intoxication would have been produced by him at the trial in answer to the main charge. (p. 237)

There is a curious optimism in the assumption that defendants would see no injustice in securing their own conviction for an offence by proffering the evidence for acquittal on another. Furthermore, it is assumed that courts would be able to distinguish between behaviour caused by the will of the defendant and behaviour caused by intoxication even when the observable action is essentially the same. It is also apparently assumed that evidence of intoxication, whilst negating the criminal intent of the defendant, establishes the cause of the offending behaviour.

Secondly, the Criminal Law Revision Committee (1980) recommended that self-induced intoxication be defined as a form of recklessness. This Committee appears to have considered it an attraction of their proposal that conviction for some offence on grounds of intoxication would follow even in cases which would lead to outright acquittal when intoxication was not an issue.

> For example, a householder who mistakenly believes that a police officer, who has entered his house to look around on finding the front door open, is a burglar about to attack him and strikes him down in self-defence would probably be acquitted on the indictment (for murder). But if his mistaken belief was due to voluntary intoxication the effect of our proposals would be that he would be acquitted of murder but convicted of manslaughter. (Criminal Law Revision Committee 1980, p. 117)

This proposal has large implications for the freedom of individuals to become intoxicated in their own homes, and, in such a condition, to defend themselves against intruders, who may subsequently turn out to be zealous policemen. Of particular interest here, however, is the apparent assumption that intoxication can induce a mistaken belief which in a sober individual appears to be an unfortunate but understandable misinterpretation of the visible evidence. Why should such a mistaken belief be attributed to the effects of alcohol?

The reasoning of these two committees demonstrates the real power of the intoxication excuse to impede legal judgements of responsibility. The intoxication excuse appeals to a commonsense presumption that alcohol diminishes the capacity for rational, responsible behaviour. This underlying presumption has bedevilled legal arguments over the intoxication excuse, and yet has been so much a part of 'common knowledge' about alcohol that its veracity has largely been unchallenged. Mitchell complains of legal argument about intoxication:

> The legal logic of the doctrine is frequently attacked but its factual premises are seldom questioned... As a consequence, both judicial pronouncements and learned commentaries are populated by imaginary creatures – 'blind drunks' who can see, 'dead drunks' who move openly among the living, intoxicated 'automatons' who perform complex, purposeful tasks and 'mad drunks' who knowingly focus their aggression on specific targets. (1988, p. 77)

Commonsense presumptions about alcohol's effects on the human will have not only underpinned lawyers' unease about the refusal to consider intoxicated offenders' mental states, but have also provided the basis of rationalisations for this refusal. For example, the treatment of intoxication as a special form of recklessness has been

justified by the argument that a defendant's knowledge of the risks
incurred by intoxication is demonstrated by the fact that it is 'common
knowledge' that alcohol precipitates aggressive behaviour (Mackay
1990). The Criminal Law Revision Committee made the following
observation about intoxicated aggression:

> The drunken man who kicks and punches a publican who tries to
> eject him from his establishment may not know what he is doing;
> and even if he has enough understanding to appreciate that he is
> punching and kicking out, he may not be able to appreciate that he
> is exposing the publican to risk of injury. (p. 112)

No evidence is cited to substantiate this claim, which is expressed as
a statement of the obvious. Nevertheless, from this unquestioned
assertion about the effects of alcohol on self-awareness and apprecia-
tion of consequences, the Committee was forced to generate complex
legal arguments in order to justify the conviction of intoxicated offenders.

Legal thinking reflects the prevalent social and moral attitudes of
its time (Mitchell 1990, p. 4). Part of this context concerns societal
disapproval of drunken behaviour. Notwithstanding the common
belief in alcohol's power to deprive the drinker of rational and
moral faculties, the unrestrained behaviour of the intoxicated individual offends societal values of self-discipline and decorum. Thus,
the Criminal Law Revision Committee was unperturbed by the prospect of convicting intoxicated offenders in cases in which their sober
counterparts would be acquitted, taking the view: 'What calls for
punishment is getting intoxicated and when in that condition behaving
in a way which society cannot, and should not, tolerate' (1980, p. 112).

Mackay (1990) observes that such moral outrage has 'tainted' judicial decision making in cases in which the excuse proffered is one of
general validity, but in which evidence of intoxication is produced.
Defences of provocation, mistake, duress, insanity and automatism
have been rejected, when evidence of intoxication is produced, despite
their foundations on evidence of these conditions which would generally satisfy the courts in cases of sober crime. Mackay argues that
'the courts have over-zealously allowed their attitude towards self-
induced incapacity to taint and infect alternative methods of exculpa-
tion which might be otherwise open to the accused' (1990, p. 37).
Thus, moral judgements are not suspended until legal responsibility is
established, but themselves inform the determination of legal responsibility. The paradoxical outcome is the acceptance of the intoxication

excuse in some cases, despite official rejection of its validity, and punitive refusal of legitimate defences in others.

Legal thinking on the intoxication excuse, therefore, has been based upon assumptions about the effects of alcohol on the human mind and will, drawn from the stockpile of 'common knowledge'. The law's interpretation has also been influenced by societal disapproval and censure of intoxication, and the perceived need for the full armoury of the law to be weighed against the depravity of the intoxicated offender.

THE INTOXICATION EXCUSE IN MITIGATION

The legal status of the intoxication excuse has dominated debate, to the neglect of two further issues. Firstly, the basic rule of denying the intoxication excuse as a defence does not illuminate fully its proper treatment. The application of that basic rule, and the sheer weight of numbers of defendants convicted of, or admitting to, their intoxicated crimes suggests that it is in the realm of sentencing that the intoxication excuse is most commonly invoked. The judgements of culpability which inform decisions about consequent punishment have less to do with the strictly legal attribution of responsibility than with the moral appraisal of offenders and their actions.

Thomas informs us:

> The overwhelming majority of offences which come before criminal courts arise from factual situations which conform to a recurring pattern and which can be categorized by reference to particular elements. This recurring pattern of common factual situations provides a basis for a corresponding pattern of sentences, which can be adjusted to accord with the detailed variations of particular cases. The conventional relationships between frequently encountered factual situations and corresponding levels of sentence constitute the foundations of the tariff. (1979, p. 30)

Circumstances involving alcohol are quite possibly the *most* 'frequently encountered factual situations' in which offenders claim to commit their offences. Indeed, we sometimes appear to have become inured to the constant repetition of this information. So, for example, Shapland (1981) presents without comment the finding that intoxication was the most frequently mentioned item of information proffered in mitigation speeches. Yet the law is somewhat reticent as to the implications of this information for sentencing decisions. Thomas merely observes that '[d]runkenness, while having little or no independent mitigating effect, may add some marginal weight to other more substantial mitigating factors' (1979, p. 209). But the reasons why this may be so are not clear. Nor is the extraordinary persistence of the intoxication excuse in mitigation explained by this directive. Thomas further observes that '[t]he victim of alcoholism will normally be considered a candidate for individualized treatment, if there are any reasonable prospects of success' (1979, p. 210). Thomas cites cases in which probation orders have been substituted for substantial terms of imprisonment on these grounds. However, Thomas also identifies alcoholism as a basis upon which 'the sentencer may impose imprisonment rather than an individualized measure in order to provide an opportunity for treatment, and he may ignore mitigating factors in determining the length of the sentence so as to ensure that the period of confinement is sufficiently long for treatment to take place' (1979, p. 44). Thomas does not remark on these paradoxical sentencing paradigms, nor explain how sentencers are to distinguish between an alcoholic ripe for probation and one requiring unmitigated imprisonment for the purpose of treatment.

This brings us to the second neglected issue: that sentencing decisions in cases involving intoxication may be as vulnerable to the vagaries of commonsense reasoning about alcohol's effects on the human will as judgements of strict legal responsibility. Perhaps, given the relative lack of guidance, such decisions may be even more vulnerable. In an effort to develop rational guidelines for sentencing intoxicated offenders, Felker instead graphically demonstrates the curious assumptions that may underpin judgements of culpability for intoxicated deviance.

> [I]ntoxication should be available as a mitigating factor to the extent that intoxication impaired the offenders [*sic*] capacity to appreciate the wrongfulness of his conduct at the time of the crime. However, if the offender's intoxication has repeatedly resulted in criminal conduct to the extent that defendant's [*sic*] decision to become drunk is equivalent to a decision to commit crime, then the offender's intoxication can be an aggravating factor unless the offender is otherwise a good candidate for rehabilitation. (Felker 1990, p. 3)

How are we to identify, or distinguish between these different consequences of drinking? How might we recognise 'a good candidate for rehabilitation' from an untreatable miscreant? Such qualitative distinctions are not necessarily self-evident from the observable offender or his behaviour. Moreover, how can we be sure that the changes in the offender's will which Felker postulates are truly caused by intoxication?

STUDYING THE INTOXICATION EXCUSE

This study is based upon a particular premise. Since it would appear that the power of commonsense wisdom confounds legal direction on the intoxication excuse, then it is necessary to understand that very commonsense wisdom itself, if we hope to influence the judgements of responsibility which spring from it. This study, therefore, is a theoretical and empirical exploration of the foundations of the intoxication excuse in mitigation and the mechanisms by which an appeal to intoxication or alcoholism may influence the judgement of an offender's culpability, and thereby the sentencing decision.

The theoretical exploration seeks to explain why the plethora of academic research and theory on the subject of alcohol has not resolved the legal dilemma over intoxicated responsibility. The relationships between lay theory, or commonsense wisdom, and judgements of responsibility are also explored. Lay theories about alcohol's effects on rationality, intentionality and behaviour are identified as powerful tools in the explanation of crime: both for offenders themselves, in the construction of neutralisations and rationalisations for their deviance, and for those who pass moral and legal judgement upon their behaviour. Finally, the social psychological processes by which mitigation achieves its purpose of reducing punishment through the appeal to these very lay theories are explored.

The empirical study involves observations of sentencing hearings in a magistrates' court, supported by interviews with magistrates – those lay theorists upon whose judgements of culpability rests the punishment of many offenders – and with probation officers, who bring their own professional theories to bear on the attempt to influence sentencing decisions. The study exposes the richness of the intoxication excuse in mitigation and considers its variety, complexity and nuances in the context of the total sentencing exercise.

Chapter 2 examines a variety of explanations of the alcohol–crime relationship, exposing their frequent reliance on commonsense assumptions, or lay theories, about the effects of intoxication on mood, mind and rationality. It is argued that existing academic theories offer deterministic, causal explanations which are not warranted by the findings of research. Chapter 3 develops a theoretical approach which avoids the unwarranted determinism of traditional approaches, while preserving their important contributions. Particular attention is paid to the role of the 'alcohol expectancies', or set of commonsense beliefs about alcohol's effects, in underpinning offenders' techniques of neutralisation and post-offence rationalisations of their behaviour. Chapter 4 explores the appeal to the intoxication excuse in mitigation, emphasising the adaptation of the private techniques of neutralisation and rationalisation for public consumption, and the social psychological processes of mitigation. Chapter 5 introduces the empirical study at City Magistrates' Court. Chapter 6 examines the construction of sentencing decisions, including the role of information about drunkenness and alcoholism in shaping the interpretation of case material. Chapter 7 explores the management of information about intoxication in pursuit of mitigation of punishment. Chapter 8 examines the role of probation officers in the sentencing decision-making process, and includes a comparison of probation officers' and magistrates' theories of alcohol-related crime and its treatment. Chapter 9 draws together the theoretical and empirical strands of the study and explores their implications for the due process of justice.

Certain points of detail should be made clear from the outset. Firstly, the study concerns itself only with male offenders. This limitation follows from several theoretical and practical observations: there is mounting evidence of gender differences in drinking attitudes and behaviour (e.g. Bardo and Risner 1985; Blane 1979; Cappell and Greeley 1987; Greeley, McCready and Theisen 1980; Harford 1983; Marsh, Dobbs and White 1986; Wechsler 1979; Wilsnack and Wilsnack 1979; Wilson 1987); there is evidence of gender differences in crime (e.g. Heidensohn 1985; Morris 1987); there is controversial evidence of gender differences in the courtroom constructions of crime and sentencing decisions (e.g. Allen 1987; Daly 1994; Eaton 1984; Edwards 1984); and there were very few female defendants relevant to the nature of the empirical enquiry. Since the interests of particular groups are not served by implying that conclusions based on data from which they are excluded may be extended to them, offenders are explicitly masculine in both the theoretical and empirical discussion. In the latter, however, care has been taken to refer to other participants in the courtroom process in terms which are neutral as to gender or, indeed, to any characteristic which might result in personal identification. In particular, the term 'magistrate' is used to refer not only to any member of the bench, but also to the particular magistrate chairing it on any occasion, thus avoiding both the gender specific 'chairman' or 'chairwoman' and the unfortunately inanimate 'chair'.

Secondly, the theoretical discussion was initially hampered by the lack of a formal term for the academic study of alcohol. Surprisingly, given the plethora of multidisciplinary research and theory in the topic, the study of alcohol is not embraced by a generic title, as, for example, are the disciplines of criminology, psychology, zoology and gerontology. The variable use of phrases such as 'alcoholism research' and 'theories of intoxication' incurred the possibility of semantic and conceptual confusion. The issue has been resolved for the purposes of this study by the adoption, where necessary, of the title 'academic alcohol theory' to denote the total enterprise of academic study of alcohol. 'Alcohol–crime theory' has also been invoked to denote the study of the particular relationship between alcohol and crime, on occasions when alternative phraseology would be cumbersome. Contributory disciplines, such as ethnography and psychology, are specified as appropriate.

Thirdly, considerable convolutions of phraseology have been avoided by the ungrammatical expedient of referring to 'intoxicated crime'. It has been pointed out to me that crime does not drink. However, the prospect of constantly repeating phrases such as 'crimes committed after the offender had been drinking alcohol' throughout this book overcame my scruples. Furthermore, common phrases such as 'crimes committed under the influence of alcohol' often imply precisely those effects of intoxication on behaviour which are at issue in this book. Finally, adoption of the phrase 'intoxicated crime' suggested the equally ungrammatical, but graphic, 'sober crime', which appeared to me to be infinitely preferable to 'crimes committed when the offender had not been drinking alcohol'. In short, while it is acknowledged that crime is neither intoxicated nor sober, on this occasion I have embraced a commonsense approach to grammar.

2 Theories of Intoxicated Crime

This chapter considers whether academic research and theory has undermined the confident ascription of criminal responsibility to intoxicated offenders. It is suggested that any concern that academic knowledge erodes the principle of free will is bolstered more by the deterministic expression of alcohol theory than by the substance of its research; and that academic theory about the alcohol–crime relationship often rests on commonsense assumptions. The chapter examines firstly the alcohol–crime association; secondly, academic interpretations of offenders' theories of intoxicated crime; and thirdly, the major emphases of academic theories of the alcohol–crime relationship.

THE ALCOHOL–CRIME ASSOCIATION

Research has repeatedly demonstrated the frequency with which alcohol consumption precedes crime commission. This statistical alcohol–crime association has been found in surveys of offenders (Washbrook 1977), studies of criminal careers (Collins 1982; Pittman and Gordon 1958) and studies of particular offences, including murder (Gillies 1976), rape (Rada 1975; Wright and West 1981), robbery (Walsh 1986), assault (Berkowitz 1986; Mayfield 1976) and burglary (Bennett and Wright 1984a). Researchers have become so accustomed to the association that failure to find it is sometimes attributed to methodological defects such as ineffective enquiry or inefficient recording (Pittman and Handy 1964), rather than to its actual absence. Collins, reviewing the accumulated literature, concludes:

> [C]onsiderable evidence suggests that alcohol is often present in or before criminal events, and that a disproportionate number of criminal offenders have alcohol problems. (1982, p. 188)

The association is particularly strong for violent crime (Collins 1982), a factor which has contributed to a concentration of research and theory on this relationship (Miller and Welte 1986; Pernanen 1982).

The repeated establishment of the alcohol–crime association reflects the preoccupation of much research with indexing the social harm attributable to alcohol misuse. Alcohol has been implicated in almost all forms of social ill, of which crime is only one. Others include domestic violence (Gayford 1975; Kantor and Straus 1987; Wilson 1982), accidents (Denney 1986; Royal College of Physicians 1987), employee absenteeism (Plant 1981; Polich 1979; Rix 1981), divorce (Blane 1979; Jacob and Seilhamer 1982), prostitution (Blane 1979), suicide (Beck, Wissman and Kovacs 1976; Blane 1979) and acute and chronic sickness (Royal College of Physicians 1987).

The repeated finding of an association between alcohol consumption and a problematic event explains very little about the relationship between the two phenomena. Nevertheless, the tendency to assume cause from association pervades much of the literature. Indeed, the presence of alcohol, where it is found, is often treated as the sole cause for criminal events which are, in their sober manifestations, recognised to be complex, multi-factored phenomena. This 'single cause assumption' (Gusfield 1981) has also been termed the 'malevolence assumption' by Hamilton and Collins who describe it as the 'tendency to see alcohol as blameworthy whenever it accompanies problematic behavior' (1982, p. 254). It is linked to a variety of deficiencies in the collection and interpretation of research data demonstrating the association:

(a) Pernanen (1982) suggests that proper examination of cultural variations in alcohol use and crime rates might challenge the assumed stability of the alcohol–crime relationship. For example, Pernanen notes that France has a very high national consumption of alcohol, but a low homicide rate, while the reverse pertains in Central and South America.

(b) The association has not been adequately contextualised within the drinking patterns of the general population. It tends to be assumed that the statistical association demonstrates an abnormal drinking pattern peculiar to offenders. However, 'impact figures' (Pernanen 1982) created by statistical assertions about the extent of alcohol consumption by offenders would signify little if they resemble the customary drinking patterns of comparable groups in the general population (Evans 1986; Pernanen 1982). For example, Kantor and Straus (1987) found that although male heavy drinkers were more likely to abuse their wives than light- or non-drinkers nevertheless the majority of heavy drinkers did not abuse their wives.

Washbrook (1977), however, attributed his finding, that a group of male prisoners appeared no more alcoholic than a group of male employees, to defects in the research methodology.

(c) Research has concentrated on convicted, and particularly imprisoned, offenders. However, Collins (1982) suggests that alcohol-involved offenders may be over-represented in the criminal justice system. Reasons for this are unclear, and probably multiple. Contributory factors may not involve a causal relationship between alcohol and crime. For example, the perception of alcohol as an indicator of culpability, noted in Chapter 1, may increase the likelihood of prosecution and harsh punishment.

(d) Research has neglected to contextualise pre-offence drinking within offenders' customary drinking patterns (Miller and Welte 1986). Bennett and Wright (1984a, 1984b) found that the frequency of burglars' pre-offence drinking closely reflected the frequency of their drinking in itself. Kantor and Straus (1987) found that although wife assaults frequently followed drinking, most occurred when neither partner had been drinking.

(e) The 'malevolence assumption' (Hamilton and Collins 1982) has also infected aspects of victim research, through findings of an association between drinking and victimisation (Goodman, Mercy, Loya et al. 1986; Hough and Mayhew 1983, 1985; Wright and West 1981). By strengthening theories of victim precipitation, this assumption imputes blame to victims, although the criminal justice system relies heavily on the assumption of 'innocent' victims (Shapland, Willmore and Duff 1985). A less emotive analysis might suggest that the association reflects situational aspects of crime, such as the likelihood of victim and offender meeting in a public drinking place.

(f) Covariation between levels of alcohol consumption and crime rates does not necessarily reflect a causal relationship. Pernanen (1982), reviewing 'natural experiments' in which the availability of alcohol was reduced through events such as price increases or strikes in the liquor industry, found an association with a reduced rate of violent crime. However, Pernanen cautions that consequences of reduced alcohol availability such as reduced levels of social interaction in public places, may explain this covariation. Smith and Burvill (1987) found that a lowered legal drinking age in Australian states was followed by a rise in juvenile crime. Violent crime, however, was much less affected than property crime, such as opportunistic car thefts, suggesting that juvenile criminal activity was influenced by the changes in opportunities for typical juvenile crime brought about by heightened interaction in public drinking places.

(g) Situational factors associated with alcohol-related offences suggest a complex causal relationship. For example, violent crime commonly occurs in or around licensed premises (Felson, Baccaglini, and Gmelch 1986; Goodman, Mercy, Loya et al. 1986; Luckenbill 1977). Such crime, however, is not only associated with drinking, but also with concentrations of young adult males (Felson, Baccaglini and Gmelch 1986; Hope 1985), city-centre locations (Hope 1985) and the physical design of pubs (Marsh and Campbell 1979).

(h) The alcohol–crime association, and covariation between alcohol availability and crime, feed an assumption that increased drinking will inevitably be accompanied by increased crime. At the individual level, however, this does not appear to be true. Indeed, very heavy or chronic drinking may suppress serious offending (Collins 1982; Hamilton and Collins 1982; Pernanen 1982; Pittman and Gordon 1958; Washbrook 1977).

Thus, cultural, situational and individual variables may all have a strong bearing on the alcohol–crime relationship, but have often been neglected in data collection and interpretation, due to the intuitive obviousness of alcohol itself as a plausible cause of crime. The exploration of attempts to explain that relationship begins with the theories of offenders themselves, who may perhaps, as experts in crime, offer some special insights into alcohol's contribution to their depredations.

OFFENDERS' THEORIES

Overview

Academic research does not generally regard the commonsense theories of lay people as a reliable source of objective truth. Nevertheless, researchers have on occasions asked offenders about their beliefs as to the influences of alcohol on their criminal behaviour (e.g. Bennett and Wright 1984a, 1984b). Such information also emerges during the course of interviewing about other aspects of offending (e.g. Athens 1980; Walsh 1986), participant observation research (e.g. Parker 1974), and the collection of biographical data (e.g. Athens 1989;

Maguire 1982). Such sources suggest four distinctions made by offenders between intoxicated and sober crime, suggesting qualitative differences in the exercise of rationality and intentionality: motivelessness, impulsivity, indiscriminateness and incompetence. These distinctions, however, imply degrees of motivation, deliberation and skill which are not generally associated with sober crime. They appeal to intuitive commonsense notions, which are accepted or discredited by researchers according to their own perspectives.

1. Motivelessness

Although the obvious purpose of robbery is to obtain money, Cordilia (1986) found that men convicted of group robbery after drinking quite often said that money was not important. Parker, during drinking sessions with a gang, observed that 'one can get into a fight for almost no apparent reason' (1974, p. 145). Burglars (Bennett and Wright 1984a, 1984b) and opportunistic robbers (Walsh 1986) sometimes assume that intoxication has caused their offence, since they do not recollect forming any prior intention. Offenders also appear to regard impulsivity and indiscriminateness as evidence of the motivelessness of their intoxicated crimes.

Such statements imply that motives for sober crime are well articulated. However, when asked generally about their criminal motives, offenders offer mundane, unambitious and often vague reasons. For example, burglars usually cite wanting money as their motive (Bennett and Wright 1984a; Walsh 1986), but, as Walsh remarks,

> few seemed to have any clear idea of what they were looking for beyond 'money', and of those who did have a definite notion of their wage and return for skill, most set their sights very low and were content with quite trivial amounts, usually £100 or less. (1986, p. 33)

Ill-gotten gains are often small (Maguire 1982; Walsh 1986). Further, the uses to which offenders put them display little ambition or deliberation, revolving around basic subsistence (Bennett and Wright 1984a) and pleasures such as drinking and gambling (Bennett and Wright 1984a; Maguire 1982; Walsh 1986; Wright and Decker 1994).

Criminal motivations have complex sources, including both historical factors in the offender's prior experience and situational factors providing the immediate opportunity for the offence (Bennett and Wright 1984a; Clarke and Cornish 1985; Cordilia 1986). Moreover, motivation to offend is generally intermittent, limited and highly dependent on the confluence of the motivation itself and an opportunity to satisfy it (Bennett and Wright 1984a; Best and Luckenbill 1982; Briar and Piliavin 1965; Cornish and Clarke 1987; Pfuhl 1980; Walsh 1986). Such episodic, situationally specific motivation is not easily distinguishable from motivation intermittently 'caused' by alcohol. Given the customary frequency of offenders' drinking (Bennett and Wright 1984a, 1984b; Miller and Welte 1986), it may be more appropriate to regard alcohol as a prevalent feature of situations in which criminal opportunities arise, or are generated by already motivated offenders.

Criminal motivations include emotional rewards – for example, excitement, relief of boredom, unhappiness and anger (Bennett and Wright 1984a; Feeney 1986; Maguire 1982); beating the system (Bennett and Wright 1984a; Pfuhl 1980); peer-group solidarity (Best and Luckenbill 1982; Cordilia 1986; Scully and Marolla 1985; Wade 1967); triumph over fear (Munro 1972); and demonstration or preservation of self-image (Pfuhl 1980; Scully and Marolla 1985; Wade 1967). Further, single offences may serve multiple purposes (Pervin 1986), which may be more or less fully articulated by the offender. For example, wanting money is compatible with also wanting excitement, although the former, being concrete, may be more easily articulated.

Intoxication itself achieves such goals, providing camaraderie (Cavan 1966; Marsh, Dobbs and White 1986), excitement (Dorn 1983; Maguire 1982; Parker 1974) and opportunities to demonstrate one's status to peers and others (Cavan 1966; Dorn 1983; Maguire 1982; Parker 1974). Thus, a cluster of activities, including intoxication, offending and gambling (Cornish 1978), satisfy similar motivations.

Attributing motivelessness to intoxicated crime, therefore, wrongly implies that motivation for sober crime is well articulated, ambitious and independent of situational contingencies. Intoxication and offending have some common motivations. Motivelessness in fact appears to be a more accurate description of the sober, non-offending activities in the lives of ordinary offenders (Parker 1974; Patrick 1973).

Life with the gang was not all violence, sex and petty delinquency. Far from it. One of the foremost sensations that remains with me is the feeling of unending boredom, of crushing tedium, of listening hour after hour at street corners to desultory conversation, and indiscriminate grumbling. (Patrick 1973, p. 80)

2. *Impulsivity*

Offenders suggest that they commit intoxicated crime 'on the spur of the moment', without prior deliberation or intent to offend. This theme emerges in accounts of intoxicated robbery (Cordilia 1986; Walsh 1986), burglary (Bennett and Wright 1984a, 1984b) and rape (Wright and West 1981).

However, impulsivity is not peculiar to intoxicated crime. Bennett and Wright (1984a) found that the idea of offending sometimes seemed to 'pop into' burglars' heads, with no identifiable precipitating factor. They suggest that with experience offending becomes mere routine, obviating the need for contemplation. Furthermore, planning has a cost in flexibility, causing difficulty in adapting to setbacks by switching targets, compared with a more opportunistic approach (Bennett and Wright 1984a). Walsh (1986) sees impulsive burglary as a popular protective strategy against the anxiety provoked by pondering the hazards of the enterprise.

Despite the apparent impulsivity of intoxicated violence, in group-drinking situations, ethnographers record keen awareness of the behavioural cues associated with aggression, careful avoidance of producing them, and defusing of volatile situations (Archard 1979; Mungham 1976; Parker 1974). For example, such fine cues as eye contact may be carefully controlled in order to avoid giving unintentional offence.

Moreover, spontaneity is an integral feature of some types of crime. For example, Zimring (1981) suggests that spontaneity characterises robbery by young offenders because they typically offend in groups, engage in little preparation and rely on numerical strength. Street robbery, furthermore, depends heavily on speed and surprise for success, allowing little time for deliberation (Feeney 1986; Lejeune 1977; Walsh 1986). Similarly, vandalism is rarely planned, but develops in playful group interaction, seizing opportunities immediately to hand (Best and Luckenbill 1982; Wade 1967). Indeed,

> [b]ecause most delinquent activities require few resources, such as special skills or equipment, many occasions can be transformed into situations for delinquency. (Best and Luckenbill 1982, p. 52)

Parker (1974) suggests that the apparently spontaneous fighting between young men in city-centre pubs must be understood in the context of situations which lack rules regulating confrontations, necessitating pre-emptive action.

Prior experiences promote readiness to seize sudden opportunities. In life history terms, Cordilia (1986) suggests that socially isolated men are highly motivated to preserve tenuous relationships with drinking companions. Wade argues: 'Little exploration of feelings of fellow members of a delinquent group need be made when past natural histories of their careers indicate predispositions to any behaviour hinting of excitement, danger, and even malice' (1967, p. 101). Experience of crime itself enables robbers (Feeney 1986; Walsh 1986) and thieves (Carroll 1982; Carroll and Weaver 1986) to identify opportunities more rapidly, and to be readier to seize them. Experience thus provides a 'pattern' (Feeney 1986) or 'script' (Forgas 1986) for an offence.

Suddenness masks the generally orderly execution of impulsive offences. The 'ethogenic approach to social psychology' (Marsh and Paton 1986), however, which is increasingly popular in criminological research, assumes that all behaviour is understandable given sufficient knowledge of the actor's perceptions and motivations. This perspective has fostered a series of studies showing logical sequences of events and behaviour leading to the completion of impulsive burglary (Wright and Decker 1994), robbery (Lejeune 1977; Luckenbill 1980), assault and homicide (Athens 1980; Felson and Steadman 1983; Luckenbill 1977), rape (Athens 1980) and vandalism (Wade 1967).

Impulsivity, therefore, reflects prior experience, a defensive psychological strategy and factors integral to certain types of crime.

3. *Indiscriminateness*

Indiscriminateness implies that intoxicated offenders commit random offences, rather than selecting offences or targets on a rational basis. Burglars may attack premises, not on the basis of prior selection, but merely because they are encountered after leaving the pub (Bennett and Wright 1984a; Maguire 1982). Cordilia (1986) suggests that intoxication distorts normal priorities to the extent that sober individuals find their intoxicated violence incomprehensible. Parker's (1974) accounts of group-drinking sessions are replete with apparently indiscriminate attacks on people and property.

Intoxicated indiscriminateness has been called illusory by anthropologists, who find that even the most outrageous drunken violent and sexual orgies are constrained by rules: for example, prohibiting violent victimisation of women and children, sexual partnership with children and kin, or the use of certain weapons (Macandrew and Edgerton 1969). Discrimination is also affirmed on occasion by offenders. For example, in Maguire's biography of a professional burglar violence is resolutely eschewed, despite considerable heavy drinking, because 'there's no profit in this game' (1982, p. 100).

Sober criminals, however, do not always practise fine discrimination. Patrick found that juvenile gang members were

> capable of both utilitarian and non-utilitarian delinquent acts. The same boys could steal objects for profit, for their own consumption, and for 'the hell of it' all in the one day. They committed thefts as the need and the mood of the moment took them without regard for the neat classifications of sociologists. (Patrick 1973, p. 200)

Bennett and Wright (1984a) found that burglars' willingness to attack different types of dwelling increased with experience. This probably reflects, not increasing indiscriminateness, but learning, for example of the much lower risk of apprehension than that anticipated by novices. This, again, given the frequency of pre-offence drinking, may explain the willingness to seize opportunities casually encountered after drinking.

Fine discrimination between types of offence and target is constrained by the limitations of available opportunities (Collins 1982; Letkemann 1973; Walsh 1986). For example, robbers profess to principles about victimising groups such as the elderly or women (Lejeune 1977; Walsh 1986), but these scruples are 'easily eroded in the attempt to select the most accessible or vulnerable target' (Lejeune 1977, p. 135).

Indiscriminateness, therefore, is not a necessary consequence of intoxication, nor is subtle discrimination practised by the majority of sober offenders.

4. Incompetence

Inadequate preparation, clumsiness and unnecessary risk taking are regarded as qualities of intoxicated crime (Bennett and Wright 1984a, 1984b; Cordilia 1986; Walsh 1986). Offenders believe that intoxication inhibits successful performance of dishonest crime and that it promotes aggressive offences (Cordilia 1986; Walsh 1986; Wright and West 1981). Walsh remarks that drinking sessions in which burglars exchange useful information

> can easily degenerate, due to boasting based on alcohol intake, into a 'dare', where nobody really *wants* to, but feel now that they *have*

to, as a result of group pressure, carry out a task which is fraught with needless risk. (Walsh 1986, p. 44)

Nevertheless, intoxicated people often competently perform complex behaviours which are particularly valued. Anthropological studies reveal the competent performance of social functions such as ceremonial duties despite intoxicated interference with basic motor functions (Marshall 1981). Blane suggests that the apparent decrease in alcohol-related problems over the life span

> may reflect not a reduction in alcohol-related problems but a more sophisticated capacity to modulate the behaviors in question so that they don't come to the attention of those whose function it is to identify such behaviors. (1979, p. 27)

Observers of offenders remark on the high value placed on personal control (Walsh 1986) and skills such as verbal quick wittedness (Campbell 1986; Parker 1974), displayed during drinking sessions.

Professional crime is a comparative rarity. For example, dwelling-house burglaries are frequently committed by juveniles (Maguire 1982), in offenders' own, often disadvantaged, neighbourhoods (Bennett and Wright 1984a; Hough and Mayhew 1983; Maguire 1982), achieving little gain (Maguire 1982; Walsh 1986) and involving needless risks (Bennett and Wright 1984a; Maguire 1982; Walsh 1986). Experienced burglars know *how* to execute careful crime, but frequently fail to implement their knowledge (Bennett and Wright 1984a; Maguire 1982; Walsh 1986). Roebuck and Johnson (1962), comparing specialist and 'jack-of-all-trades' offenders, found that the latter displayed gross incompetence throughout their criminal careers, despite their comparative sobriety.

The technical sophistication of much crime is low. Common, rather than specialised knowledge and skills are very frequently applied to criminal activity (Letkemann 1973), and learning involves the mastery of psychological defences against anxiety at least as much as technical ability (Carroll and Weaver 1986; Lejeune 1977; Walsh 1986). Preparation is often minimal (Bennett and Wright 1984a; Lejeune 1977; Maguire 1982; Walsh 1986), equipment basic (Walsh 1986) and success reliant on victims' or observers' naiveté rather than on subterfuge (Bennett and Wright 1984a; Buckle and Farrington 1984; Lejeune 1977; Lejeune and Alex 1973; Murphy 1986; Steffensmeier and Terry 1973; Walsh 1986).

Maguire (1982) suggests that burglars' customary lifestyle, favouring hedonism, profligacy and dare-devilry, militates against the consistent use of knowledge and skill. Bennett and Wright (1984a) found that unnecessary risk taking was itself prompted by rewards such as the certainty of gain, excitement and convenience.

Incompetence, therefore, is not a necessary consequence of intoxication, nor is it a distinctive quality of intoxicated crime.

The Appeal to Common Sense

These observations suggest that levels of motivation, preparation, discrimination and skill in sober crime are over-estimated in subjective comparisons with intoxicated crime. Offenders generally seem to weigh opportunities and risks in a rough and ready way, rather than with objective precision, opting for 'what seems reasonable at the time' (Bennett and Wright 1984a; Clarke and Cornish 1985; Cornish and Clarke 1986). Thus, Coid (1986a), reviewing sober and intoxicated rape, concludes that the most significant finding is probably their essential similarity.

In making their distinctions between intoxicated and sober crime, offenders appeal to commonsense beliefs about alcohol's effects, rather than to special insights derived from experience. Indeed, the intuitive reasonableness of their claims is reflected in the difficulty, in much of the literature, of distinguishing fully between offenders' theories and the assumptions of the researchers.

Taylor (1972) criticises the frequent tendency of academics to discredit offenders' accounts in favour of their own theories, or to accept them only under special conditions such as guaranteed privacy. Such responses smack of academic arrogance. Nevertheless, the dilemma is real. Firstly, offenders may be motivated, under any conditions, to offer self-justificatory or self-excusatory accounts, rather than to acknowledge fault or failure to themselves or to others (Maguire 1982). Secondly, offenders' accounts reflect the ignorance of lay people generally about alcohol. Fitzmaurice and Pease (1986) also note that offenders' theories of crime usually reflect popular beliefs, rather than special insight. Thirdly, people appear often to have little or no knowledge of the 'real' reasons for their actions, invoking instead reasons which, although incorrect, strike them as plausible (Nisbett and Wilson 1977). Thus, offenders may offer intoxication as a primary explanation when it appears to be either the most desirable or the most likely reason for their behaviour, on the basis of commonsense beliefs about alcohol's effects on rationality. Furthermore, when directly asked to compare their intoxicated and sober crimes, offenders may bring to mind occasions with distinctive features, such as arrest, which may be attributed to intoxication.

Researchers appear to respond to offenders' accounts with acceptance or qualification, according to their particular personal beliefs, theoretical perspectives and research focus. This can lead to notable contradictions.

(a) Personal Beliefs

Researchers' willingness to believe in the irrationality and incompetence of intoxicated offenders' behaviour contrasts strikingly with their confidence in the reliability of their own intoxicated reasoning. Participant observers produce confident commentary after heavy drinking sessions with their subjects (Archard 1979; Hobbs 1988; Parker 1974). Hobbs, investigating the police, recalls:

> For the most part I spoke, acted, drank, and generally behaved as though I was not doing research. Indeed, I often had to remind myself that I was not in a pub to enjoy myself, but to conduct an academic inquiry and repeatedly woke up the following morning with an incredible hangover facing the dilemma of whether to bring it up or write it up. (Hobbs 1988, p. 6)

Maguire's (1982) repeated endorsement of burglars' denunciation of intoxicated crime as irrational contrasts oddly with the respectful biography of a successful professional thief whose accounts are replete with references to heavy drinking which go unremarked by the author. Maguire's concept of 'professionalism' appears to disqualify the possible relevance of intoxication to his analysis.

(b) Theoretical Perspective

Berkowitz (1986) disputes Luckenbill's (1977) assertion of the significance of onlookers in violent interactions. No assaulter in Berkowitz' study believed that the presence or absence of an audience influenced his offence. This, however, ignores the evidence from experimental research that people fail to recognise the effects of an audience on their behaviour (Latané and Darley 1970), which suggests that the responses of Berkowitz' assaulters were predictable but unreliable. By contrast, Berkowitz argues that assaulters increased their violence in response to signs of their victims' pain, *although themselves unaware* of this stimulus. Berkowitz' selectivity as to which 'unconscious' responses he recognises complements his theoretical preference for the psychodynamic explanation of wilful harm inflicted by 'explosive' men with weak ego defences.

Similarly, Cordilia (1986), favouring a symbolic-interactionist perspective, explains intoxicated-group robbery as the attempt to prolong intense, but tenuous relationships, although when interviewed offenders did not articulate their motives in this way.

(c)   Research Focus
Researchers sometimes appear 'blind' to their subjects' obvious intoxication when offending. Maguire's (1982) disregard of intoxication when examining 'professionalism' has been mentioned. Athens' (1980) analysis of violent crime, derived entirely from offenders' accounts, achieved detailed explanations of the motives for and execution of offences without invoking alcohol as a cause, although the majority mentioned being heavily intoxicated. Athens himself does not comment on the prevalence of intoxication in these accounts. For both offenders and researchers, focusing on the sequence of events and decisions leading to an offence appears to render intoxication superfluous to causal explanations of crime.

Is academic theory itself capable of generating explanations of intoxicated crime which are of higher quality than those of offenders? We turn now to examine three main varieties of academic theory: dispositional; situational; and substance focused. Each is illustrated with a particular theoretical conceptualisation of the alcohol–crime relationship.

DISPOSITIONAL THEORIES

Overview

Dispositional theories of deviance attempt to link the development of deviant behaviour to distinctive experiences or personality characteristics. They therefore primarily concern the processes of initiation, development and change during drinking and criminal 'careers'. Research emphasises methods such as longitudinal studies, cross-sectional surveys, studies of special populations, such as prisoners or alcoholics in treatment, and personality measurement.

(a) Life Experiences

The development of individual drinking problems has been studied by
longitudinal comparisons of drinking patterns between early and later
adolescence (e.g. Marsh, Dobbs and White 1986), adolescence and
young adulthood (e.g. Ghodsian and Power 1987) and youth and later
adulthood (e.g. McCord and McCord 1962). The manifestation of
drinking problems has been studied through cross-sectional population surveys (e.g. Hauge and Irgens-Jensen 1987). Collectively, such
studies suggest that although early and later drinking problems are
statistically linked, individual drinking patterns fluctuate so considerably over the life span that 'no reliable predictive statement can be
made about a given individual even in the presence of extensive
information about the person's drinking behavior, personality and
life history' (Blane 1979, p. 28; Collins 1982; Zucker 1979). Despite
the instability of individual drinking patterns through the life cycle,
there is in general a marked shift from comparatively common problematic drinking in young adulthood towards unproblematic drinking
in maturity (Blane 1979; Collins 1982; Sadava 1987). Drinking problems are experienced differently in youth and middle age (Hauge and
Irgens-Jensen 1987; Zucker 1979). Similar fluctuations, and the
tendency towards desistance after young adulthood are found in
criminal careers (Briar and Piliavin 1965; Collins 1982; Hirschi and
Gottfredson 1983).

Multiple life history factors are implicated in the development of
drinking problems. These include, for example, ethnicity, religion and
culture (Blane 1979; Goldman, Brown and Christiansen 1987; Greeley, McCready and Theisen 1980; Zucker 1979), parental relationships
and models (Goldman, Brown and Christiansen 1987; Greeley,
McCready and Theisen 1980; Zucker 1979), family size (Zucker
1979) and socio-economic status (Blane 1979; Collins 1982; Zucker
1979). Such factors, however, interact with each other to exert their
relative influences in complex combinations (Collins 1982; Cox 1987;
Sadava 1987; Zucker 1979). Furthermore, the salience of different
factors to an individual's drinking pattern changes over the life span,
for example in the relative influence of parental and peer group
models (Zucker 1979). Finally, the influence of historical factors is
heavily modified by the individual's contemporary social position and
drinking environment (Blane 1979; Collins 1982; Harford, Wechsler
and Rothman 1983; Hauge and Irgens-Jensen 1987; Hope 1985;
Nusbaumer, Mauss and Pearson 1982; Sadava 1987; Zucker 1979).
Again, similar factors have been found to predict persistent

delinquency (Farrington 1987; Loeber and Dishion 1983; West and Farrington 1977).

(b) Personality Characteristics
The 'alcoholic personality' concept has been discredited by the failure of research to link alcoholism convincingly to distinctive personality characteristics (Cox 1987; Fingarette 1988). Nevertheless, the concept retains its attractiveness. Some theorists continue to argue the import-ance of personality factors in alcoholism (e.g. Ludwig 1988).

It is unclear how far some measures of personality which character-ise alcoholics, such as low self-esteem, depression, anxiety, high field dependence and external locus of control, are a cause, and how far a consequence of alcoholism (Cox 1985, 1987; Heather and Robertson 1985). Cox argues that 'the intense negative affect observed among alcoholics is largely a consequence of long-term alcohol abuse' (1985, p. 215).

The suggestion in some research that individuals prone to develop drinking problems are more sensitive to alcohol's effects than others (Cappell and Greeley 1987; Cox 1987; Sher 1987), nevertheless begs the question how such individuals come to value those effects. For example, Sher (1987) notes that individual susceptibility to alcohol's tension-reducing effects appears to be unrelated to personality meas-ures of anxiety proneness.

Personality characteristics which do appear to predict problematic drinking, such as impulsivity, non-conformity and low self-control, do not self-evidently explain its onset. Despite the consistent finding of these personality characteristics, 'there is no uniform evidence that substance users and abusers were maladjusted or psychologically dis-tressed prior to their substance use' (Cox 1985, p. 215). These person-ality characteristics also resemble characteristics such as troublesomeness, aggression and anti-social behaviour, which have been found to predict delinquency (Farrington 1987; Loeber and Dishion 1983).

Thus, adolescent problem drinking and delinquency appear to be part of a cluster of non-conforming behaviours which may have com-mon psychosocial foundations (Collins 1982; Sadava 1987; Zucker 1979). Although the intensity of offending during later criminal careers appears to covary with periods of heavy drinking, this is not in itself evidence of a causal effect of frequent intoxication on crim-inality (Collins 1982, 1986). Collins (1982) suggests that in fact ado-lescent delinquency may precede drinking, and adult criminality may exacerbate drinking problems. This perspective has received scant attention, perhaps because it runs counter to the commonsense cause and effect relationship between drinking and crime.

Dispositional explanations of the relationship between acute intoxication and specific criminal events are largely of two types: that intoxication exacerbates the factors which predispose individuals to commit crime; or that there is an underlying common cause of both drinking and offending (Pernanen 1982).

Approaches of the former type usually rely on assumed pharmacological effects of alcohol, such as disinhibition (Pernanen 1982). More detailed attempts have difficulty encompassing the varied strands of relevant research. For example, Blum (1982) suggests that the probability of violence among alcoholics is enhanced by the stressfulness of social situations caused by their external locus of control, field dependency and impaired abstract reasoning. This argument, however, overlooks evidence that violence is *suppressed* among very heavy drinkers (Kantor and Straus 1987) and that the offences of chronic alcoholics are typically non-violent, drunkenness offences (Pittman and Gordon 1958; Washbrook 1977).

Blum's account suggests predictability of offending from the combination of personal attributes and the effects of alcohol. However, both intoxicated and sober individuals vary considerably in their responses to different situations (Pervin 1986; Toch 1986). For example, males may confine their violence to domestic situations (Fagan, Stewart and Hansen 1983), but even there not all provocative situations will result in violence (Dobash and Dobash 1984).

Approaches of the latter type usually identify personal attributes which are thought to underlie both excessive drinking and criminality. The concept of 'undersocialisation', examined below, falls into this category. Such common cause conceptualisations may offer explanations of the apparent covariation of drinking and offending careers, or the transfer of deviance from offending to drinking in later life, since both behaviours are thought to stem from the same psychosocial sources. Once again, however, explanations of the relationship between acute intoxication and specific criminal events tend to appeal to alcohol's assumed effects.

Undersocialisation   The concept of 'undersocialisation' (Bahr and Caplow 1974) is not a unified theory, but is invoked to a greater or lesser extent by several alcohol and crime theorists. It is also a popular lay concept, expressed in terms such as 'inadequacy', 'inability to cope', 'dependency' and 'poor self-control'. Underpinning the various manifestations of the undersocialisation concept is the theme that drinking and offending are maladaptive solutions to the failure to develop sufficient psychological resources to respond competently to the demands of conventional social life.

Undersocialisation is popularly applied to explanations of the skid-row lifestyle, which is characterised by chronic drinking and offending. For example, Pittman and Gordon explain the shift from property crime to chronic drunkenness offences in terms of undersocialisation.

[T]he criminal career is generally divided into two distinct phases. The first covers the earlier years of life, generally when the man is under 40 years of age, and is marked by arrests and incarcerations for offenses that are seemingly unrelated to excessive use of alcohol. However, these arrests and incarcerations mean that their attempted criminal careers have been unsuccessful. They then drop out of active crime, not only because of ineptness and age, but also through the emergence of the new pattern of adaptation to societal norms and requirements which is reflected in increased drinking and life on Skid Row. In terms of their perception of the life situation, drinking forms a part of a new pattern of gratifying psychological needs, replacing the unsuccessful attempt to achieve that gratification in a career of crimes against property. (Pittman and Gordon 1958, p. 542)

They continue:

The penal institution is thus functional for those inebriates who show long and continuous histories of incarceration, in that it meets, although in a socially disapproved way, the basic psychological needs of their personality structure. Incarceration, on the other hand, is dysfunctional in the sense that it provides the situation in which the developing dependency can be fixed in the personality pattern where it is already evident as an inability to develop autonomy in adulthood. (1958, p. 546)

The undersocialisation concept lies at the heart of some theoretical accounts of intoxicated crime. For example, Cordilia's (1986) symbolic-interactionist analysis of robbery arising in a group-drinking context appeals to the generation of intense, tenuous relationships between socially isolated individuals in a drinking situation.

Control theory (Briar and Piliavin 1965; Gottfredson and Hirschi 1990; Hindelang 1973; Hirschi 1969; Wiatrowski, Griswold and

Roberts 1981) provides an example of a rigorous theoretical account, complemented by considerable research, of the release of criminality through the failure of socialisation experiences to develop strong internal controls, or 'commitments to conformity' (Briar and Piliavin 1965). Nevertheless, since crime is not continuous even among poorly controlled individuals, it is necessary to examine specific criminal events (Clarke and Cornish 1985) to determine the factors which motivate the individual to act on the coincidence of his weak self-control and the opportunity to offend (Briar and Piliavin 1965; Hirschi 1969; Shover 1985).

The undersocialisation concept implies that the deviant lifestyle is less demanding than the conventional one. Individuals who have failed to achieve adequate levels of socialisation for competent performance in conventional life turn to deviance as an easier route to survival. However, both alcoholic and criminal lifestyles make heavy demands on individual resources (Archard 1979; Cook 1975; Healy 1988; Phillimore 1979; Shover 1985; Walsh 1986; Wiseman 1970). Cook, observing the frequent use of the word 'inadequate' in social workers' reports on skid-row men, remarks impatiently:

> These 'judgements at a distance' do not reflect in any way the qualities the men need to survive on skid row. The resourcefulness and energy required on skid row can at times be considerable, and hordes of the passively inadequate men described could not survive at all. (Cook 1975, p. 164)

Significant skill deficits are deficits for criminal competence as much as for conventional activities. Roebuck and Johnson (1962) attribute the failure of 'jack-of-all-trades' offenders to progress in professional crime to their clumsiness, poor self-discipline, frequent apprehension, indiscriminate choice of crime and isolation from more sophisticated criminals. The single area of relative social competence displayed by these offenders was their comparative sobriety!

The popularity of the undersocialisation concept is accompanied by a tendency to regard its explanatory power as self-evident. Bahr and Caplow (1974) challenge such theoretical complacency, after finding that skid-row drinkers were more sociable, had more friends and more family and community ties than abstainers, whose histories were marked by non-attachment.

A condition such as 'undersocialization', cannot be the major factor in the development of a certain behavior if it appears most consistently in the lives of those who do not exhibit the behavior. The heavy drinkers in our sample may indeed be undersocialized in comparison with the general population, but this deficiency cannot be the explanation for their excessive drinking if it is even more characteristic of abstainers and moderate drinkers on the Bowery. (Bahr and Caplow 1974, p. 256)

The point, that skid-row life is more tolerable if the individual participates in its major social activity, is often taken to imply 'escape' from poverty and degradation through intoxication. There are, however, positive benefits to be derived from participation in skid-row drinking, including a degree of sociability and support unavailable to the abstainer (Bahr and Caplow 1974; Peterson and Maxwell 1958; Rubington 1958). This incentive encourages the adaptation of individual drinking behaviour to the predominant pattern of the drinking group (Rubington 1958; Wallace 1965). Filtering information through the theoretical lens of undersocialisation may encourage its attribution to behaviour which is in reality a product of this 'social organisation of deviance' (Best and Luckenbill 1982). Four examples of such misinterpretation demonstrate this point:

(a) Skid-row drinking patterns are shaped by the tension between chronic poverty and the desire to maintain drinking (Archard 1979). Loose drinking groups are formed for the procurement and consumption of alcohol, avoiding police interference (Archard 1979; Cook 1975; Peterson and Maxwell 1958; Rubington 1958). Such transient relationships, driven by economic and situational necessity, may appear to reflect inability to sustain social ties.

(b) Skid-row men have neither the financial resources nor the opportunities to make long-term plans or provisions. Feeding, clothing, drinking and shelter are day-to-day activities, funded by the small financial and material resources available from casual work, state and charitable welfare, small-scale theft and begging (Archard 1979; Cook 1975; Healy 1988; Peterson and Maxwell 1958; Phillimore 1979; Wiseman 1970). Analyses of these activities, however, show each to require a degree of enterprise, persistence and skill which is masked by the superficial appearance of passive receipt of hand-outs.

(c) The suppression of serious offending among chronic heavy drinkers may appear as the result of incompetence exacerbated by physical and mental deterioration (e.g. Pittman and Gordon

1958). However, opportunities for large-scale or organised crime are simply absent in the environments and social groupings within which skid-row men move (Archard 1979; Pernanen 1982; Wiseman 1970).

(d) Failure to remain in treatment facilities may appear to the providers as evidence of inadequacy and lack of commitment to rehabilitation (Archard 1979). However, skid-row men appear to employ a different definition of treatment resources as, for the most part, a means of maintaining their lifestyle, rather than changing it. Such facilities provide short-term detoxification, shelter, food and escape from police surveillance to restore the physical and psychological stamina required by the rigours of skid-row life (Archard 1979; Healy 1988; Wiseman 1970).

SITUATIONAL THEORIES

Overview

Situational perspectives recognise that criminal activity requires 'the confluence in time and space of the target and offender in the absence of effective deterrents' (Gottfredson 1984, p. 3). Thus, they are primarily concerned with the analysis of specific drinking and criminal events, examining the contributions of situational factors to the production of crime: the human (Garofalo 1987; Gottfredson 1984; Hough and Mayhew 1983, 1985; Lejeune and Alex 1973) and physical (Bennett and Wright 1984a; Maguire 1982; Mayhew, Clarke, Sturman and Hough 1976) targets of crime; and the development of criminal opportunities (Bennett and Wright 1984a; Clarke 1980; Clarke and Cornish 1985; Hope 1985).

Drinking behaviour is heavily influenced by situational factors. For example, it varies according to the public or private nature of the drinking context (Harford 1979, 1983; Marsh, Dobbs and White 1986), presence and number of drinking companions (Harford 1983; McCarty 1985), models for drinking behaviour (McCarty 1985; Nusbaumer, Mauss and Pearson 1982; Zucker 1979) and gender of drinking companions (Harford 1983; Wilsnack and Wilsnack 1979). Harford (1983) suggests that different factors such as drinking context and type of drinking companion interact in complex ways to modify drinking behaviour. Nusbaumer, Mauss and Pearson (1982), however, argue that the detailed attention to social situational factors neglects the special reinforcements for heavy drinking provided in the design and management of public licensed premises.

Bennett and Wright (1984a), by contrast, argue that situational research in criminology has concentrated narrowly on immediate factors in the physical environment, to the neglect of relevant social situational factors such as the presence and behaviour of peers. Similarly, Hope (1985) argues that an analysis of city-centre disorder should include a broad examination of situational and socio-cultural factors concerning the leisure preferences of those who congregate in city centres, physical factors concerning the design of city centres and drinking places, and issues in the management of licensed premises.

Such arguments encourage a theoretical perspective in which alcohol itself may be viewed as a situational factor, defining the context of social interaction (e.g. pub), its nature (e.g. leisure) and the range of anticipated behaviour (e.g. disinhibited) (Cavan 1966; Gusfield 1987). Both alcohol (Barrett 1985; Harford 1979; McCarty 1985; Sadava 1987) and crime (Campbell 1986; Clarke and Cornish 1985; Cornish and Clarke 1986; Forgas 1986; Pervin 1986; Toch 1986) theorists argue that individual perception and cognition are crucial to the explanation of the influence of situational factors on behaviour. Thus, situational analyses of crime must be highly crime specific in order to identify important aspects of decision making (Cornish and Clarke 1986).

The pursuit of research into broad categories of crime such as assault obscures fine differences between sub-categories of offences under that heading. Situational analyses of violent interactions (e.g. Felson and Steadman 1983; Luckenbill 1977) are primarily accounts of escalating mutual aggression between males, often arising in a public drinking setting. Examining domestic violence, Dobash and Dobash (1984) found that during an attack female victims repeatedly attempted to *appease*, rather than to incite, a male aggressor. They suggest that this signifies a crucial distinction between domestic assaults and public violence between males and that the intention to attack is formed by the aggressor prior to the interaction itself, rather than emerging within it. Any role played by alcohol in a premeditated assault must differ, at least in the initial stages, from that implied when violence is an unplanned outcome of a situationally inspired aggressive interchange.

Situational perspectives thus usefully present alcohol as a contributor in conventional decision-making processes, rather than attributing qualitative alterations in rationality to its effects. They aid an understanding of the variability of individual behaviour in different situations. Paradoxically, however, analyses of intoxicated crime tend to imply the inevitability of criminal, in particular violent, outcomes of drinking episodes in provocative situations.

Symbolic Interaction

Symbolic interaction has provided a major theoretical contribution to the analysis of criminal events, particularly violence, on which much of its attention has focused (Felson and Steadman 1983), and which has particular attractions for theories of intoxicated crime. The theory stresses the importance of the establishment, management and pre-servation of self-image in social interaction (Felson and Steadman 1983). Thus, it has an affinity with lay explanations of violence as the result of 'macho posturing', 'refusal to climb down', and 'face saving'.

Luckenbill's (1977) study of 'situated transactions' resulting in homicide illustrates this genre of research and theoretical analysis. Creating detailed reconstructions of incidents of criminal homicide from content analysis of the official documentation in each case, Luckenbill concluded:

> Transactions resulting in murder involved the joint contribution of the offender and victim to the escalation of a 'character contest', a confrontation in which at least one, but usually both, attempt to establish or save face at the other's expense by standing steady in the face of adversity. (1977, p. 177)

Luckenbill's study illustrates an earlier point: that a research focus on the sequence of events and decisions prior to an offence obviates the necessity of invoking alcohol as a contributory causal factor. Indeed, Luckenbill asserts that the analysis is generally applicable to hom-icidal assaults irrespective of alcohol involvement. Other research, however, has established alcohol involvement as one of only two factors which reliably distinguish fatal from non-fatal assaults, the other being the presence of a weapon (Pittman and Handy 1964). Indeed, this is the only substantive difference between alcohol-related and sober crime to emerge during an extensive literature search. The discrepancy therefore seems important.

One possible explanation is methodological. Despite the advantages of crime specificity, exclusive concentration on homicide might itself obscure vital differences between fatal and non-fatal assaults (Bank-ston 1988). Had Luckenbill's study included non-fatal assaults, alcohol involvement might have emerged as a distinctive factor in homicide. Certainly, alcohol is a prevalent situational feature in Luckenbill's account. Thus, Luckenbill's analysis may embrace the significance of alcohol without explicitly identifying it. For example, a fatal outcome might be attributed to alcohol's disinhibiting or aggression arousing effects, resulting in greater attacking force by an intoxicated aggressor, or greater resistance in an intoxicated victim. Such an explanation would also usefully account for Luckenbill's failure to identify a decision to use lethal force, but only a 'working agreement' between participants to use violence itself.

However, an appeal at this stage to alcohol's assumed effects is premature. Felson and Steadman (1983) found that although both victim aggression and victim intoxication were related to the severity of a violent assault, these two factors were themselves unrelated. This finding contradicts the prediction that resistance will be greater among intoxicated victims through disinhibition or aggression arousal. Further, if alcohol fails to intensify victim aggression, by implication it may equally fail to intensify assailants' attacks.

Alternative explanations may be suggested for Luckenbill's failure to identify a decision to use lethal force. One possibility is again methodological. Possibly Luckenbill's data was drawn predominantly from homicides in which fatality was indeed an unpremeditated, even unforeseen outcome of a violent incident. Alternatively, a clue might lie in Luckenbill's observation that the homicides were characterised by prior 'rehearsals', in which aggressive interactions involving the participants had occurred. The failure of previous strategies to prevent a recurrence of aggression might prompt assailants to use greater, if not explicitly lethal, force on the fatal occasion. The availability of such alternative explanations demonstrates that the stage has not yet been reached when only an appeal to alcohol's effects can explain a fatal outcome.

Symbolic-interactionist accounts which attempt to include detailed analysis of alcohol's effects encounter difficulties deriving, paradoxically, from the complementary attractiveness of some of alcohol's effects to the theoretical perspective itself. Such attraction may encourage theorists to stress these effects disproportionately to their demonstrated impact on behaviour. Thus, symbolic interactionists have stressed particular pharmacological effects of alcohol on perception and cognition, such as field dependency and subjective feelings of power and control (Campbell 1986; Cordilia 1986; Gibbs 1986). Gibbs (1986) has developed a sophisticated model of the contribution of these effects to the development of bar-room violence, drawing on earlier work by Pernanen (1976, 1982). The theoretical attractiveness of such effects stems from their conceptual affinity with key symbolic-interactionist concepts of role-taking, situational identity, and defence of self-image. These perceptual and cognitive changes are seen to enhance the subjective importance of immediate self-presentational roles, assumptions of mastery over people and events, and situational cues to aggression, whilst simultaneously impoverishing the sophistication and range of the behavioural repertoire.

However, Pernanen (1982) cautions that these effects have been found in experimental studies of the effects of comparatively low doses of alcohol on behaviour such as competitiveness in card games. Theoretical extrapolation to violence under conditions of heavy intoxication relies on two assumptions: that perceptual and cognitive changes occur incrementally with dosage; and that competitiveness and violence are part of the same behavioural repertoire. Empirical support for these assumptions is unavailable (Pernanen 1982). The distortion of empirical evidence, encouraged by its affinity with a theoretical perspective, results in analyses which imply that aggression, escalating into violence, is a virtually inevitable outcome of increasing intoxication. For example:

> [V]iolence is the product of certain kinds of interpersonal interactions, and alcohol affects perception and cognition in ways that make the occurrence of these kinds of interactions more likely. The bar is the context within which these interactions occur, and it features environmental qualities that can shape both drinking and the expression of aggression. (Gibbs 1986, p. 137)

But '[a]lcohol-related violence is rare in relation to the number of man-hours devoted to drinking' (Evans 1986, p. 146; also Blum 1982; Smith and Burvill 1987). Bankston (1988), criticising this weakness in interactional analysis, recommends a form of control theory, situationally applied, as a more useful theoretical framework. Control theory, by focusing on the erosion of constraints on violence in aggressive situations, would alert the analyst to features of alcohol use situations affecting the release of conventionally inhibited behaviour, such as heightened interaction, crowding, physical design, drinking companions, drinking styles, bystanders and pub management (Cavan 1966; Harford 1979, 1983; Harford, Wechsler and Rothman 1983; Hope 1985; McCarty 1985; Marsh and Campbell 1979; Pernanen 1982; Zinberg 1984). Once again, there is a beguiling affinity between this theoretical frame and concepts of disinhibition and aggression arousal, so that alcohol might be seen to contribute directly to the weakening of behavioural controls.

At this point, however, the conceptual distinction between 'escalatory' and 'erosive' situational factors becomes difficult to sustain in practice, since both the pertinent situational variables and the behavioural outcome are the same in both cases. Furthermore, this approach offers no clearer identification of the (literally) 'decisive' element in the use of force, again implying inevitability through the progressive erosion of controls. Thus, other situational approaches have problems in explaining intoxicated crime in common with symbolic interaction.

Theoretical approaches such as these risk invoking alcohol as an all-purpose explanatory tool. For example, Gibbs (1986) claims that alcohol may explain *both* variation *and* consistency in individual responses to different situations. Cordilia (1986) suggests that alcohol 'magnifies' the significance of situational cues, enhancing individual responses. Such appeals to alcohol's effects explain everything and nothing. In attempting to retain sufficient flexibility to acknowledge the indeterminateness of behaviour in alcohol use situations, theoretical statements about alcohol's effects may become so general that they explain little or no more about behaviour than theories of sober crime.

SUBSTANCE-FOCUSED THEORIES

Overview

Substance-focused theory and research primarily concerns the identification of changes in mood and behaviour directly attributable to the pharmacological effects of alcohol. It has already been seen that dispositional and situational theories of alcohol-related crime often appeal to these assumed effects.

Substance-focused research emphasises methods such as clinical observation and testing, measurement of physiological responses of light, heavy and non-drinkers to varied alcohol doses, and behavioural observation and subjective self-reports under the same conditions. A major tool in such experimental research has been the balanced placebo design methodology, in which subjects' beliefs about whether or not they have consumed alcohol are manipulated independently of the actual administration of alcohol or placebo doses. Substance-focused theories relate experimental findings to 'real world' conditions, by drawing on the contributions of ethnographic observations of drinking behaviour in natural environments.

Substance-focused research has pursued the precise specification of conditions in which particular mood and behavioural changes will result from alcohol ingestion. However, it has been impossible to identify specific effects of alcohol on the brain and central nervous system which induce responses with potentially straightforward links to criminal behaviour, such as aggression (Brain 1986; Evans 1986). Others, such as sexual responsiveness, appear in fact to be suppressed (Coid 1986a). Alcohol's physiological effects appear to be generalised and indeterminate as to behavioural consequences (Pernanen 1982). Ironically, this genre of research has convincingly demonstrated the significance of non-pharmacological factors in intoxicated behaviour, and in particular the role of 'expectancies', or subjective beliefs about the effects of alcohol.

The central concept underpinning substance-focused explanations of the alcohol–crime relationship is 'loss of control'. Unlike dispositional theories, which postulate low self-control as an individual characteristic, substance-focused theories suggest that episodic loss of control is itself induced by alcohol's pharmacological effects. Lay theory encapsulates this notion in the observation that some individuals 'can't hold their drink'. This key concept underpins the relevance of substance-focused theories both to drinking and criminal careers, through a concern with chronic inebriation, and to drinking and criminal events, through a concern with acute intoxication. Thus, the loss of control assumption pervades substance-focused conceptualisations of alcoholism and disinhibition.

1. Chronic Inebriation: Alcoholism

The loss of control concept in theories of alcoholism implies that chronic inebriation destroys the ability to regulate drinking itself voluntarily. Its significance in theories of alcohol-related crime is largely connotative: by implication, control over other behaviour is also lost (e.g. Kessel and Walton 1989), or 'desperate' crime results from the need to continue drinking (e.g. Cameron 1964).

Disease theory (Jellinek 1960) hypothesises: that chronic inebriation damages cell tissues so that alcohol's presence in the bloodstream triggers involuntary drinking; that alcoholics perpetuate drinking in order to avoid the discomfort of withdrawal; and that this loss of control over drinking is permanent. These hypotheses have been disconfirmed by clinical and observational research. Initial alcohol consumption does not trigger involuntary drinking in alcoholics (Mendelson and Mello 1979; Wilson 1987); alcoholics may tolerate self-imposed withdrawal (Archard 1979; Fingarette 1988; Healy 1988; Mendelson and Mello 1979); and alcoholics may resume non-problematic drinking (Armor 1980; Polich 1980). The extent of drinking by alcoholics following detoxification is influenced by their social circumstances, such as marital status (Armor 1980), and the degree of tolerance of drinking in their environment, as, for example, in 'dry' or 'wet' hostels (Cook 1975; Rubington 1958).

Ethnographic studies reveal alcoholic drinking to be a controlled activity. In skid-row drinking groups, the 'runner' does not consume the bottle instead of returning to the group. Consumption itself is moderated by sipping, passing on, pauses and conversation (Archard 1979; Peterson and Maxwell 1958; Rubington 1958). Crude spirit consumption is an intermittent response to economic necessity and does not cause continuous reliance on the practice (Archard 1979; Cook 1975; Peterson and Maxwell 1958). The novice must practise consuming it slowly, in small sips, made palatable with orange juice (Archard 1979; Cook 1975).

Such evidence of voluntary self-regulation has presented academic alcohol theory with the problem of explaining why alcoholics continue or resume heavy drinking in the face of the obviously disastrous consequences. Sober alcoholics frequently describe drinking as pleasurable (Mendelson and Mello 1979). However, simple enjoyment is an inadequate explanation, since despite their affirmations, direct observation of intoxicated alcoholics reveals progressive dysphoria, anxiety, agitation and irritability (Barrett 1985; Mendelson and Mello 1979). This discrepancy cannot be explained by the deleterious effects of alcoholism on memory, rendering alcoholics incapable of recalling their aversive experiences (Mendelson and Mello 1979; Wilson 1987). Notwithstanding the self-serving selectivity of such memory impairment, sober alcoholics do nevertheless recognise the long-term damaging consequences of their drinking (Wilson 1987).

Cox (1987) suggests that changes in the affective consequences of intoxication during alcoholic drinking careers produce concomitant changes in the motivation for drinking: alcoholics drink to offset negative affect. But drinking is a manifestly unsuccessful strategy for accomplishing this. Such reasoning begins to suggest that alcoholic drinking is irrational behaviour caused by alcohol's ruinous effects on the alcoholic's ability to assess his own internal emotional states. Mendelson and Mello (1979), concluding that the explanation for persistent alcoholic drinking is as yet unknown, suggest that common-sense assumptions about what constitutes a 'positive' or 'aversive' experience may require radical reappraisal.

These problems lead to a temptation to resort to the loss-of-control assumption, which pervades some academic expositions, despite attempts to retain notions of rationality and self-direction. For example, Ludwig (1988) argues that alcoholics simply refuse to believe that they will never be able to resume drinking without suffering aversive consequences. Notwithstanding a measure of clinical evidence, already noted, to support this alcoholic obstinacy, Ludwig's explanation of the phenomenon is itself infused with the loss-of-control assumption.

> [T]he attractive but controversial hypothesis of state dependent learning is probably overly simplistic, ignoring such alternative explanations as the disinhibiting effects of alcohol on the frontal cortex of the brain (which could explain why conscience has wryly been defined as 'a substance readily dissolvable in alcohol'), the influence of different discriminative stimuli as determinants of specific behaviors, and the ability of alcohol to unleash a whole array of conditioned responses. Whatever the true explanation, the problem remains clear. Virtually all psychotherapeutic approaches eventually falter once alcohol begins circulating in the brain, unlocking a highly predictable repertoire of the attitudes and behaviors associated with drinking. (Ludwig 1988, p. 61)

Much of the controversy about alcoholic loss of control has centred on the concept of 'craving'. Jellinek (1960) postulated irresistible craving as a defining characteristic of alcoholism. Other theorists object that the concept of craving is meaningless: if craving is irresistible, then it is defined simply by drinking; if it is not, it merely states the known fact that alcoholic drinking behaviour is variable (Fingarette 1988; Mendelson and Mello 1979).

This sterile academic dispute revolves around the question whether internal states can be said to exist if there is no behavioural evidence for them. Common sense, however, suggests, by introspection, that people frequently experience desires which they refrain from indulging. Ludwig's (1988) graphic biographical accounts of craving experiences describe situations with which drinking is commonly associated, and in which the desire to drink therefore is generally regarded as unremarkable: whilst pondering an acute dilemma, watching sport on television, staying in a hotel, finishing a game of golf and flying. Arguably, the difference for the alcoholic derives from a conflict of interests: he simultaneously wants to drink, anticipating immediate pleasure, and also to abstain, anticipating longer-term misery. Cornish offers a similar explanation of compulsive feelings associated with gambling.

> If there is little evidence that the gambler is forced into ever more intense involvement by the compelling nature of the reinforcement itself, the subjective feelings of pressure or compulsion undoubtedly experienced by some heavy gamblers can still be given an alternative explanation. Where people have begun to gamble at an early age, for example, such feelings are particularly likely to arise as rival sources of reinforcement (wife, or family) begin to make their appearance in the gambler's life. At this stage, and not before, the gambler would become aware of conflicts of interest such as those between the earlier and smaller reinforcements provided by gambling and those larger and later ones provided by people and events outside the gambling situation. These conflicts might be responsible for belated attempts at 'impulse-control'...and the subjective feelings of 'loss of control' frequently reported as symptomatic of the 'compulsive' gambler...(Cornish 1978, p. 208)

Despite experiences of aversive consequences, motivations for drinking persist, partly, at least, due to their very mundanity. They may become conditioned by association with particular situations (Barrett 1985; Fingarette 1988; Ludwig 1988; also Kaplan 1983 on drug use). Once motivated to drink, the alcoholic must choose which action – drinking or abstinence – will achieve greater satisfaction. This choice is not so starkly obvious as the evidence of aversive intoxication experiences and long-term damage suggests that it should be. For example, confidence in successful abstinence and the perception of relative gain from abstinence over drinking may be crucial factors in the decision (Orford 1980; also Sutton 1978 on smoking). Barrett also points out that evidence of the ultimately aversive consequences of alcoholic intoxication obscures the simple fact that

> people continue to use psychoactive drugs not because they neces- sarily 'feel good' or 'euphoric' but only that they 'feel' *better* soon

after taking the drug than they did immediately before. (Barrett 1985, p. 133)

It is unnecessary to 'feel better' on every drinking occasion. Intermittent success is sufficient to maintain an established habit (Cox 1985; Ludwig 1988; also Cornish 1978 on gambling). Further, alcoholics do not generally experience strong rewards for abstinence. The comparative sociability of the alcoholic over the abstinent skid-row lifestyle (Bahr and Caplow 1974) has already been noted. Polich (1980) found that, four years after treatment, abstainers and non-problem drinkers fell substantially below general population norms on measures of social adjustment such as employment, personal satisfaction and psychiatric symptoms, even though they fared better than continuing heavy drinkers.

Social rehabilitation, then, was not a common outcome even for those who were in remission at the four year follow-up. (Polich 1980, p. 105)

For the alcoholic, then, sobriety may be, if not an aversive state, then not a particularly positive one either. Once this is recognised, the alcoholic's decision to drink appears similar to any other mundane choice: a subjective balance of the perceived costs, risks and benefits of the different options within the actor's environment (Fingarette 1988; Ludwig 1988; Sutton 1978; Wilson 1987). Fingarette makes a point similar to one raised by the earlier review of offenders' theories of intoxicated crime: that it is a mistake to compare alcoholics' decisions to a standard of rationality to which sober decision makers do not generally conform.

The general truth is this: Human beings do not always respond wisely and with foresight; we often drift, unwitting, into a tangled web of decisions, expectations, habits, tastes, fears, and dreams. The chronic heavy drinker is no exception – no more mysterious, no less vulnerable. For the person challenged by personal problems, heavy drinking is one of the culturally available responses, however imprudent and self-destructive. (Fingarette 1988, p. 103)

2. Acute Intoxication: Disinhibition

Like undersocialisation, 'disinhibition' is not a unitary concept, but has been applied to a range of suppositions about alcohol's destabilising effects on moral self-control (Lang 1981). These include disruption of higher-order mental processes, triggering of aggression, arousal of sexual responsiveness and reduction of anxiety (Adesso 1985; Lang 1981). Academic theories of disinhibition, therefore, have obvious connotative links with lay notions such as 'Dutch courage'. Indeed, the fact that it is not easy to trace authoritative academic origins for such hypotheses, despite the considerable effort that has gone into testing them, suggests that they may be derived directly from lay notions.

The results of research into alcohol's disinhibiting effects have been comprehensively reviewed (e.g. Adesso 1985; Brain 1986; Cappell and Greeley 1987; Coid 1986a, 1986b; Evans 1986; Lang 1981; Macandrew and Edgerton 1969; Woods and Mansfield 1981). They repeatedly show that intoxication does not inevitably lead to disinhibited behaviour, is not culturally uniform in its behavioural consequences, does not trigger aggression, does not enhance sexual responsiveness and does not uniformly reduce anxiety. Furthermore, subjects' self-reports of mood changes after alcohol consumption frequently conflict with the evidence of physiological measurements.

Thus, in relation to alcohol's tension-reducing capacity, for example, Cappell and Greeley observe 'a huge gap between the apparent faith in the (tension reduction theory) and the quality of the evidence to support it' (1987, p. 44). Instead, 'there have been numerous observations of how complex are the relationships determining alcohol's credentials as an anxiolytic agent' (p. 44). Cappell and Greeley identify two points of key relevance to alcohol–crime theory. Firstly, subjects vary considerably in their experience of tension reduction, according to factors such as gender, dose, the nature of the anxiety-provoking stimulus and their customary drinking patterns. Secondly, mood enhancement is demonstrated only at low alcohol doses, with increases in anxiety and tension at higher doses. Alcohol–crime theory, however, has generally assumed that alcohol's effects are uniform and incremental.

A third issue appears more immediately compatible with alcohol–crime theory. Conflict situations appear particularly successful in eliciting tension reduction after alcohol consumption (Cappell and Greeley 1987). Contemplation of an offence appears to arouse conflicting feelings, as offenders weigh the anticipated gain against uncontrollable hazards (Carroll and Weaver 1986; Walsh 1986). Intoxication is one strategy employed by offenders for coping with such conflict (Walsh 1986). Nevertheless, it is unclear what in the nature of conflict makes it amenable to alcohol's tension-reducing effects, or in what circumstances intoxication will be preferred to other anxiety-reducing strategies (Cappell and Greeley 1987; Sher 1987). Volpicelli (1987), however, argues that tension-reduction theory is fundamentally misguided in assuming that alcohol consumption precedes anxiety reduction, claiming that the evidence suggests that tension reduction itself elicits alcohol consumption. This interpretation would complement the frequent observation that offenders rapidly spend the proceeds of crime on alcohol (Bennett and Wright 1984a; Maguire 1982; Walsh 1986). Here, however, alcohol–crime theory based on disinhibition through tension reduction encounters the problems of continuing disagreement among alcohol theorists about the correct interpretation of the research evidence, and selection between attractive but opposing alternatives.

Pernanen sees two alternatives for theory building. Theory may assume that 'given a detailed enough specification of "external" predisposing and situational determinants, a satisfactory explanation can be given by a listing of these and a specification of their internal relationships' (Pernanen 1982, p. 27). Alternatively, explanations may be developed which are explicitly premised 'on the perceiving/cognizing individual and his/her structuring of the situation' (Pernanen 1982, p. 27). The research reviewed above appears to have been primarily guided by the former principle, although the direct applicability of such precisely specified relationships to 'messy, real-world decisions' (Abelson 1976) in which individual and situational factors are themselves highly variable, complex and fluid, seems questionable. Its results might more usefully be regarded as helping to define the crucial variables, and their inter-relationships, whilst constructing explanations of the latter type.

Paradoxically, the intensive efforts to specify precise relationships between alcohol's pharmacological effects and mood and behavioural changes have provided clear evidence of the crucial importance of cognition in the production of these changes. The balanced placebo design methodology, in which subjects' beliefs that they have consumed alcohol are manipulated independently of the administration of alcohol or placebo doses, has demonstrated that responses depend heavily on the belief in, rather than the fact of, alcohol ingestion. These 'expectancy' effects, or the influence of subjective beliefs about alcohol's effects, have emerged in studies of tension reduction (Cappell and Greeley 1987), aggression (Evans 1986; Goldman, Brown and Christiansen 1987), sexual responsiveness (Coid 1986a; Goldman, Brown and Christiansen 1987), mild forms of disinhibition such as laughter and sociability (Lang 1981) and alcoholic craving (Fingarette 1988; Goldman, Brown and Christiansen 1987; Marlatt, Demming and Reid 1973).

Expectancy effects have considerable implications for alcohol–crime theory. For example, as seen earlier, intoxicated aggressiveness has been attributed to perceptual and cognitive impoverishment. However, since expectancy effects occur independently of alcohol's presence, individuals who do not believe that they have consumed alcohol may remain apparently immune to the implied psychological consequences of their deteriorating information-processing capacity (Lang 1981).

Expectancy theory has particular advantages for the different theoretical approaches reviewed in this chapter. Firstly, the variability of intoxicated behaviour may be explained by postulating expectancies, themselves modified by dose, setting and individual differences, as mediating factors between consumption and response (Goldman, Brown and Christiansen 1987). Secondly, learned expectancies may explain the links between prior life experiences and later alcohol-related behaviour (Adesso 1985; Douglas 1987; Goldman, Brown and Christiansen 1987; Greeley, McCready and Theisen 1980; Heath 1981). Thirdly, the significance of situational factors for alcohol-related behaviour may derive from learned associations, or expectancies (Adesso 1985; Goldman, Brown and Christiansen 1987; Ludwig 1988).

CONCLUSION

Academic theories of intoxicated crime, at their heart, contain appeals to lay theories just as do those of offenders. Their reliance upon appeals to assumed pharmacological effects of alcohol has been exposed repeatedly in this review. Moreover, they tend towards deterministic analyses of the alcohol–crime relationship which are not justified by the fruits of empirical research. This is not to say that these endeavours have no virtue.

Dispositional perspectives offer clues to the significance of life experiences through their impact on individual exposure to cultural, social, familial and situational traditions of alcohol use. Personality factors may be thought to influence individual motivations to use alcohol in particular ways, either habitually, as the establishment of a drinking style or pattern, or situationally, as a response to specific events. Situational perspectives highlight the importance of alcohol itself as a situational factor, defining the social qualities of particular drinking occasions. Indeed, these perspectives enrich contemporary theoretical interest in the situational aspects of crime, through their illumination of features of common criminal events.

The major contribution of substance-focused theory and research to alcohol–crime theory has been its demonstration of the importance of cognition in mediating mood and behavioural changes consequent on alcohol consumption. Theory and research concerning alcohol expectancies may have considerable implications for the development of theories of intoxicated crime. The inclusion of expectancy theory would shift the theoretical focus to the effects which the individual is *motivated to achieve* in the situation in which drinking takes place, his *belief* in alcohol's ability to produce those effects, and how he learns to *interpret* alcohol's generalised pharmacological effects as specific changes in mood, facilitating desired, but prohibited behaviour. Such a shift in theoretical emphasis would support the confident attribution of criminal responsibility, by implying the motivated use of alcohol in the commission of crime.

3 Techniques of Neutralisation: the Appeal to Alcohol

Is it possible to develop an explanation of alcohol-related crime which avoids the excessive determinism of existing approaches, while preserving their insights? In this chapter, a theoretical framework will be suggested and explored which draws on the promising notion of the 'alcohol expectancies' in order to show how offenders may invoke commonsense beliefs about intoxication to facilitate and legitimate their behaviour. Beginning with an examination of expectancy theory itself, the analysis moves on to explore its application to the neutralisation and rationalisation of offensive conduct.

THE ALCOHOL EXPECTANCIES

In their exposition of alcohol expectancy theory, Goldman, Brown and Christiansen explain the term 'expectancy' in the following way:

> The term expectancy, rather than attitude or belief, is usually invoked when the author refers to the anticipation of a systematic relationship between events or objects in some upcoming situation. The relationship is understood to be of an if–then variety; *if* a certain event or object is registered *then* a certain event is expected to follow... (1987, p. 183)

The alcohol expectancies are a specific variety of such cognitions about causative relationships (Goldman, Brown and Christiansen 1987). They define a range of moods and behaviours which are susceptible to change through intoxication. Thus, they enable individuals to anticipate and interpret the effects of alcohol on their own and others' behaviour. Importantly, alcohol expectancies are *common*, rather than idiosyncratic beliefs (Brown, Goldman, Inn and Anderson 1980; Goldman, Brown and Christiansen 1987). They constitute a body of common or lay knowlege about alcohol, and, as such, they provide a set of premises for social judgements about intoxicated behaviour and personal responsibility under intoxication.

Reviewing research, Goldman, Brown and Christiansen (1987) found considerable agreement about the nature of alcohol expectancies. For example, Brown, Goldman, Inn and Anderson (1980) identified six different alcohol expectancies which were shared by adults with drinking histories ranging from abstinence to alcoholism: that alcohol positively transforms experiences, enhances social and physical pleasure, enhances sexual performance and experience, increases power and aggression, increases social assertiveness and reduces tension. However, the earlier review of substance-focused research has already exposed the factual inaccuracy of these alcohol expectancies.

Moreover, the alcohol expectancies identified by these researchers are mutually contradictory. For example, alcohol is apparently believed to enhance sociability, to arouse aggression *and* to reduce tension. Similarly, Christiansen and Goldman (1983) identified seven alcohol expectancies among adolescents, which embrace blatant contradictions: for example, the beliefs that alcohol both enhances and impedes social behaviour, both improves and disrupts cognitive and motor functioning, and both arouses and relaxes. Furthermore, individuals may hold different expectancies for the effects of alcohol on themselves from those which they hold for others (Goldman, Brown and Christiansen 1987).

Like many varieties of lay theory, the alcohol expectancies constitute 'common knowledge', but they do not necessarily reflect objective truth or reality (Furnham 1988). Yet it is to be noted that the alcohol expectancies identified above are entirely permissive. They do not insist that mood and behaviour on each drinking occasion will necessarily change in the ways which they postulate as possible effects of alcohol. Nor do they disqualify any sober moods and behaviours from manifesting themselves under intoxication. The alcohol expectancies, therefore, permit a wide range of moods and behaviours to be interpreted as the results of intoxication. They therefore will not be proven false by non-manifestation of specific behaviours in individual experience or observation of intoxication on particular occasions.

The apparent contradictions between different alcohol expectancies may arise, at least partly, from a tendency to think of alcohol's effects in terms of specific situations. Lay theories may be flexible belief systems, influenced by the perception of specific situations. Roizen (1981) reports survey data suggesting that people may hold general, and apparently contradictory, beliefs that alcohol causes feelings of aggression, romance, friendliness and sleepiness, but rarely claim that alcohol produces any one of those feelings on each drinking occasion.

> In this observation would seem a nice demonstration that alcohol is not linked to its various effects in lockstep fashion in popular opinion but is instead regarded very much as a matter of the particularities of the drinking event. That most of us might agree that alcohol may help us to be **friendly** does not, then imply about common opinion that alcohol always or even usually will have this effect. (Roizen 1981, p. 241)

Brown, Goldman, Inn and Anderson (1980) identified expectancies by measuring subjects' responses to statements such as 'Having a few drinks is a nice way to celebrate special occasions', 'After a few drinks it is easier to pick a fight' and 'Alcohol helps me sleep better'. In order to decide on their agreement or disagreement with such statements, individuals may bring to mind occasions when alcohol has been associated with such outcomes. Picking a fight tends to occur on different occasions and in different situations to falling asleep, although drinking may precede both events. Such situational specificity may enable people to disregard the inconsistency of their alcohol expectancies. In everyday life, commonsense wisdom enables us to manage varieties of concrete, real-world situations. We are rarely called upon to ponder the logical rigour and internal consistency of our everyday belief systems. These points illustrate the theoretical utility of regarding alcohol as a situational variable, identified in Chapter 2.

The theoretical framework which is developed here has at its centre the notion that it is these expectancies, rather than a set of objective truths, which offer the key to understanding the alcohol–crime relationship. Yet, if they do not necessarily reflect objective truths about the effects of alcohol, where do the alcohol expectancies come from? The significance of cultural and social learning in the transmission of beliefs about and attitudes to alcohol has been stressed in much academic alcohol theory and research (Adesso 1985; Douglas 1987; Galizio and Maisto 1985; Goldman, Brown and Christiansen 1987; Greeley, McCready and Theisen 1980; Gusfield 1987; Lang 1981; Pernanen 1982; Wilson 1987). Such theorists argue that a significant amount of learning about alcohol's apparent effects on behaviour occurs prior to direct experience of drinking. Whilst culture may provide a basic conceptual framework for anticipating and interpreting alcohol's effects on mood and behaviour, individual experience modifies these notions in particular ways. Individual experience includes both vicarious learning from the examples of others and direct experience of alcohol consumption. Of the former, Wilson asserts:

> Vicarious learning or modeling is a robust form of cognitive learning that is seminal in the development of social behavior, including drinking. Complex behavior patterns and attitudes are acquired through observation of social models without any reinforcement of overt behavior... (1987, p. 343)

Direct experience of alcohol consumption further increases the specificity of expectancies, leading, for example, to distinctions between expectancies for different dosages (Goldman Brown and Christiansen 1987; Wilson 1987) and drinking situations (Wilson 1987). Individual physiological differences (Goldman, Brown and Christiansen 1987; Wilson 1987) and differences in the personal values placed on the anticipated effects (Goldman, Brown and Christiansen 1987) may also contribute to this process of specific individual expectancy development. Thus, Goldman, Brown and Christiansen (1987) suggest that heavy-, light- and non-drinkers are not distinguished by qualitatively different alcohol expectancies, but by the differing strengths with which they hold common expectancies. As Adesso concludes:

> It does seem, then, that the two processes of social learning and experience with a drug contribute to the development of expectancies about the effects of a drug. This is precisely what social learning theory would predict: with increased experience one develops more specific expectancies from the generalized expectancies acquired through social learning processes. (1985, p. 183)

Goldman, Brown and Christiansen claim that 'expectancy patterns can successfully predict drinking behavior at all levels of the drinking continuum, from beginning drinking in adolescents through alcoholism' (1987, p. 207). This claim, which is supported by other reviewers of the research evidence (e.g. Adesso 1985; Wilson 1987), raises an immediate concern for the theoretical framework proposed here. Curiously, these theorists fail to remark upon the general inaccuracy and contradictoriness of alcohol expectancies, despite their confidence in the influence of those beliefs on behaviour. It appears that alcohol expectancy theory has, like other academic theories, moved towards a deterministic position, in which individual behaviour is seen to be as much governed by cognitive expectancies as it was earlier thought to be by alcohol's pharmacological effects. This deterministic position produces the apparent irrationality of fixed beliefs about alcohol's effects, because it fails to contextualise those beliefs in the cultural, situational and individual circumstances within which they develop, are maintained and invoked.

Alcohol expectancies do appear to be successful in the prediction of aspects of drinking careers. Goldman, Brown and Christiansen (1987) claim them to be more powerful predictors than the types of dispositional variable identified in Chapter 2. This is perhaps to be expected. The relevance of the research inspired by dispositional theoretical perspectives to the fuller understanding of expectancy development becomes apparent when considered in the light of the importance of social learning and experience. Individual life history and personality characteristics will themselves have a bearing on the exposure to, experience of, and development of beliefs and attitudes concerning alcohol. In this context, the greater predictive strength of the alcohol expectancies may reflect their status as a distillation of the influence of such factors on specific expectancy development.

However, alcohol expectancies do not determine behaviour in any specific drinking situation. Yet, since they are methodologically derived from batteries of statements which encourage situationally specific responses, they are closely tied to individuals' beliefs about the effects of alcohol in particular situations. It is now well accepted in psychological attitude theory and research that 'the more closely the measures of an attitude correspond to specific features of the situation in which a behavior will be performed, the better the predictability of the behavior' (Goldman, Brown and Christiansen 1987, p. 186).

The predictive power of alcohol expectancies might usefully be considered in the light of Pernanen's aforementioned 'perceiving/cognizing individual and his/her structuring of the situation' (1982, p. 27). In particular, theoretical development here will follow Barrett's advice that 'drug-taking behaviour is not reflexive. Rather, it is a goal-directed, purposeful, operant response' (1985, p. 127).

Such a theoretical position suggests that individuals are not passively driven by their alcohol expectancies, but acquire a sophisticated degree of control over alcohol's generalised effects to produce desired changes in mood and behaviour in particular situations. In this light, the predictive power of alcohol expectancies reflects the identification of situations in which particular beliefs about alcohol's effects become salient, and may be invoked to anticipate, interpret and legitimate changes in mood and behaviour associated with alcohol in those situations.

The remainder of this chapter considers the potentially purposeful exploitation by offenders of the alcohol expectancies, or lay theories about alcohol in the legitimation and explanation of intoxicated crime. This will be examined from two perspectives: pre-offence neutralisation and post-offence rationalisation. It is argued that the significance of lay theories about alcohol in the legitimation of criminal activity lies in the implications of these beliefs for judgements of personal responsibility.

It should be noted that the criminological literature is not entirely clear or consistent in distinguishing between 'neutralisation' and 'rationalisation'. However, since the following discussion examines different stages in the offending sequence, it is useful to distinguish clearly between them. The distinction indicated by Minor (1981) has been adopted. 'Neutralisation' refers to a personal rationale for legitimating a proposed course of criminal conduct. 'Rationalisation' refers to a personal rationale constructed by an offender for excusing himself for crime after its commission. Rationalisation is thus to be distinguished from 'mitigation', which here refers to a formal 'account' (Scott and Lyman 1968) of a criminal offence offered publicly, in order to reduce judgements by others of culpability and consequent punishment.

NEUTRALISATION

The role of alcohol in offence neutralisation will be considered from three perspectives: its pharmacological effects; its situational significance in moral decisions; and its invocation in techniques of neutralisation.

Pharmacological Effects

Goldman, Brown and Christiansen (1987) observe that the mechanisms which have often been postulated to explain the development of alcohol expectancies, such as classical conditioning, vicarious learning or causal attribution, do not themselves require any pharmacological effects. Expectancies are held to develop through the repeated association between alcohol consumption and particular behavioural consequences, whether or not alcohol directly produces that effect. However, this should not be taken to imply that the pharmacological effects of alcohol are superfluous to a full understanding of alcohol-related behaviour.

The failure of research to identify precise pharmacological mechanisms for the causation of intoxicated disinhibition was noted in the previous chapter. However, people do commonly believe that alcohol produces alterations in mood consistent with disinhibited behaviour (Goldman, Brown and Christiansen 1987; Roizen 1981), and use alcohol to facilitate these changes (Cavan 1966; Gusfield 1987; Lang 1981; Macandrew and Edgerton 1969). But whatever mood change an individual seeks or anticipates through intoxication, it seems unlikely that alcohol's pharmacological effects alone can be relied upon to achieve it. Alcohol's pharmacological effects are highly susceptible to individual variables such as age, gender and health (Bardo and Risner 1985; Barrett 1985; Blum 1982). Although the common belief that alcohol disrupts intellectual functioning is justified (Berglas 1987), the manner in which it does so is complex. The extent of interference with different cognitive and motor functions depends both on their complexity and specific sensitivity to disruption by alcohol and also the motivation and personality of the drinker (Blum 1982; Lang 1981; Woods and Mansfield 1981).

Evidence further suggests that mood changes consequent upon alcohol consumption are susceptible to situational influences. For example, solitary and group drinking lead to different affective changes (Blum 1982; Hartocollis 1962; McCarty 1985), alcoholic withdrawal experiences are related to the number of situational cues for drinking (McCarty 1985), and specific behaviour changes are more predictable in institutionalised settings involving unambiguous roles and authority (Blum 1982).

It appears that alcohol has a generalised effect on internal physiological arousal, but the specific emotional definition attributed to this experience by the drinker is guided by external cues (Blum 1982; Lang 1981; Marshall 1981; Zillman 1978). However, it is not suggested here that individuals merely respond passively to the combined experience of internal arousal and external cues. Individual motivation must also be considered in the interpretation of intoxicated mood changes. It is to be remembered that balanced placebo design experiments demonstrate the failure of subjects to respond to environmental cues for disinhibition when they do not believe that they have consumed alcohol, despite alcohol's direct effects on internal arousal. Pharmacologically induced arousal without awareness of alcohol consumption, therefore, does not cause a mood alteration despite the presence of salient situational cues (Lang 1981).

The experience of an emotion requires *both* arousal *and* an available explanation for it (Lang 1981; McCarty 1985). In drinking situations, individual arousal is potentially influenced by multiple situational factors of the kinds identified in Chapter Two, such as alcohol itself, peer group behaviour, crowding and physical design features. However, individuals may not identify all of these disparate sources of arousal, but 'collapse' them into a single emotional attribution, the experience of which may be enhanced as a result (McCarty 1985; Zillman 1978). McCarty explains:

> Individuals tend to combine undifferentiated physiological sensations. Consequently, all sensations are attributed to one specific salient stimulus rather than partialed out among the actual sources. The perceived strength of the salient stimulus is enhanced, and emotional behavioral reactions may be amplified as a result of the transfer of excitation. (1985, p. 271)

Reviewing experimental evidence that intoxicated individuals may attribute arousal *either* to drug ingestion *or* to situational stimuli, McCarty (1985) seems to imply that the 'misattribution' of arousal to external stimuli is a mistake. However, the attribution of arousal to a drug may itself be purposeful, in permitting individuals to ignore other, less convenient, sources of discomfiture.

Attitudinal research reveals a remarkable human talent for altering the perception of internal states of arousal so that they complement the emotional condition implied by behaviour (Brickman 1978; Dienstbier 1978; Eiser and Van Der Pligt 1988; Zanna and Cooper 1974). Individuals prefer to experience consistency between their internal emotional states and external behaviour, to the extent that they will redefine their internal states in order to produce such consistency where this is easier than altering behaviour. This perspective has been fundamental to theories of attitude formation and change (e.g. Festinger 1957). It was noted in Chapter 2 that alcohol appears to reduce tension in conflict situations. Perhaps alcohol consumption could facilitate the achievement of consistency between internal arousal and external behaviour in situations involving moral conflict.

For example, Dienstbier (1978) found that subjects, confronted with a moral dilemma over whether to cheat in a test, were more likely to cheat when they were able to attribute sensations such as heart acceleration and flushing to the side-effects of a pill. In

Dienstbier's experiments, the pill was a placebo, but the ability to attribute the physiological signs of conflict to its effects reduced the inhibitory influence of such arousal on moral infractions. Zanna and Cooper (1974) found that subjects required to write an essay expressing opinions contrary to their personal beliefs did not demonstrate the reduction of inconsistency through attitude change usually observed in such exercises, when they were able to attribute signs of tension to the effects of a pill. Again, the experience of conflict appeared to be reduced or negated when arousal could be attributed to drug ingestion.

It is unnecessary for individuals to be fully aware of this process of redefining emotional arousal; indeed they frequently appear to be unaware of it (Brickman 1978; Eiser and Van Der Pligt 1988; Fitzmaurice and Pease 1986; Zanna and Cooper 1974). Nevertheless, the 'appropriate' emotional definition of internal arousal may have to be learned by individuals engaging in a new behaviour (Brickman 1978), as in the case of novice drug users learning to experience disorientation as pleasurable (Best and Luckenbill 1982; Zinberg 1984).

Physiological arousal is often diffuse and non-specific (McCarty 1985). Dienstbier (1978) argues that certain emotions may be alike in their underlying physiological arousal, so that different emotional attributions may be made for similar arousal experiences. Again, this process may be purposeful. For example, fear may be eliminated if the arousal it engenders may be re-attributed to excitement (Dienstbier 1978).

Applying such an analysis to alcohol, it may be hypothesised that the drinker may be enabled to define the experience of arousal through intoxication as a specific mood change, facilitated by features of drinking situations. Moreover, such situations may facilitate an emotional attribution consistent with rule-breaking behaviour. It was noted in Chapter 2 that drinking and offending offer some common emotional rewards, such as excitement, camaraderie and status enhancement. Drinking situations thus facilitate the translation of arousal into definitions of mood which are also consistent with offending behaviour.

This analysis of the achievement of consistency between mood and offending behaviour does not require the prior intention to commit crime. It is a product of a coincidence of emotional rewards offered by two different activities. This may account in part for the apparent impulsivity of some intoxicated offending, such as that of youthful peer groups. Following intoxication, mood is already consistent with subsequent behaviour, as individuals seize opportunities for further excitement. Nevertheless, it is also possible that individuals intending to offend might exploit this coincidence of intoxicated and criminal moods, and drink purposefully to achieve 'Dutch courage' (Bennett and Wright 1984a, 1984b; Walsh 1986). For example, while drinking, a husband dwelling on his wife's faults, may experience sufficient 'aggression' to enable him subsequently to assault her. Such an analysis complements the aforementioned finding of Dobash and Dobash (1984) that the intention to attack is formed prior to the aggressive encounter between husband and wife.

Repeated experiences of an anxiety-provoking event reduces the degree of anxiety which it elicits (Volpicelli 1987). Thus, the importance of alcohol as a facilitator of mood and behaviour consistency may diminish as the offender acquires criminal experience. The two activities of drinking and subsequent offending may then, over time, simply become part of an established 'routine' (Bennett and Wright 1984a, 1984b), or 'scripted' activity (Forgas 1981, 1986). Nevertheless, once mastered, the technique of using alcohol for achieving mood and behaviour consistency may be invoked when required. The alcohol expectancy for the desired mood change having been learned and strengthened through experience, it is available for exploitation on subsequent occasions according to need.

Thus, intoxication provides a means of achieving consistency between emotional states and behaviour, which may facilitate moral infractions: firstly by enabling arousal to be attributed directly to alcohol rather than to moral conflict; and secondly by facilitating the re-attribution of arousal to emotions consistent with proscribed behaviour. The thrust of these arguments avoids the pitfalls of deterministic reasoning. For example, it would not be suggested here that an intoxicated individual would show greater sexual curiosity (Coid 1986a, 1986b; Goldman, Brown and Christiansen 1987; Lang, Searles, Lauerman and Adesso 1980) because his expectancy for sexual disinhibition *causes* him to lose his customary guilt. Rather, it would be suggested that the convenient re-attribution to intoxication of the arousal caused by conflict between sexual guilt and temptation permits him to show that curiosity which he is *motivated* to indulge.

Drinking Situations and Moral Decisions

The influence of situational factors on behaviour has already been identified. Situational features also guide moral interpretations of behaviour (Dienstbier 1978). People discriminate between situations in terms of the moral rules to be applied to them (Campbell, Bibel and Muncer 1985). The mere presence of alcohol in a situation endows it with a particular moral meaning in setting it apart from serious, non-leisure occasions (Gusfield 1987). Thus, events and behaviour acquire different moral significance according to whether they occur in drinking or sober situations.

Definitions of drinking situations, however, themselves vary widely (Roman 1982), including, for example, recreation, religious ceremony and business transactions. There is no singular emotional, spiritual or attitudinal state which can encompass the range of situations in which alcohol is present, or the moral expectations and judgements of behaviour within them. Indeed, in many drinking situations, particularly recreational ones in public places, there is considerable ambiguity as to the moral meaning of behaviour. Cavan remarks on the central contradiction inherent in interactions between strangers in public drinking places:

> As strangers, they should be treated with the reserve and restraint that drinking is at the same time expected to diminish. (1966, p. 43)

Cavan observes that such interactions are guided by a series of implicit norms and conventions which permit the simultaneous loosening of behavioural reserve and maintenance of social distance. Nevertheless, the constant ambiguity in these social relationships increases the unpredictability of interactions.

> Thus, while sociability is available to all in the public drinking place, there is little to guarantee that encounters between the unacquainted, once begun, will proceed in a neat and orderly fashion. Rather, from the onset their career is problematic, subject to a variety of contingencies that make them always tentative and often superficial. (Cavan 1966, p. 63)

Unpredictability is enhanced by the dislocation of public drinking situations from social roles which generally inform behaviour, such as parent, spouse, or employee (Campbell 1986; Cavan 1966). Public drinking situations commonly acquire the status of 'time out' (Macandrew and Edgerton 1969) from these customary roles and their constraints on behaviour. This situational dislocation from social roles protects the integrity of individuals' 'sober' identity (Campbell 1986; Cavan 1966; Gusfield 1987; Macandrew and Edgerton 1969). Furthermore, loose structures for conveying authority and prescribing social behaviour within the drinking situation itself (Blum 1982; Gusfield 1987; Hope 1985; Luckenbill 1977) create a precariousness in the establishment and maintenance of orderly conduct, particularly where actors are unfamiliar with each other (Felson, Baccaglini and Gmelch 1986).

The unpredictability of public recreational drinking situations has encouraged the development of strategies for bringing behaviour under control at numerous social levels: law and public policy (Gusfield 1987); social rituals and sanctions applied on drinking occasions (Zinberg 1984); integration between drinking places and community social life (Plant 1981); authority and rules invoked within drinking establishments for dispute settlement (Cavan 1966; Gibbs 1986); and the careful, rulebound conduct of interactions (Cavan 1966). However, this should not obscure the point that moral ambiguity, and its associated unpredictability and risks, are precisely those features of public drinking situations which are often valued, sought and created within them. A view of problematic behaviour in drinking situations, as merely a product of poor controls, requiring improvements in management and design, erroneously assumes that people unequivocally wish for the elimination of this moral ambiguity. However, the fun, excitement and enjoyable risks to be derived from the moral ambiguity of public recreational drinking situations are undoubtedly part of their attraction. 'Time out' behaviour is thus motivated behaviour, licensed by the presence of alcohol in the drinking situation (Cavan 1966; Macandrew and Edgerton 1969).

Indeed, overt attempts to control actual or threatened rule infractions appear to be a major, if not the main, immediate cause of the eruption of disorderly behaviour in public recreational drinking settings (Felson, Baccaglini and Gmelch 1986; Marsh and Campbell 1979; Pernanen 1982). Attempts at control, even in volatile situations, may therefore be made in a non-confrontational manner, avoiding explicit condemnation of the offending behaviour. Thus, Cavan remarks that 'activities handled in unequivocal terms in most settings may, in the public drinking place, be treated with a tact and finesse that seem unwarranted by their nature' (1966, p. 69).

In ambiguous situations such as these, alternative definitions for rule-breaking behaviour may be invoked which remove the potential moral opprobrium. In particular, behaviour may be defined as 'play' and 'having fun', and perpetrators may define themselves as 'pranksters' (Coid 1986b; Wade 1967). Thus, for example, behaviour which in a bus queue would be considered sexual assault, at a party is 'a bit of fun' (Coid 1986b). Such occasions also require others to respond to the behaviour in a manner appropriate to its situational moral definition. Thus, a 'victim' of unsolicited sexual approaches at a party who calls the police may be regarded as a 'spoilsport' (Coid 1986b). These situational moral definitions and expectations of behaviour are closely connected to the kinds of intent attributed to it. The attribution of, for example, intent to offend sexual privacy is itself dependent on the situational cues informing participants of the nature of the occasion and the kinds of behaviour, or 'scripts' (Abelson 1976; Forgas 1981, 1986), appropriate to it.

Drinking situations thus become situations of 'non-responsibility'. Within such situations, the dynamics of group behaviour may play a vital role in the transformation of 'time out', which merely implies permissiveness, into criminal activity. In situations of *collective* non-responsibility, the abdication of *individual* responsibility is a notable feature of group crimes such as rape (Coid 1986a; Wright and West 1981), vandalism (Wade 1967) and robbery (Cordilia 1986).

Thus, the presence of alcohol signifies a change in a situation's moral meaning, with implications for the kinds of behaviour which will be deemed appropriate and the kinds of intent which will be attributed to actors. The moral definition of drinking situations may be ambiguous, particularly in public recreational drinking settings. This moral ambiguity facilitates unpredictability, 'non-responsibility', the redefinition of offensive behaviour in non-pejorative terms and the development of group dynamics in which individual moral responsibility is abdicated.

Techniques of Neutralisation

It has now been seen that neutralisations of the moral offensiveness of behaviour are available through the diversity and ambiguity of drinking situations. Under what circumstances might an individual invoke alcohol itself as a neutralising technique? It will now be argued that the selective invocation of alcohol as a technique of neutralisation may be linked to a range of factors: its power to overcome moral objections to the offence; the individual's readiness to offend; his preference for the available offending opportunities; and his prior experience. These factors are mediated by the alcohol expectancies, or lay theories, about alcohol.

1. Overcoming Moral Objections

Neutralisation is only necessary in circumstances in which the individual has some moral objection to the deviant behaviour under consideration. The individual who experiences no guilt or moral ambivalence about engaging in a certain behaviour has no need of self-excusatory devices to overcome it (Minor 1980). Yet, theories which suggest that offenders are committed to deviant norms (e.g. Moran 1971) are repeatedly confronted by research evidence that offenders appear to subscribe to conventional moral standards (e.g. Ball-Rokeach 1973; Shover 1983). This implies that the majority of individuals contemplating an offence will experience a degree of conflict between their internal emotional state and the behaviour under consideration, and will be motivated to achieve consistency between them, either by avoiding the behaviour or by altering their emotional state to achieve compatibility with it.

In drinking situations, it may be unnecessary to invoke alcohol itself to achieve neutralisation. Other techniques may be available and preferable (e.g. Minor 1981; Sykes and Matza 1957). Three conditions have been suggested on which a neutralisation technique may depend for its success: it must be acceptable to its user (Agnew and Peters 1986); the user must perceive the situation to be one in which it is applicable (Agnew and Peters 1986); and there must be time to generate it (Minor 1981). Alcohol has particular attractions for meeting such conditions. Firstly, common cultural beliefs about its effects on rationality, mood and behaviour legitimate its invocation by individuals (Lang 1981). Secondly, the multiplicity and inconsistency of these beliefs facilitate the use of neutralisations invoking alcohol in a wide variety of situations and for diverse behaviours. Thirdly, the fact of prior consumption, and the familiarity of the alcohol expectancies, facilitate the immediate invocation of the intoxication excuse as an opportunity for deviance arises.

The generation of successful neutralisations by the uninitiated in deviance can require considerable psychological effort, ingenuity and practice (Best and Luckenbill 1982; Carroll and Weaver 1986; Cornish and Clarke 1986). The availability of 'common knowledge' about alcohol's effects provides a ready stock of neutralisations for immediate use. Thus, the alcohol expectancies, or lay theories, provide potentially powerful neutralisations for behaviour about which the individual experiences moral conflict. Evidence of their effectiveness has been found in the release of sexual responsiveness among high sex-guilt individuals (Lang, Searles, Lauerman and Adesso 1980),

violence among individuals with rigid religious backgrounds (Roebuck
and Johnson 1962) and wife assault among men who morally repudi-
ate it (Kantor and Straus 1987).

2. Readiness to Offend

Cordilia (1986) draws attention to the complex and variable relationship between historical and situational factors and the generation of
motivation to offend. Historical factors in the individual's experience
may lead in themselves to motivation, or to the individual encountering situations within which motivation is generated. These differences
reflect differences in the quality of the motivation, or readiness to
offend.

In the first case, in which motivation arises through prior experiences, this may represent only a provisional readiness to engage in
certain behaviour given the occurrence of a particular kind of situation. Pfuhl describes this as a state of willingness, which 'means no
more or less than that one is available for participation in a deviant
act' (1980, p. 70). Clarke and Cornish argue:

> Readiness involves rather more than receptiveness: it implies that
> the individual has actually contemplated this form of crime as a
> solution to his needs and has decided that under the right circum-
> stances he would commit the offence. (1985, p. 167)

Alcohol may be related to this type of provisional readiness in two
ways. Firstly, life experiences and personality characteristics, identified in Chapter 2 as creating 'risk' or 'vulnerability' to heavy drinking
and crime, may be reframed here as background influences in the
generation of provisional readiness to offend. Such factors enable the
individual to contemplate moral infractions more easily. Individual
biographies influence exposure to and perception of deviant behaviour and the evaluation of the non-deviant alternatives (Clarke and
Cornish 1985; Pfuhl 1980). For example, Athens (1989) argues that
brutalising experiences contribute to readiness to respond to threat
with violence. Repeated exposure to intoxicated violence may also
strengthen the expectancy for this consequence of drinking, rendering
it unsurprising and comparatively easy to apply to one's own behaviour.

Secondly, readiness is linked to self-concept in that it requires the
ability to perceive oneself as one who would engage in the deviant
behaviour under consideration (Briar and Piliavin 1965; Clarke and
Cornish 1985; Pfuhl 1980). Alcohol, via the alcohol expectancies, has

the capacity to facilitate episodic changes in self-concept, by licensing proscribed behaviour as the product of intoxication rather than personal moral failing. In this sense, the alcohol expectancies may provide the individual with provisional 'permission' to offend, in the form of statements such as 'If I were drunk I wouldn't care', or 'If I were drunk I would react to that sort of provocation with violence'.

Provisional readiness to offend may persist over time without being acted upon (Carroll 1982; Pfuhl 1980). However, once an acceptable neutralisation has been mastered, motivation to commit the contemplated offence may itself be enhanced (Minor 1981). Furthermore, provisional readiness interacts with situational factors, and may be perpetuated by repeated exposure to the temptation to offend. For example:

> [V]iolent episodes between intimates have no exact point at which they begin or end; instead, they form an integral part of a continuing relationship. The factors associated with a man's use of violence against his wife are present most of the time, and the specific factors leading to any particular event may occur days, months or even years before the event itself. (Dobash and Dobash 1984, p. 272)

Within certain relationships, such as marriage, alcohol may already feature as a symbol of power and control (Blum 1982; Kantor and Straus 1987). The link between intoxication and marital violence may thus develop, and acquire increasing salience, over a series of hostile interchanges.

In the second case, Cordilia's (1986) analysis suggests that the motivation for an offence may be generated within situations which offer the opportunity for it. Motivation here is more closely related to the formulation of intention to commit a specific offence, as, for example, in Luckenbill's (1977) situationally inspired 'working agreement' between aggressors to use violence.

Individuals may go to greater or lesser efforts to create opportunities to offend in the situations in which they find themselves. Drinking situations provide opportunities to 'display' readiness to offend, for example, by discussing targets for burglary (Bennett and Wright 1984a, 1984b; Walsh 1986), or by projecting hostility (Parker 1974). Furthermore, such interactions facilitate the learning of perspectives which permit offending behaviour, by exposure to examples, neutralisations, opportunities and encouragement (Best and Luckenbill 1982; Pfuhl 1980).

Intoxication is one of a range of techniques employed by offenders 'to manipulate their beliefs to make them compatible with intended courses of action' (Bennett and Wright 1984a, p. 142). Others include: contemplation of gain (Walsh 1986); concentration on the urgency of need (Walsh 1986); anticipation of heightened self-esteem and respect of others (Walsh 1986); exaggeration of skill (Lejeune 1977; Walsh 1986); minimisation of risks (Lejeune 1977); refusal to plan or to contemplate failure (Bennett and Wright 1984a; Walsh 1986); and redefinition of fear as enjoyment (Lejeune 1977; Wade 1967). A particular attraction of alcohol in this process may be its legitimation of potential failure as the result of intoxicated incompetence, without reflection on the individual's public image as a competent operator (Berglas 1987). Equally, intoxication may enhance the excitement of success through the experience of overcoming an intellectual handicap (Berglas 1987).

3. Preference

Garofalo (1987) suggests that 'target attractiveness', or the instrumental or symbolic value of the target to the offender, is an important aspect of offence decisions. Offenders' preferences may reflect moral scruples about certain offences or offence targets (Maguire 1982; Munro 1972), or pragmatic considerations, for example, to do with anticipated victim behaviour (Walsh 1986) or the disposability of property (Garofalo 1987). Nevertheless, the frequent abdication from such moral or pragmatic stances, arising from factors such as the vagaries of opportunity and the urgency of need was noted in Chapter 2. Lay theories about alcohol's effects on rationality and morality provide non-pejorative explanations for behaviour which contradicts preferences, for example by invoking indiscriminateness or impulsivity.

4. Prior Experience

Repeated experience of an offence alters the perception of its moral significance, reducing the need to neutralise guilt or fear (Carroll and Weaver 1986; Feeney 1986; Jacobs 1989; Minor 1980; Pfuhl 1980). Such shifts in perception will reduce the importance of neutralisations based on beliefs about alcohol. Another consequence of experience, moreover, may be that the offence becomes part of the series of scripted activities connected with drinking situations and established in the offender's repertoire. Thus, offending 'routines' (Bennett and Wright 1984a), 'patterns' (Feeney 1986) or 'scripts' (Forgas 1986) arising in drinking situations may acquire the mundane 'mindlessness' (Langer 1978) of other, non-deviant behaviours commonly associated with drinking.

Experience of intoxication may also influence the perception of alcohol itself (Blum 1982; Zucker 1979). It has been seen that heavy drinkers hold conventional alcohol expectancies, but with particular emphases. The experience of success in acting out a particular expectancy, for example, for increased assertiveness under intoxication, is likely to reinforce that expectancy, perpetuating the association between intoxication and a particular type of offence, in this case aggressive.

RATIONALISATION

It may not be possible to draw a rigid distinction between pre-offence neutralisation and rationalisation after the event. An offender may have more time after an offence to construct a rationalisation (Minor 1981), but, once mastered, this may serve as a neutralisation for subsequent offences. For example, Walsh (1986) observes that burglars concentrate on their last offence and the intensity of their need in order to perpetuate their feelings of self-justification for future offending. Nevertheless, it does not follow that techniques for neutralisation and for rationalisation are the same in all cases. For example, a rationalisation is likely to take into account the outcome of the offence. Thus, rationalisations may differ for successful and unsuccessful offences, with the latter type being constructed to compensate injured pride. The relationship between a rationalisation constructed following an unsuccessful offence and the neutralisation of subsequent offences may then depend on the prediction of future success. For example, intoxication may be invoked as a rationalisation for failure which does not reflect on the offender's general, sober competence (Berglas 1987).

Although rationalisations must be plausible, at least to the offender, they may be constructed in ways which do not reflect the real reasons for an offence (Semin and Manstead 1983), since their primary purpose is self-excusatory. In this respect, rationalisations may fall broadly into two types. Firstly, they may justify or excuse the offender's *act*. For example, a murderer 'may select as an event leading to his violence one which places the brunt of responsibility for the murder on the victim' (Luckenbill 1977, p. 197). Alternatively, rationalisations may justify or excuse the offender's *condition*. For example, Cook (1975) observes that alcoholics describe their problems in terms of the incurability of alcoholism, the inevitable failure of attempts at sobriety and the inexorable escalation of the appetite for alcohol.

Taylor (1972) suggests that a full understanding of offenders' rationalisations for their behaviour requires an examination of four issues: the range of justifications available for particular offences; the role of others in defining the acceptability or unacceptability of the available justifications; the variables affecting the acceptance and development of alternative rationalisations; and the significance of alternative rationalisations for the offender's self-image and behaviour. The following discussion will examine offence rationalisations from these aspects, under the briefer headings of availability, acceptability, alternatives, and self-image.

Availability

It has been seen that offenders do not appear to possess special insights into the causes of crime. Although rationalisations may not reflect real reasons for actions, offenders' explanations conform to cultural beliefs about the causes and justifications for behaviour (Semin and Manstead 1983), or 'vocabularies of motives' (Taylor 1972). Cultural beliefs about alcohol circumscribe the motivational statements which may invoke alcohol (Pernanen 1982). Thus, for example, in Jewish culture, in which alcohol use is integrated with religious ritual and symbolism, motivations for drinking do not invoke the intoxicating effects of alcohol *per se*, whilst in Irish culture drinking motivations concern emotional release through the direct effects of alcohol (Greeley, McCready and Theisen 1980). Sykes and Matza's (1957) observation that delinquents' self-justificatory accounts are based on legal defences to crimes, probably reflects less the legal expertise of offenders than the fact that legal defences are themselves rooted in cultural beliefs about the causes and moral justifications of behaviour.

Offenders' rationalisations are thus socially learned. For example, Scully and Marolla argue:

> We view rape as behavior learned socially, through interaction with others; convicted rapists have learned the attitudes and actions consistent with sexual aggression against women. Learning also includes the acquisition of culturally derived vocabularies of motive,

which can be used to diminish responsibility and to negotiate a non-deviant identity. (1984, p. 530)

Whilst it is difficult to develop personal rationalisations for deviance independently of such deep-rooted cultural beliefs, it may also be advantageous to adopt the available vocabularies of motive. For example, observing the common tendency for sex offenders to explain their behaviour in terms of sudden loss of self-control, Taylor remarks:

It is *others* who have led him to cite such motives, but most import-antly it means that he can now represent his motives to himself in such deterministic terms before engaging in the action or before deciding upon whether to continue it. (1972, p. 27)

Jacobs takes this argument further, implying that rationalisation skills may be highly developed at the cultural level, in order to sustain justifications for activities which have unpleasant social consequences:

Given the complexity, magnitude, potential dangers, and relentless occurrence of crashes and casualties, it is a tribute to our capacity for repressing unpleasant truths that we continue to think of auto-mobile injuries as aberrational and perceive driving to be safe compared with other (actually safer) modes of transportation, such as airplanes. (Jacobs 1989, p. 16)

Rationalisations which link intoxication and offending are facilit-ated by their common vocabularies of motive. The similarity of many incentives and rewards for both drinking and offending reduces the necessity to construct special rationalisations for offending. Explana-tions for drinking may be adopted or adapted in the development of offence rationalisations. In this context, it may be noted that academic theories of both drinking and crime themselves draw upon similar explanatory concepts. Thus, academic accounts of delinquency and drinking often appear interchangeable. For example:

Because delinquent behavior is typically episodic, purposive, and confined to certain situations, we assume that the motives for such behavior are frequently episodic, oriented to short-term ends, and confined to certain situations. (Briar and Piliavin 1965, p. 36)

[M]ost adolescent drinking is episodic and opportunist in character. Those who drink tend to drink when and where they can and few will have the routine drinking habits associated with regular adult drinkers. (Marsh, Dobbs and White 1986, p. 13)

Similarly, although it has been strongly argued that there are no theoretical concepts which satisfactorily explain the age–crime relationship (Hirschi and Gottfredson 1983; Rowe and Tittle 1977), academic theorists have usually attempted to construct explanations invoking factors such as marriage, employment, or loss of confidence, which are held to alter the personal motivations of offenders (e.g. Collins 1982; Shover 1985). Such factors are similarly invoked by alcohol theorists to explain the age variation in drinking patterns (e.g. Blane 1979; Sadava 1987; Zucker 1979).

Thus, drinking and crime are semantically linked, facilitating the adoption and adaptation of common vocabularies of motive for the purpose of explaining one behaviour in terms of the other.

Acceptability

The foregoing discussion suggests that offenders' rationalisations are derived from culturally available explanations of the causes and justifications of behaviour. Indeed, the most useful rationalisations will be constructed for their social, rather than purely personal, acceptability. Cameron (1964) found that although non-professional shoplifters might in fact employ sophisticated techniques for stealing, they differed markedly from professionals in the inadequacy of their excuses upon arrest. It appeared that non-professional shoplifters, through their failure to perceive themselves as criminals liable to be held to account in public, had devised rationalisations with a severely limited currency, plausible only to themselves.

Interaction with other offenders facilitates the learning of a repertoire of rationalisations (Best and Luckenbill 1982). These rationalisations may be adapted to complement the circumstances of the preceding crime. For example, Parker (1974) observed that, following apparently impulsive fights, the gang would spend some time developing the appropriate rationalisations, such as 'teaching a lesson' to a rival gang, or 'self-defence' against an aggressive stranger. Notably, Parker's gang do not appear to have found it necessary to invoke intoxication in the rationalisation of violence, although drinking had almost invariably taken place beforehand. They drew instead on perceptions of the social relationships between themselves and their victims. In only one instance, in which an argument developed within the gang itself, does Parker record that intoxication was invoked as a cause of the aggression. Here, however, rationalisation provided grounds, not for justification, but for tolerance and forgiveness.

The rehearsal of rationalisations among drinking or offending companions promotes not only the individual's personal repertoire, but also peer group solidarity (Parker 1974). To this extent, the acceptability of rationalisations shared between peers will be related to the needs of the group. For example, despite the public commitment of Alcoholics Anonymous to continual sobriety, 'slipping' appears to be quite common amongst its members (Fingarette 1988). Confession and re-affirmation of commitment in the style of Alcoholics Anonymous meetings appears to reinforce group identification (Antze 1987).

Peer group rehearsals may also reflect the translation of unpleasant emotional concomitants of an offence into a non-pejorative, and even attractive experience. In the aftermath, fear may be redefined as thrill, and unnecessary risk-taking or incompetence as part of the hilarity of the occasion (Lejeune 1977). In this sense, rationalisations may assist the learning of re-attribution of arousal, discussed earlier: the individual who has learned to say with hindsight, 'I was excited, not scared' may learn to say 'I *am* excited, not scared' in later, similar situations. Thus, rationalisations may assist neutralisation of subsequent offending.

Alcohol, therefore, will not be invoked indiscriminately, simply because of its conveniently wide applicability. Rather, the intoxication excuse will be applied selectively and purposefully as a rationalisation for offences for which other, perhaps morally more persuasive, explanations are unavailable or unnecessary. Ladouceur and Temple (1985) found that although convicted offenders reported consumption levels prior to their offence similar to their typical drinking pattern, they differed markedly in their perceptions of their intoxication. Rapists and burglars were more likely to report feeling very drunk at the time of their offence than were non-violent sex offenders and assaulters. A possible explanation for these differences in the subjective experience of intoxication might derive from the necessity, perceived by offenders, for special rationalisations for abhorrent or incompetent crimes, in order to deflect responsibility on to an external agent.

Alternatives

The discussion so far has pointed to the essentially social nature of rationalisation. Even though they may be invoked for personal self-justification, rationalisations draw on cultural vocabularies of motive, are learned and rehearsed among social groups, and are most usefully developed with consideration of potential audiences. Cultural vocabularies of motives develop in accordance with the social need for them. For example, Morgan argues:

> Historically, when physical chastisement against wives was seen as a common prerogative of husbands, an alcohol-related or any other type of disinhibitory 'excuse' was not needed... However, in the last half of the 20th century, with relations within the family in flux, husbands attempting to retain dominance can no longer justify acts of violence and aggression as an automatic right. The mediating influence of disinhibitory alcohol behavior then is seen as a much easier association to make. (1981, p. 414)

Alternative rationalisations are invoked according to the perceived expectations of different potential audiences (Scott and Lyman 1968). For example, the exaggeration of violence in accounts of aggressive incidents among young male peers 'may be acceptable within a social group which tacitly recognises the legitimacy of adding a sense of "excitement" to routine events' (Marsh and Campbell 1979, p. 7).

Social subgroups may develop alternative rationalisations for the different purposes of justifying behaviour to their own satisfaction or of explaining that behaviour to outsiders. For example, in the first case, Peterson and Maxwell (1958) observe that 'winos', as one of the most vilified groups on skid row, share a range of justifications for drinking wine, including assertions that its effects are more deadening and longer lasting, that it is more easily digested and that it suppresses appetite more successfully than other beverages. In the second case, Wallace (1965) reports that skid-row men offer explanations of their lifestyle to outsiders which serve to counter social opprobrium by condemning conventional standards, glorifying skid row, and producing biographies adapted to appeal to the preconceptions of the investigator.

Personal rationalisations require some social reference group within which they may be developed and sustained. Best and Luckenbill (1982) remark on the stress and disorientation experienced by solitary offenders, resulting in increasing difficulty in effectively utilising their limited, inflexible stock of rationalisations to sustain their lifestyle. Cameron (1964) suggests that the childishness of the excuses offered by non-professional adult shoplifters is linked to the development of rationalisations for stealing among juveniles, upon which mature offenders fall back in the absence of a contemporary peer group within which to generate more appropriate alternatives. Taylor (1972) notes that the isolation of sex offenders prevents them from developing alternative vocabularies of motive, resulting in the persistence of claims to intoxicated loss of control or overwhelming biological drives.

Self-image

It has been argued that cultural and social beliefs and attitudes circumscribe the available range of rationalisations, their acceptability, and the generation of alternatives. Individual motivations, however, are likely to influence the selection, utilisation and adaptation of rationalisations from among this cultural stock. Thus, for example, Snyder, Stephan and Rosenfield (1978) suggest that a variety of personal motives, such as desire for accuracy, to present oneself in a particular light, or to avoid disbelief, may compete against the general tendency for individuals to take credit for good outcomes of their actions, but to blame external causes for bad ones. In the case of rationalisations for deviance, the significance of the behaviour for the individual's estimation of his own moral character may crucially influence the selection and invocation of self-excusatory devices.

Cameron (1964) illustrates the crucial impact of a deviant attribution on self-image and behaviour in the finding that non-professional shoplifters almost universally desist abruptly upon initial arrest. These 'snitches', having sustained hitherto a belief in their respectability, despite the regularity, deliberation and skill of their stealing, had no rationalisations capable of deflecting the sudden acquisition of the identity of 'thief'.

In developing a typology of criminal identities, Irwin (1970) acknowledges that in reality these characterisations overlap, are ambiguous, and frequently contradicted in the behaviour of offenders. Nevertheless, Irwin argues that such identities are meaningful to offenders, and subtly influence individual self-images. The major themes identified by Irwin in the identity of 'thief' – the quest for the 'big score', the moral code of responsibility and loyalty to peers, and the importance of 'coolness' and skill – are echoed by Walsh (1986) in his study of burglars. Such self-characterisations, albeit that they appear romantic and removed from realities of offenders' behaviour, nevertheless offset the severely pejorative terms in which they also frequently describe themselves (Walsh 1986).

Reference to one's personal drinking pattern is often a core aspect of self-concept. Athens' (1980) enquiry into the self-perception of violent offenders at the time of their offences, shows that offenders repeatedly explained their self-images, whether positive or negative, by reference to their drinking patterns. The selective utilisation of rationalisations invoking alcohol may therefore derive from individual motivations either to sustain a valued self-image or to acknowledge self-criticism. In this context, it is notable that rationalisations invoking alcohol may be either self-laudatory (e.g. a 'hard drinker') or self-deprecatory (e.g. an 'alcy').

Taylor (1972) argues that sex offenders are highly motivated to sustain rationalisations which appeal to loss of control, given the alternative necessity of coming to terms with socially abhorrent sexual preferences as an integral aspect of their own characters. Similarly, Shover remarks that persistent, yet incompetent, ageing criminals resorted 'alternately with resignation or desperation to the belief that it was "too late" for them to accomplish anything in life' (1985, p. 215).

The investment of offenders in the maintenance of a self-image which is, at least to some degree, non-deviant, accounts for the attractiveness of the intoxication excuse as a personal rationalisation for abhorrent behaviour. After all,

> if people have been brought up to believe that one is 'not really oneself' when drunk, then it becomes possible for them to construe their drunken changes-for-the-worse as purely episodic happenings rather than as intended acts issuing from their moral character. (Macandrew and Edgerton 1969, p. 169)

McCaghy suggests that the personal significance of such rationalisations has been ignored in the interpretation of sex offenders' invocations of the intoxication excuse as purely public denials of responsibility.

> We do not wish to naively imply that persons may not use their explanations of deviance as manipulatory devices while fully intending to resume their deviant behaviour. Nor do we claim that denials or excuses involving drinking represent, either totally or exclusively, the intent or ability of individuals to avoid further deviance. We do wish to suggest, however, that the confrontation between society and the deviant may produce corrective efforts by the deviant which are misinterpreted because of society's emphasis

on his accepting full responsibility for his deviance. (McCaghy 1968, p. 49)

Taylor (1972) further points out that a degree of tolerance is extended by prisoners only to those sex offenders for whom the offence could plausibly be attributed to temporary loss of control. Such stringent criteria for minimal social acceptance 'suggests that it might be foolish to persuade the sexual deviant that he acted with consciousness and awareness' (Taylor 1972, p. 36).

CONCLUSION

This chapter has revealed the potential ubiquity of the intoxication excuse. Neutralisations for moral infractions which invoke alcohol may be pharmacologically, culturally, situationally, or cognitively derived. Common expectancies for alcohol's effects and social definitions of drinking situations involve the relaxation of moral boundaries. These are not notions peculiar to offenders, but deeply embedded in our cultural stock of common knowledge.

Thus, the secret of most successful techniques of neutralisation and rationalisation for alcohol-related crime is not that they are unusual, esoteric or idiosyncratic, but rather that offenders have mastered the art of exploiting and manipulating this stock of common knowledge. They do so, not because they are driven by the consequences of their intoxication or alcoholism, but because they have an incentive to do so: the facilitation, justification and perpetuation of their offending activities.

4 Responsibility and Mitigation

In the previous chapter, in drawing a distinction between rationalisation and mitigation, it was suggested that mitigation is a formal 'account' (Scott and Lyman 1968) of a criminal offence offered publicly in order to reduce judgements by others of culpability and consequent punishment. This definition now requires deeper inspection, in order to determine the similarities and differences between accounts offered in everyday life and mitigation in the courtroom.

MITIGATION: THE APPEAL TO LAY THEORIES

Scott and Lyman explain their concept of accounts in the following exposition:

> An account is a linguistic device employed whenever an action is subjected to valuative inquiry. Such devices are a crucial element in the social order since they prevent conflicts from arising by verbally bridging the gap between action and expectation. Moreover, accounts are 'situated' according to the statuses of the interactants, and are standardised within cultures so that certain accounts are terminologically stabilized and routinely expected when activity falls outside the domain of expectations. (1968, p. 46)

These elements of everyday accounts can be perceived in courtroom mitigation. Scott and Lyman's definition points out the likelihood that certain cultural conventions for the construction of accounts will be followed in courtroom mitigation, while special features will derive from the specific situation in which they are presented. A weakness of their definition when applied to courtroom mitigation may lie in their specification of conflict prevention as the function of account rendering. In the courtroom, following conviction for an offence, mitigation is less concerned with prevention of conflict than with reduction of punishment. Shapland's explanation of everyday accounts lessens this discrepancy.

[O]ffence has been given to someone and the person giving the offence accounts for giving that offence and attempts to forestall punishment, i.e. he performs remedial work on the situation. (1981, p. 43)

'Remedial work', according to Shapland, involves the restoration of equity to the harmed victim: by compensation; by some equivalent harm to be suffered by the offender; or by justification of the harm suffered by the victim. However, Shapland continues:

Although restoring equity to the victim is important, the offender must also portray his current relationship to the rules which his conduct appears to have broken and do penance, whether directly to the victim, or separately, for breaking the rules as well as harming the victim. (1981, p. 44)

Mitigation recognises the inevitability of punishment. Within this constraint, however, the similarities between accounts and mitigations are sufficient to warrant the observation that 'the content of the mitigation speech is a special case of what would be said in everyday life' (Shapland 1981, p. 43). Therefore, much may be learned about courtroom mitigations by a consideration of everyday accounts, or accounts in lay life. Two aspects of accounts require consideration for this purpose: their basic types and their specific features.

Types of Accounts

Accounts fall into two basic types: justifications and excuses (Scott and Lyman 1968; Shapland 1981; Shaver 1985). In the courtroom sentencing exercise, the primary judgement is that of relative moral culpability or blameworthiness, rather than absolute responsibility. Full denial of responsibility, therefore, is not an optional strategy in the attempt to mitigate punishment. Within this constraint, courtroom mitigations observe the general rules of construction and presentation established in everyday accounts and rooted in commonsense assumptions about cause, responsibility and moral blameworthiness.

1. Justifications

Justifications are accounts in which one accepts responsibility for the act in question, but denies the pejorative quality associated with it. (Scott and Lyman 1968, p. 47)

This type of account asserts that 'contrary to the perceiver's opinion, the action taken was a *positive* one' (Shaver 1985, p. 162). Shaver (1985) suggests that such an assertion may be achieved by arguing either that the act did not in fact possess the morally reprehensible nature originally perceived in it, or that its reprehensibility was outweighed by some larger social purpose which it served.

In the context of courtroom mitigations, such arguments would be heavily constrained by the fact of conviction and the inevitability of punishment. The presumption of personal accountability in this context, in which the judgement to be made concerns the extent, and not the fact, of culpability suggests that mitigation by justification is a high-risk strategy, liable to be perceived as evasion of personal responsibility or assertion of commitment to a reprehensible morality. Some justificatory techniques, such as 'condemnation of the condemners' or 'self-fulfilment' (Scott and Lyman 1968) may be altogether impermissible in these circumstances. Others, such as denial of either the injury or the victim (Scott and Lyman 1968), may require strategic presentation to achieve acceptability. For example, Shapland, Willmore and Duff (1985) point out the heavy reliance of sentencing proceedings on the assumption of the 'blameless' victim. In Schafer's words:

> The norm-delineated functional role of the victim is to do nothing to provoke others from attempting to injure his ability to play his role. At the same time, it expects him actively to prevent such attempts. This is the victim's functional responsibility. (1968, p. 152)

In these circumstances, scapegoating of the victim would require measured argument if it were not to amount to outright denial of responsibility, a stance which might antagonise sentencers considering punishment. Nevertheless, the scapegoating of rape victims is an example of the frequently successful appeal to lay theories about the causes of sexual violence which implicate victims as provocateurs (Scully and Marolla 1984).

2. Excuses

> Excuses are accounts in which one admits that the act in question is bad, wrong, or inappropriate but denies full responsibility. (Scott and Lyman 1968, p. 47)

Excuses appeal to circumstances such as accident or mistake, or to forces such as temporary incapacity or duress (Shapland 1981).

Except in some extreme cases, such appeals do not challenge the presumption of personal accountability, but seek to reduce moral censure. Thus, they address themselves to the judgement of moral blameworthiness or culpability with which the sentencing court is concerned. They further allow for expressions of remorse, gestures of atonement and the acceptance of punishment, the specific 'remedial work' with which the sentencing court is concerned. Excuses, therefore, are a less risky strategy in mitigation.

Characteristics of Accounts

Certain characteristics of accounts are subject to particular constraints in the context of courtroom mitigations: impression management; negotiation; intelligibility; and credibility.

1. Impression Management
Scott and Lyman remark:

> Since individuals are aware that appearances may serve to credit or discredit accounts, efforts are understandably made to control these appearances through a vast repertoire of 'impression management' activities. (1968, p. 54)

Above all, the offender must demonstrate the sincerity of his account, showing proper regard for the correctional process (Shapland 1981). For example, in apologising, the offender must show genuine distress caused by the victim's suffering (Shapland 1981). In the courtroom, the expectation of sincerity extends to the defence solicitor proffering mitigation on the offender's behalf.

> That involves, above all, trying consistently with fair and proper means to reduce the level of punishment which may come to your client but, secondly, and this is important, assisting the court to arrive at what seems to be the least punishment consistent with justice. No-one will doubt that in seeking to persuade to the mitigation of punishment, the major requirement is to convince the court that you are there to assist, as indeed you are. (Napley 1983, p. 164)

Impression management is a complex task for defendants in the courtroom. Firstly, unfamiliarity with courtroom procedure and etiquette (Carlen 1976; McBarnett 1983; Parker, Casburn and Turnbull 1981), physical design features of the courtroom (Carlen 1976) and the offering of mitigation through a third party are disruptive situational influences on the display of behaviour which usually accompanies an account. Secondly, defendants experience multiple motivations connected with the court appearance itself: for example, to speed the processing of their case, to avoid publicity and to protect their employment (Bottoms and McClean 1976). Thus, motivation to atone for the offence itself, however sincere, is necessarily in competition with these situational motivations.

Furthermore, the offender's perspective on his offence may itself be influenced by features of the criminal justice process. For example, Schafer (1968) found that offenders' remorsefulness and wish to make reparation varied in relation, not only to features of their offences, but also to their anticipated sentence. In respect of offenders facing imprisonment, Schafer observes:

> Their orientation was such that they could not understand their wrongdoing in terms of social relationships, not even in terms of the victim. Their understanding of incarceration seemed limited to what they viewed as merely a normative wrong that has to be paid to the agencies of criminal justice, but to no one else. Their reluctance to go beyond this isolated and narrow attitude was not due to some deviant logic, but to a lack of understanding of the referent factors of their crime. (1968, p. 83)

Bottoms and McClean (1976) suggest that much of the behaviour of defendants at court should be interpreted as impression management techniques for dealing with these situational aspects of the court appearance, rather than for accounting for the offence. They identify certain self-presentational styles, such as 'the respectable first-timer', 'the strategist', 'the rights assertive' defendant, and the 'passive respondent'. The notable point about these self-presentational styles is that they are derived from recognisable roles in everyday life. Furthermore, they are selected to complement the type of person which the defendant perceives himself, or may be perceived by others, to be in everyday life. For example, the 'respectable first-timer' may be either 'a remorseful one-time loser', or a 'mistakenly indicted citizen'. But in either case, qualification for this self-presentational style requires an established identity in everyday life, thus excluding teenagers from attempting it (Bottoms and McClean 1976). The offender's perspective on his offence may itself thus be influenced in the attempt to integrate his account with the self-presentational styles available to him in the courtroom.

2. Negotiation

In everyday accounts, the offender is attempting to negotiate for himself absolution from, or reduction of, censure. Negotiation in everyday accounts is generally implicit. It does not require assertion, since it is inherent in the rendering of the account itself. But whilst negotiation is an intrinsic feature of the everyday account, a large part of negotiation in the courtroom is separated from the mitigation speech. Courtroom negotiations are frequently explicit, whether at a low-key, consultative level between participants, as when solicitors confer with court clerks (Parker, Casburn and Turnbull 1981), or in the form of overt pressure to alter the course of the proceedings, as in plea bargaining (Baldwin and McConville 1977). This severance of negotiation from mitigation creates a paradoxical relationship between the necessary sincerity of the mitigation itself and communications outside it which reveal a distinctly pragmatic approach to the 'true facts' of the case. For example, Gusfield observes that 'the decision to prosecute on a particular charge is much affected by the ability of the defendant to create organizational problems for the prosecution by taking the case to trial' (1981, p. 161).

It is to the offender's advantage to grasp this severance of negotiation from mitigation. For example, Baldwin and McConville, studying plea bargaining in the Crown Court, remark:

Many of the defendants we interviewed, and particularly the recidivists among them, regard this kind of dealing as a standard, if somewhat underhand, method of administering justice and it is to some of them a much more realistic and acceptable way of proceeding than, say, taking their chance with a jury. (1977, p. 25)

However, negotiations to reduce judgements of responsibility and culpability may require a shift in the offender's perspective on the nature of his offending behaviour. For example, an offender offering mitigation based on an appeal to intoxicated impulsivity, however sincerely he may believe in that 'cause' of his offence, may nevertheless discover that success depends not merely on contrition, but on demonstrable reform. Mosher observes of American justice:

Treatment strategies have begun to incorporate the criminal justice system into the treatment methods themselves. Providers view the coercive arm of the law as helpful to their work. The threat of criminal prosecution serves to encourage a breakdown of the 'denial' of the problem, generally considered the first step toward successful treatment. The criminal law actually encourages clients to admit to an alcohol problem which needs to be cured, for otherwise they may be found morally responsible for criminal behaviour. (1981, p. 453)

3. *Intelligibility*

Scott and Lyman (1968) argue that successful accounts are adapted to the social circle within which they are offered. Acceptable 'vocabularies of accounts' become routinised within cultures, subcultures and social groups, according to their established 'background expectancies', or 'those sets of taken-for-granted ideas that permit the interactants to interpret remarks as accounts in the first place' (Scott and Lyman 1968, p. 53). This argument suggests that successful accounts must be intelligible in the social context within which they are offered, rather than that in which the offence itself was committed. It further suggests that intelligibility is constrained by the availability and acceptability of alternative 'vocabularies of accounts' within that social context. A clear relationship emerges here between everyday accounts and certain qualities of personal rationalisations for offences, as considered in Chapter 3.

In the courtroom, the immediate intelligibility of mitigation is vital. There is rarely time available to express novel or unusual explanations for behaviour. As has been seen already, offenders do not in any case possess special insights into crime causation and they develop personal rationalisations which reflect cultural conceptual traditions and 'vocabularies of motives'. Furthermore, the stock of lay theories of intoxication provides convenient explanations of deviant behaviour. Thus, Critchlow (1985) found that whilst information about intoxication did not generally negate attributions of responsibility for offensive behaviour, it did have a significant impact on judgements of severely antisocial acts. Critchlow attributes this effect to the unavailability of conventional explanations for highly unusual behaviour.

> When judging an act that violates expectancies, an observer searching for reasons may seize upon alcohol intoxication as a cause of the behaviour, thereby reducing attributions of responsibility, blame, and causal role. (Critchlow 1985, p. 271)

Howard and Clark (1985) found similarly that courts were likely to favour an insanity verdict when crimes involved impetuous passion or lacked an obvious motive, thus defying conventional explanations of behaviour. Sommer, Burstein and Holman (1988) found that censure of the behaviour of mentally ill people was reduced when it appeared bizarre or self-destructive. Thus, Best and Luckenbill remark that it is easier to attribute responsibility to an actor if he 'announces or can be presumed to have motives consistent with conventional explanations for intentional action' (1982, p. 216). Intoxication, like mental illness, offers a ready explanation for a range of extraordinary behaviours, accessible through the store of common knowledge.

Mitigation requires causal thinking (Fitzmaurice and Pease 1986). Shaver's (1985) 'working definition' of responsibility usefully makes this point. According to Shaver, responsibility is

> a judgement made about the moral accountability of a person of normal capacities, which judgement usually but not always involves a causal connection between the person being judged and some morally disapproved action or event. (1985, p. 66)

Information about an offender's history, personal circumstances, or state of mind, advanced in mitigation must appeal to readily intelligible, plausible causes of crime. As Scott and Lyman (1968) point out, certain general explanations usefully provide plausible causes of a variety of specific behaviours and outcomes. For example, 'having family problems' may explain criminality, heavy drinking, or depression.

> The person offering such an account may not himself regard it as a true one, but invoking it has certain interactional payoffs: since people cannot say they don't understand it – they are accounts that are part of our socially distributed knowledge of what 'everyone knows' – the inquiry can be cut short. (Scott and Lyman 1968, p. 53)

Thus, Napley suggests a useful appeal to lay versions of the undersocialisation theory of criminality.

> Many people, despite their age in years, have not, in fact, grown up; they have not faced up to the responsibilities of life and, if this is so and you can demonstrate it, you can make a plea in mitigation in a highly effective way; it is something which judges and experienced magistrates know and to which they will be receptive. Properly presented and cogently argued, they may accept it as an explanation. (1983, p. 166)

The appeal to popular figures of speech is also exemplified in the appeal to 'sickness'. In this metaphor 'sickness' is invoked to describe the most unattractive, distasteful and frightening aspects of social life. Wiseman's account of skid row illustrates the pervasive imagery of sickness.

> [T]o social workers, psychiatrists, psychologists, and many sociologists, Skid Row is seen as a prime manifestation of social pathology. Like a cancer embedded in healthy tissue, Skid Row is viewed as a potential danger to an entire city. The physical deterioration of the buildings and resultant lowering of property values of adjacent areas is but one aspect of this threat. The social and psychological deterioration of its residents, inevitably resulting in added cost to the city for police surveillance and humane care, is the other. (1970, p. 5)

Cook offers a powerful example of an account which appeals to this metaphor:

> For the hard core of skid row drinkers the Camberwell 'spike' can still represent the final downfall. As one hard-liner put it: 'I felt sick, really sick, sick from drink, sick from "skippering", and sick of life. In fact I felt so bad that I walked from the East End to the "spike". That was really admitting defeat.' (Cook 1975, p. 131)

In this context, the flexibility of lay theories about alcohol's effects provides a range of plausible explanations for different behaviours. As Lang points out, in excuses for intoxicated conduct, 'social acceptance of such drinking attributions is critical to the maintenance of their use' (1981, p. 91). A special advantage of lay theories of intoxication derives from the readiness of individuals to attribute various 'well-known' effects of alcohol to others, despite having no personal experience of such results from drinking (Roizen 1981; Sharp and Lowe 1989a).

4. Credibility

Scott and Lyman (1968) suggest two reasons for the rejection of an account: illegitimacy, due to its inadequacy for a grave offence or its unacceptability in the group to which it is offered; and unreasonableness, due to its appeal to an unusual explanation beyond common theories of plausible causes. As has been seen, the intoxication excuse, by appeal to lay theories, provides a plausible explanation for a variety of behaviours. Its legitimacy, however, is linked to the gravity of the offence, the type of account being offered and the frequency with which it is invoked by an individual. Examples of its circumscription by each of these factors may be given:

(a) Offence Gravity

McCaghy (1968) observes that some deviant behaviours are perceived to be so bizarre or despicable that no explanation which attempts to portray them as reasonable will be accepted. Intoxication, for example, is unlikely to succeed in mitigating sexual molestation of children if the appeal merely suggests that such behaviour falls into the 'normal' range of pardonable disinhibited lapses from social decorum. Successful invocation of the intoxication excuse in these circumstances involves 'deviance disavowal' (McCaghy 1968): repudiation of the behaviour, and of other perpetrators of that behaviour, whilst asserting exceptional loss of control induced by intoxication in the offender's own case.

(b) Type of Account

Scully and Marolla (1984) found that convicted rapists offered one of two types of account: admission, in which the use of unacceptable force to obtain sex was acknowledged; or denial, in which either sexual contact with the victim was denied, or was acknowledged but not defined as rape. Appeals to intoxication varied according to the type of account. Admitters cited alcohol as a cause of their loss of sexual control. Deniers, however, used intoxication as a source of victim discreditation and scapegoating. They did not regard intoxication as having affected their own judgement or behaviour, since their denial required the assertion of self-control and ability to recall events accurately. These differences in the appeal to alcohol's effects occurred without noticeable evidence of differences between admitters and deniers in the actual use of alcohol prior to the offence.

(c) Frequency of invocation

Repeated recourse to the intoxication excuse progressively weakens its credibility (Berglas 1987; Nusbaumer 1983). Turner remarks that

> because a deviant role is negatively valued and deviants are subjected to discriminatory treatment, disavowal of deviance is the usual response. But like all roles, a deviant role can sometimes be the lesser evil in a situation of limited choice. (1972, p. 313)

The appeal to alcohol's effects in these circumstances may shift from deviance *disavowal*, through invocation of episodic intoxicated loss of control, to deviance *avowal*, through embracement of an alcoholic identity. Thus, Nusbaumer explains:

> Ultimately, the illness model allows for greater reality negotiation on the part of deviant drinkers. They may choose to negotiate reality by openly avowing their deviance through self-labeling and adopting a repentant–deviant role that allows for the conditional acceptance of continued deviant behavior. (1983, p. 229)

Macandrew and Edgerton describe the extreme form of this as a shift from invocation of the 'time out' excuse to the 'ineligibility' excuse.

> Every society has come up with some version of Ineligibility in order to account for and to deal with certain of those classes of troublesome or potentially troublesome persons (the profoundly mentally retarded, for instance) who are considered chronically or permanently incapable of living up to their society's minimal standards of competence. Since it is presumed of these people that 'they know not what they do' or that they are incapable of doing otherwise than they do, the approach that we have termed Ineligibility consists in setting them off as a class apart and granting them one or another form of *long-term* or *permanent immunity* from the demands of their society's accountability system. (Macandrew and Edgerton 1969, p. 167)

At this point, however, it is pertinent to note a particular implication of these identified qualities of accounts in the special context of courtroom mitigation. The discussion of intelligibility identified a relationship to the conditions for rationalisation construction in terms of acceptability, availability and alternatives. Thus, mitigations based on the intoxication excuse resemble personal rationalisations which appeal to alcohol's effects. Personal rationalisations, however, were also observed to be intimately linked to self-concept.

In the courtroom, the contrivance of the intoxication excuse is revealed through the situational constraints on the general qualities of account rendering. Defendants' situational motivations, the constraints on impression management, the severance of negotiation from mitigation, the need for rapid intelligibility, and the shifting criteria for credibility all convey a deep ambiguity to defendants' appeals to intoxication, despite the advantages. It does not necessarily follow that offenders do not at some level believe their appeals to alcohol's effects. They subscribe to the same stock of commonsense wisdom about alcohol's effects as does their audience. More deeply, however, self-exculpatory rationalisations based on intoxication may have formed a crucial aspect of their defence of personal self-concept. In this respect, belief, however wilfully induced in the first instance, has played an important role in the success of personal rationalisations.

Thus, Cook (1975) draws attention to the genuine ambivalence of skid-row drunks about their condition. The strategic appeal to a 'full-blown medical model' (Cook 1975, p. 117) in court is underpinned by a series of real personal rationalisations which derive from that model. Similarly, Scully and Marolla, whilst observing that 'rapists have learned the advantage to be gained from using alcohol and drugs as an account' (1984, p. 539), also allude to their ambivalence. A successful appeal to some form of 'sickness' absolves from public blame. Nevertheless, to believe in some temporary 'sickness' at the time of the offence protects a non-deviant identity and predicts recovery of a normal condition. Thus,

> Admitters asserted a non-deviant identity despite their self-proclaimed disgust with what they had done. Although admitters were willing to assume the sick role, they did not view their problem as a chronic condition, nor did they believe themselves to be insane or permanently impaired. (Scully and Marolla 1984, p. 540)

MITIGATION: SPECIAL ASPECTS

Shapland (1981) points out some basic differences between everyday accounts and courtroom mitigations. Everyday accounts usually involve some direct conversational exchange between two or more people, while mitigation is a speech delivered with little verbal interchange or response. Neither the victim nor the offender may be involved in the presentation or response to mitigation. The person who receives and responds to the mitigation is a third party, the sentencer, who represents, not the victim personally, but society. The offender's mitigation may be offered by a third party whose own ideas about an appropriate account for the offence will influence the representation of the offender's original account. The offender's established legal responsibility for the offence precludes certain forms of complete justification; punishment is inevitable; mitigation must therefore aim to achieve leniency rather than deliverance from punishment.

This last point generates the essential thrust of mitigation. Although the construction of accounts in mitigation follow the established rules governing those in everyday life, the essential aim of reducing punishment constrains their selection and presentation. Mitigation seeks to achieve that purpose by changing the audience's perception either of the offence or of the offender. It may be suggested, however, that a change in the perception of an offence in itself consequentially alters the perception of the offender, by modifying the judgement of his responsibility. Fitzmaurice and Pease argue:

> Mitigation or aggravation entail by necessity a re-estimation of the liability to be punished through a consideration of factors which are concerned with a more global assessment of the 'morality' of the accused... (1986, p. 125)

In the absence of interaction and exchange between the sentencer and the person offering mitigation, the latter may assume a need to challenge the most severe potential judgement of the offence and offender (Shapland 1981). Mitigation, therefore, attempts to shift the audience's perception, from a hypothetical 'worst case scenario', towards a more moderate one by appealing to 'special' information about the particular offender. Successful mitigation, then, attracts attention to special information about a case, thus reducing the audience's reliance on rigid stereotypical responses to categories of offences and 'provoking mindfulness' (Palmerino, Langer and McGillis 1984; also Fiske and Neuberg 1989) in respect of individual offenders.

There is some evidence to suggest that this may be an effective strategy. For example, Stalans and Diamond (1990) note that when asked general questions about crime and punishment, lay people suggest that the courts are too lenient, but, when exposed to information about specific cases, they moderate their criticism of judicial sentencing. Ellsworth (1978) observes a similar incongruity between lay judgements about abstract issues and specific cases. When presented with a detailed case, substantially fewer subjects favoured capital punishment than when responding to an abstract question about their support for that measure. Similarly, Austin, Walster and Utne (1976) cite evidence to suggest that jurors take a defendant's own suffering into account when considering punishment. The perception that an offender has himself suffered, either through the commission of the offence itself, or through other misfortunes appears to reduce severity. The authors suggest that such information increases feelings of liking for the offender.

There is, then, some evidence that increasing attention to the individuality of a case can reduce the harshness of general lay judgements of criminal responsibility. Sentencers appear to reach their decisions by constructing explanations of crime from which to infer the 'moral quality' (Hogarth 1971) of a case. Successful mitigation manipulates this process by pointing out information which increases sentencers' attention to, and reasoning about, the circumstances in which a particular offence has been committed.

However, this general principle for successful mitigation is not entirely straightforward in practice. Firstly, individualised reasoning is not an easy option. It is cognitively demanding, and difficult in comparison with simpler, stereotypical styles of case processing.

[P]unitiveness in attitudes and beliefs is associated with a fairly simple (concrete) way of organizing information in the process of judgement. The thought processes of punitive magistrates appear to be characterized by stereotyped or compartmentalized thinking. Individual bits of information are organized in a relatively fixed way with little or no integration. In contrast, non-punitive magistrates appear to use information in a more complex and subtle way. Their thought processes are characterised by flexibility, autonomy and creativity. Their tolerance for conflict and ambiguity are higher, and their capacity for abstract thought or conceptualisation is enhanced. They appear to be much more involved in the sentencing process and find it a more difficult and demanding task. (Hogarth 1971, p. 319)

Sentencers may, therefore, need some persuasion to utilise individualised styles of reasoning, if the goal of mitigation is to be accomplished. The likelihood that they will apply themselves to such taxing individualised reasoning may be enhanced by factors such as training and experience (Bond and Lemon 1981). Carroll and Payne (1977) compared decisions about parole cases made by criminal justice experts and college students. They found basic similarities in the reasoning processes and judgements made, but experts used more information and combined different information more flexibly than students. Similarly, Lawrence and Homel found differences in the reasoning processes of experienced and novice magistrates.

Major experience/inexperience differences occurred at the levels of what magistrates brought to the cases and their reasoning. Experts had more patterned approaches, and were directed by their treatment objectives to assess cause of the defendant's behaviors, and their prospects of responding to treatment and individualized approaches. Although the novice knew and responded to ritualized evidence-gathering procedures, he seemed to work with single details. (Lawrence and Homel 1986, p. 180)

Secondly, there may be instances when it is not to the intoxicated offender's advantage to increase attention to his case. For example, in a minor American court, Mileski found that the majority of offenders incarcerated for intoxication and breach of the peace were processed in batches, with very brief consideration of their case: 'a trip to jail, then, very often is a result of one impersonal contact with the judge' (Mileski 1969, p. 78). Nevertheless, Mileski also found that defendants charged with intoxication rarely focused attention upon themselves by proffering excuses. Those who did so in fact attracted more severe punishment. Mileski relates this finding to the pressure of time in a busy court, suggesting that 'the court disproportionately uses the sanction of jail as a defense against the injection of extra information during the courtroom encounter' (1969, p. 62).

Thirdly, there are no clear rules governing the type of information to be advanced in mitigation (Shapland 1979). Shapland found considerable diversity in the mitigating factors advanced by different barristers in similar cases. This did not appear to be due to discrepant information, but to different techniques for its presentation. Shapland argues that mitigation speeches do not attempt to invoke the entire range of mitigating factors available in specific cases, but to select those which are considered to be most persuasive. Thus, selectivity may be the

result of a particular structuring of the mitigation speech, whereby only a few important factors are given in some detail, rather than all possible mitigating factors being mentioned at least briefly, with more emphasis given or time spent on the more important ones. (1979, p. 161)

Nevertheless,

there is no general agreement on what is mitigating or what kind of character is mitigating, so that what may be mitigating in one case may be aggravating in another. (Shapland 1981, p. 82)

Some types of information, such as stupidity, unemployment or intoxication, are essentially ambiguous as to their mitigating or aggravating potential (Carroll and Payne 1977; Corbett 1987; Critchlow 1985; Ewart and Pennington 1987; Hawkins 1983a; Shapland 1979, 1981), and therefore require strategic presentation in the context of other information to portray the offender's moral character in a certain light. Some evidence suggests that the particular interpretation of such ambiguous information is related to the type of offence (Carroll and Payne 1977) and to the range of sentences between which sentencers are choosing (Softley 1980).

The potential ambiguity of the intoxication excuse is aptly illustrated by Felker (1989), who suggests that information about a defendant's intoxication might influence all potential purposes of sentencing. Felker suggests that by treating it as an aggravating factor, courts might seek to deter potential intoxicated offenders. Where an offender shows no sign of reducing his alcohol consumption and, thereby, his threat to public safety, incapacitation might appear appropriate. Punishment might be mitigated through evidence of intoxicated impulsivity, or aggravated through evidence of deliberate intoxication for Dutch courage. Rehabilitation might be invoked for the provision of treatment, or, alternatively, sentence length might be increased in cases of severe alcoholism in order to facilitate that treatment. The absence of conscious irony in this analysis is remarkable. Felker apparently perceives no oddity in such manipulation of a single item of information to infer quite different judgements of moral culpability justifying alternative sentencing goals.

CONCLUSION

This analysis of mitigation suggests that it is usefully understood as a social psychological process, rather than as a specific element in the courtroom encounter between sentencer and offender. Within the cultural and situational constraints of accounts rendered in the courtroom, mitigation of punishment will be achieved through a social psychological process of sympathetic identification with the offender, resulting from increased attention to individual features of his case.

Such a perspective raises the question whether, as a social psychological process, mitigation of punishment will be achieved through the mitigation address alone, or through other features of the courtroom encounter which provoke sentencers' 'mindfulness' (Langer 1991) to and individualised reasoning about particular cases. This theoretical perspective on mitigation, and the question it raised, underpins the empirical study of sentencing decision-making at a magistrates' court, where judgements of responsibility for intoxicated crime sprang from the well of common knowledge about alcohol and its effects upon mind, mood and behaviour.

5 Introduction to City Magistrates' Court

The theoretical discussion of the previous chapters suggests a rich vein of enquiry into the judgements of responsibility and culpability for intoxicated offending formulated in the courtroom setting. How do lay theories about alcohol's effects inform the decision-making process? What are the implications of information about intoxication and alcoholism for judgements about responsibility, moral blameworthiness and the delivery of punishment?

RESEARCH METHODOLOGY

The empirical study began with the approval and agreement in principle to assist the project of the clerk to the justices at a magistrates' court and the chief probation officer of the area covered by the court. The provincial city in which the court was located has been given the title, simply, of 'City', in order to preserve confidentiality. There were four components to the research methodology: observation in the court itself; a survey of court files; extended interviews with magistrates and probation officers; and brief, focused post-sentence interviews with magistrates concerning specific cases.

Courtroom Observation

Observation covered proceedings in two types of court: the daily 'plea' courts, in which decisions were taken across the range of the court's criminal business, including adjournments, bail, committals to the Crown Court and sentencing; and a weekly, later twice weekly, sentencing court, which dealt with sentencing in the more complex cases in which Social Enquiry Reports (henceforth SERs) had been required. Notes were taken on a total of 252 cases during the course of courtroom observation. The majority of these were cases in which sentence was passed by the magistrates. A small number, mostly recorded during the early, tentative phase of study, did not proceed as far as sentence, but were transferred to another court, discontinued, taken to trial and acquittal, or committed to Crown Court. The cases also included a number of sober cases. 'Sober', here, should not be taken as an assertion of fact about an offence. A sober case was one in which there was no mention at any point in the proceedings of a defendant's alcoholism or intoxication at the time of his offence; it does not follow that he was in fact sober. The inclusion of unsentenced and sober cases in data collection, despite the study's focus on sentencing decision making in alcohol-related cases, stemmed from certain reasoning which informed data collection from the outset.

The decision to record proceedings verbatim was influenced by Shapland's (1981) study of the construction of mitigation speeches. In order to understand most fully the structured use of specific information about alcohol, it was important to understand not only the precise manner in which that information itself was offered, but also the context in which it arose. However, since the research was concerned, not merely with the semantic construction of one particular form of courtroom address, but in the *process* of mitigation and decision making, this reasoning extended to the verbatim recording of all participants' contributions to the proceedings. It was not, therefore, possible to wait until the end of a case to determine whether to record it, but necessary to commence immediately. Similarly, it was not possible to wait until reference to alcohol was made in a case before starting to record.

This reasoning and its consequences resulted in particular advantages to the eventual analysis. By virtue of recording the majority of hearings observed, a range of information about the general conduct of court business was gathered which contextualised and facilitated the specific interpretation of the sentencing process. Examples of decision making in sober cases were also collected with which to compare the treatment of alcohol-related cases. Furthermore, the methodology meant that the accumulation of decisions prior to final sentence was noted in several cases which proceeded through a series of adjournments for different reasons: for example, for legal consultation, preparation of SERs or psychiatric reports, or deferment of sentence. The ability subsequently to trace the progress of cases over what could turn out to be a substantial period of time was in fact an unanticipated, but valuable, spin-off from the protracted period of observational study.

Court File Survey

The court file survey involved examination of the files on all cases which had been recorded. This facilitated the checking of the accuracy of recording of factual detail, collection of full criminal histories and reading of correspondence, notes and reports, including the brief police statement concerning the offence. It also facilitated the tracking of cases during periods in which their progress through the court was not directly observed.

Interviews with Magistrates and Probation Officers

Semi-structured interviews were conducted with 20 magistrates and 15 probation officers. All interviews were tape recorded and subsequently transcribed for analysis.

1. Magistrates
The 20 magistrates (11 male and 9 female) comprised a sixth of the 120-strong bench. They were recruited for this part of the research for the most part by the simple expedient of asking all magistrates who participated in post-sentence interviews whether they would be willing to undertake this extended, and more general, interview. Towards the end of interviewing, when it was becoming difficult to find willing magistrates who had not already been interviewed, one of the court's administrative staff assisted with introductions to some magistrates who had not been encountered thus far. The gender balance was intended, but fortunately no special effort was actually required to achieve it.

The broad aim of the interviews was to gain the 'flavour' of City bench: the traditions and perspectives which appeared to bind a disparate group of people together and to guide their collective decision making. There were, however, three specific aims: to draw out magistrates' views on their role; to examine their attitudes towards the probation service, which provides access to treatment-based sentencing options; and to identify some of the lay theories of intoxication, alcoholism and crime which underpinned their judgements of responsibility.

This last exercise involved a sequence of questions asking magistrates for their explanations of hypothetical instances of alcohol-related deviance: why do chronic alcoholics break the law?; what do you think are the reasons for pub violence?; why is drinking so often a feature of marital disputes?; why do people drink and drive? This does not purport to be an intensive or exhaustive study of a body of lay theories, or, indeed, of the theories entertained by this particular group of people. However, it does not necessarily need to be such, for the purposes of this investigation. As a series of 'top of the head' explanations of potentially very complex issues, these questions may have successfully elicited some of the simple 'commonsense' explanations which magistrates invoked in situations requiring them to make swift judgements. In such pressured decision-making situations, theories which draw on intuitively obvious, immediately accessible, 'top of the head' explanations are potentially the most likely to be utilised to make sense of complex and ambiguous information.

2. Probation Officers

During courtroom observation, it became clear that probation officers were active and respected contributors to decision-making processes at City court. This conclusion was later confirmed during interviews with magistrates. It was important, therefore, to consider the perspectives of probation officers, not least since they were the primary 'gate-keepers' of the pathways into treatment for alcohol-related offenders. The 15 interviews with probation officers (8 males and 7 females) included the 3 senior- and 12 main-grade officers who were involved in the criminal work of the City probation team at the time of interviewing. Due to staff changes, more main-grade officers were in fact involved in the study as a whole during the courtroom observation exercise.

These interviews sought to clarify the professional theories which informed probation officers' decision making in the areas relevant to the study. Three areas of enquiry were pursued. Firstly, probation officers were exposed to the same sequence of questions on intoxicated deviance and responsibility as were magistrates. Most of the remaining questions focused directly upon probation officers' 'theories of office' (Drass and Spencer 1987), in relation to two spheres of their professional activity. Given the importance of SERs in the sentencing exercise, particularly in relation to treatment-based options for alcohol-related offenders, probation officers' views on the task of report preparation were sought. Similarly, given the probation order as the primary tool for delivering treatment-based services, it was important to understand how officers perceived probation supervision, which assumes especial importance in their theories of office since it is, quite literally, the activity by which they are defined as professionals in the criminal justice system.

Finally, it was of interest to discover how the work entailed specifically by involvement with alcohol-related offenders related to these general perspectives on the professional role and tasks of probation officers. There was a danger here in becoming tedious by repeating questions which had already been asked in general terms with specific reference to alcohol-related offenders. Moreover, supplementary questions in this form rarely produced responses which were more informative than the initial, general observations. In the end, the purpose was best served simply by inviting officers to comment on what they liked and what they did not like about any aspect of their work with alcohol-related offenders.

Post-sentence Interviews

The post-sentence interviews were conducted towards the end of the courtroom observation period, with any magistrates who were interested and willing. This meant that sometimes all three magistrates included themselves in the interview, while at other times one of their number took on the task of representing their combined views. Sometimes, it seemed that this 'composite' perspective offered by a single magistrate might have been an attempt to preserve the apparent unity of the ultimate decision in the face of real differences of opinion. This hypothesis arose on a very few occasions when there was difficulty in following the logic of the argument which was presented. However, in the interests of diplomacy, given magistrates' sensitivity to the privacy of the 'retiring room', care was taken to do no more than ask for clarification in general terms. In any case, given the explicit focus on theories of intoxicated crime and their relationship to sentencing decisions, it would have been impertinent to exploit an opportunity to indulge curiosity about the detail of magisterial relationships.

Twenty-eight post-sentence interviews were conducted. Magistrates' responses were recorded in writing as they spoke. Questions were devised to prompt magistrates to talk about the case as fully as possible, covering, for example, their opinions on the seriousness of the offence, the offender, the information provided and their satisfaction with the outcome.

CITY MAGISTRATES' COURT

It is a well-established research finding that magistrates' courts vary widely, both in their styles of conducting courtroom business (Burney 1979; Darbyshire 1984; Parker, Casburn and Turnbull 1981) and in their sentencing patterns (Burney 1985; Parker, Casburn and Turnbull 1981; Parker, Sumner and Jarvis 1989; Softley 1980; Tarling 1979). Therefore, while this study focuses on the invocation of widely accepted lay theories about alcohol, the impact of that appeal upon sentencing decisions must be contextualised within the culture of the particular court which was studied.

It was, in fact, a special advantage of City court's participation in the research that its magistrates were open to persuasion through mitigation. The study was enriched, in consequence, by the opportunity to observe, not only the semantic construction of arguments involving information about alcohol but also the influence of those arguments on sentencing outcomes. Several studies have pointed to differences in the decision-making styles of magistrates, which have real implications for sentencing outcomes (Bond and Lemon 1979, 1981; Hogarth 1971; Lawrence 1984; Lawrence and Homel 1986). Others indicate the importance of court traditions and culture (Burney 1979) and the impact of situational factors (Rumgay 1995). Following the findings of such research, it will illuminate the observation of City magistrates' treatment of specific alcohol-related cases to highlight three broad aspects of the court's functioning and approach to decision making: the use of custody; the conduct of court business; and structured decision making.

The Use of Custody

Sentencing at City court was perceived by all court personnel to be generally non-punitive, and in particular to show a stable tradition of low use of custody. Home Office statistics in fact showed a declining use of custody over the years preceding the research, in line with a general decline in the numbers of defendants sentenced for indictable offences, which reflected the general trend in England and Wales. Compared to other magistrates' courts, City's use of custody reflected the middle of the range. Strictly speaking, therefore, it was not excessive in its resort to custody, but neither was it unusually sparing.

However, at the time of the research, this reduction in the use of custody had reached a point at which custodial sentences were imposed at a rate of fewer than one per week. Among a bench of 120 strong, therefore, the experience of participation in a custodial sentence would indeed be infrequent for individual magistrates. Several magistrates in interview commented on the rarity of their personal experience of imposing custody, attributing this, in common with other court personnel, to a prevailing reluctance among their ranks to invoke this sanction.

Moreover, a genuinely sparing approach to the use of custodial sanctions was indicated during courtroom observation, during which 22 defendants were sentenced to immediate custody. In these cases, magistrates did not routinely invoke the full extent of their powers. For example, 14 of these defendants were sentenced to periods of 28 days or less. Yet these custodial sentences included cases which were at the top of the range of seriousness at magistrates' court level, such as 2 drug suppliers who received 21 days, and a defendant awarded 3 months for 15 offences of dishonesty and 1 of GBH. Even in 6 cases involving the breach of suspended sentences, magistrates explored alternatives unsuccessfully for 2 unco-operative defendants, reduced the period to be served in 2 instances, and did not activate the suspension, which was due to expire the following day, in another. It thus emerged during observation that City magistrates were parsimonious in their imposition of custodial sentences, even in high-tariff cases.

Furthermore, in several cases, the imposition of custody made little or no difference to defendants' situations at the time. For example, a sentence of 28 days was imposed for theft and destruction of a motorcycle on a defendant who was already serving a longer sentence received at the Crown Court. Four defendants received nominal sentences of 1 day and were released at the close of court business, for offences of theft, begging and drunkenness.

Indeed, a collective magisterial aversion to imprisonment emerged in the course of asking for views on City court's use of custody. Most appeared complacent about the possibility that they were less reliant on custody than some other courts.

> We're always thought of as a soft bench. I remember going to a training exercise fairly early on and one of the stipendiaries was full of contempt for the soft approach of the (City) magistrates.

> I think we're softer. I think that's brought about by these strange intellectual exercises we have to go through if we ever want to send anybody to prison these days.

Complacency, however, did not simply reflect the indifference to the sentencing traditions of other courts which is remarked upon in the research literature (Parker, Sumner and Jarvis 1989; Tarling 1979). Almost all magistrates, during interview, spontaneously deplored imprisonment, although no question directly invited an expression of opinion on the prison system. Indeed, magistrates appeared confident of the representativeness of their views on this issue.

[Our former clerk] was very strong on this, that we should never deprive a person of their liberty unless there just was no other way. To deprive a person of their liberty was the worst thing you could do to them. You mustn't do it unless there just was nothing else to do. I was trained by him and so I suppose I've gone along with that view.

I'm all for keeping them out of prison. Prison's going to do them nothing but harm.

The more I know about prison, particularly the lack of rehabilitation, the less I want to send people [there].

Given their parsimonious approach to the use of custody, and the extent of magistrates' personal antipathy to it, the frequency with which they referred to it in interview was puzzling. City magistrates often spoke of imprisonment as a real, and even regular, sentencing consideration. They also apparently believed that many of the sentences they passed were direct alternatives to custody.

Bending over backwards not to send people to prison, because the prisons are overcrowded. There has been a change in thoughts about the usefulness of prison for certain crimes, and we've been exhorted by the powers that be to look very carefully at this. And I agree with them.

We're much more encouraged from on high to cut out prison wherever possible...Much more emphasis now on trying to find non-custodial sentences.

One magistrate remarked impatiently on the frequency of discussion about a sanction which was not willingly invoked:

When we have meetings and we talk about custody, I say: 'Well, when was the last time any of you sent someone to prison?' And they all look round and they can't remember. We don't do it. Then people come round and spend 45 minutes telling us not to send people to prison and why we shouldn't do that and I'm thinking: 'We're already doing this, what are they lecturing us for?'

Magistrates' pre-occupation with custody begins to become explicable in the light of comments such as the following:

I do remember being upset on one occasion, but I really was able to accept that we had done everything to avoid this and that if we didn't do it then we were going to look very foolish.

Paperwork coming from everywhere saying do not send everybody to prison. But nevertheless, that must be the sanction at the end of the day, providing it's there as a punishment, in some cases.

In any bench of our size there will be perhaps 20 who take it seriously, in the sense that they take a deeper interest in it. It's not just in here once a week or fortnight, going home and forgetting all about it. They're genuinely interested in how the judicial system works at our level, and indeed at Crown Court level. People who read about it, people who follow it as I do...There's a number of other people – a big majority it may be said – who perhaps tend to see this as another contribution to their community, but don't look at it in that sort of depth. And I do think that because of that we don't grasp the nettle sometimes.

Comments such as these are vital clues to City magistrates' utilisation of custody. They suggest that custody was a part of these magistrates' 'working reality'. The fact that imprisonment was a real option in their sentencing repertoire, the consequent potential for its use, and the belief that their public duty conferred certain obligations upon them created conditions in which custodial sentencing was an ever-present hypothetical possibility. Therefore, they could not permit their personal antipathy to prison to alter its status as the most significant sanction in their working reality as magistrates.

The Conduct of Court Business

City court conducted its business in a predominantly democratic style. Interactions in the courtroom were generally mutually respectful, favouring a co-operative, problem-solving approach. Negotiation and compromise, rather than openly adversarial engagements, characterised courtroom encounters (see e.g. Darbyshire 1984; Parker, Casburn and Turnbull 1981 for observational comparisons of these styles). Democratic styles of conducting court business have been associated with reduced severity of punishment, particularly the imposition of custody (Anderson 1978; Parker, Casburn and Turnbull 1981).

The democratic, mutually respectful code of conduct extended to the probation service, which enjoyed a recognition as a professional participant in courtroom proceedings which is denied it in some courts (Darbyshire 1984). This recognition was explicitly conveyed in a curious small ceremony, called 'presenting the reports', which was an idiosyncratic feature of City court's operation. In sentencing hearings for which SERs had been prepared, the clerk would ask for the reports to be 'formally presented' by the probation officer at the appropriate point in proceedings, between prosecution and mitigation. The task minimally required the officer to address the bench with the words: 'I am presenting Social Enquiry Reports prepared on the defendant by [my colleague]'.

Probation officers new to City court were invariably caught at a loss when first asked to present reports, finding the request incomprehensible, and would complain that the ritual was unnecessary and embarrassing in its superfluity. However, it soon became a 'scripted' routine to which they gave no thought; so much so, that it did not seem to occur to established officers to give new colleagues prior warning of the practice. Furthermore, established officers learned that this superficial task enabled them to proffer additional comments or advice, simply by providing them with a formal opportunity to speak. This ritual could enable experienced probation officers powerfully to influence proceedings, particularly given the sensitivity of its occurrence between prosecution and mitigation addresses, and the willingness of the court to receive their professional interventions.

City magistrates' enthusiasm for the assistance of probation officers was evident in their remarks about SERs.

I always like to have SERs. We're very often very much discouraged from asking for them because it delays matters and people would rather get things dealt with and I can quite see that... I just feel very hamstrung if there aren't reports and I don't know anything about the person and I'm just having to guess whether he is somebody who's really inadequate or whether he's somebody who is never going to appear again. It's very difficult sometimes to deduce that from what you hear.

They're our right hand, the probation service. They do the ground work, we read the report. They get closer to the client than we do. It would be silly just to throw it out.

The professional recognition and influence of probation officers at City court affected the presentation of mitigation by defence solicitors. Usually, probation officers' assessments and recommendations were useful to their quest for mitigation of punishment. However, on occasions when they were not, defence solicitors tended to refrain from strong criticism of SERs or pressing of alternatives before the magistrates, despite at times taking probation officers to task informally. Research by Anderson (1978) similarly noted the attenuation of defence solicitors' arguments in a court at which social work opinion was valued.

In these circumstances, the 'moral flavour' of a case, or its 'moral quality' (Hogarth 1971), conveyed in probation officers' assessments could be a powerful influence on the sentencing decisions at City magistrates' court.

Example 5.1 The defendant, aged 45, admitted three thefts. In one case, he had stolen the wallet of a man who had bought him a drink in a pub. The other two offences involved shoplifting of a few foodstuffs and a bottle of vodka. The defendant's previous convictions dated back nearly 30 years, involving, for the most part, offences of shoplifting and drunkenness. He was in breach of a probation order imposed two months earlier.

The SER detailed a disrupted background, noting in particular the breakdown of a long-standing relationship and the subsequent loss of contact with his children. The defendant's history since that time had been characterised by homelessness, alcoholism and periodic imprisonment. His offending was 'inextricably linked with his use of alcohol'. Requesting the revocation of the current probation order, the writer concluded:

> His alcohol abuse contributes to a chaotic lifestyle in which he is unable to follow through appointments or sustain often good intentions and this in the past has led to further frustration and disappointment in himself and a tendency to blame others for his problems, in particular helping agencies.

The defence solicitor found 'nothing to gainsay the probation officer's comment about revoking that order':

> The offences are part of a long standing cycle. The current offences ought to be looked at, not as offences committed to fuel a drinking problem, but out of desperation because of social security

problems. Why does he offend? He finds himself in a state of crisis, that leads him to drink and that leads to his committing offences. I invite you to make the inevitable prison sentence as short as possible so that he can get out and start to try to sort his problems out.

The defendant was sentenced to a month's imprisonment concurrently for each of the thefts, and a further consecutive month as a consequence of revocation of the probation order.

Example 5.2   The defendant, aged 40, admitted the theft of a book from a bookshop. His previous convictions, dating back nearly 20 years, almost entirely concerned shoplifting. He was in breach of a conditional discharge, a suspended sentence and a probation order, all imposed for similar offences.

The SER described a successful educational and academic career, disrupted through the defendant's drug addiction. It detailed the loss, after long illnesses, of both parents, and the breakdown of a relationship, with subsequent, and continuing, problems in sustaining contact with the children. The offence was committed after his mother's death, which had been followed by acrimonious family arguments. Recommending a community service order, the writer pointed to the defendant's shame and remorse, his use of supervision 'to discuss his difficulties with frankness and insight', and 'his determined efforts to address his difficulties and rebuild his future'. The defence solicitor endorsed and enlarged upon these comments, claiming to know the defendant better than the probation officer. The defendant was made the subject of a community service order.

The histories of these defendants were essentially similar, at least in the details presented as significant: the disruption of long-term relationships, with consequent unhappiness and unsettlement, and long offence histories attributed to chronic substance abuse. The difference between them lay in their apparent responses to these personal problems. The first defendant stole 'items he thinks he needs and cannot afford' (SER); the second defendant's offending was an irrational expression of drunken despair. The first blamed external problems for his predicament; the second was ashamed and remorseful. The first defendant was unreliable and demanding on probation; the second was co-operative. These moral inferences were conveyed to the court through the mitigation addresses and SERs, reinforced by the unanimous defeat of the defence solicitor and probation officer in the first case, and their equally unanimous optimism in the second.

In particular, this optimism led to the discovery of an alternative to custody for a defendant who was, in fact, already in breach of more 'alternatives to custody' than his imprisoned counterpart.

Structured Decision Making

The response of the justices' clerk, whose views were sought on City magistrates' parsimonious use of custody, was forthright:

> It isn't a matter of being inclined or disinclined to use custody, it's a simple fact that they are currently being told to use it as a last resort. That's the current state of the law and that's what they're here to carry out. They have to leave their prejudices outside the door – whatever their prejudices are.

The vehemence with which this assertion was made was striking. The justices' clerk's intention to ensure that magistrates followed the prescribed decision-making procedures was clear. Moreover, if the level of awareness among magistrates of these procedures is an indication of success, then the clerk seemed to be enjoying some measure. In interview, magistrates frequently referred spontaneously to the increasing training provided for them, and in particular to the structured decision-making procedures they were required to follow in individual cases.

> One sees the sentencing process as a series of steps and having reached one conclusion you then progress to the next. This is what I mean by thinking sequentially. There's no room for intuitive process. It's not to say that you may not have a very strong feeling one way or another, but that reflects a personal view. And I think one has too be very careful that doesn't become the dominant thing. Sentencing process, to me, ought to be a gradual progression from point A to the objective.

> We have structured decision making here ... You are supposed to think of the offence first, how serious is it (on a scale of) nought to ten. Having made that decision, are there any mitigating factors that can be taken into account from the point of view of the offender. And do it in a structured way.

> We've had this extra training where we must look at the offence ... We mustn't make a quick judgement ... Now there's the question of being asked not to take their previous record into account.

This awareness, and endorsement, of the structured approach to sentencing decisions among City magistrates contrasts strongly with some other observations of sentencers' behaviour (Ashworth 1987; Burney 1985; Parker, Sumner and Jarvis 1989). Parker, Sumner and Jarvis remark:

> Rather than determining the sentencing process, the legal framework operates as a resource for the achievement of other objectives ... and thus, conversely, on occasion as a handicap which has to be overcome in order for those objectives to be met. (1989, p. 84)

It would be naive to suggest that City magistrates never considered the application of law in the light of their own preferences in individual cases. Nor is it claimed here that City magistrates diligently followed the procedural rules in all cases. Nevertheless, the inference in Parker, Sumner and Jarvis' comment that magistrates in the pursuit of their own objectives were antagonistic towards the proper application of sentencing law does not appear to apply to City court.

CONCLUSION

The point of this brief introduction to the culture of City court is to highlight reasons for magistrates' openness to mitigation. Personal antipathy to custody is not to be disregarded, although it cannot be relied upon by itself to produce low rates of incarceration (Hogarth 1971). It combined, however, with a democratic, problem-solving style of conducting court business, recognition of probation officers as professional contributors to that process and a structured approach to sentencing decision making which focused attention on case-specific detail.

These features of City court's culture and operation produced a decision-making environment in which the magistrates were open to the social psychological process of mitigation to be achieved by the provocation of mindfulness of, or individualised reasoning about, cases. Nevertheless, in the pressured environment of the courtroom, 'short cuts' to decision making are inevitable. Thus, at City court, sentencing decisions emerged from the interplay of the tensions between susceptibility to the social-psychological process of mitigation through individualised attention and the necessary simplifications of complex information-processing tasks under pressure of time. As will be seen, appeals to intoxication and alcoholism offered many advantages in the management of these tensions.

6 Simple Schemata and Offender Characterisations

From the brief examination of the decision-making environment, we turn now to explore the decision-making process. This chapter is primarily concerned with strategies for simplifying the information-processing task in the courtroom. Some simplifying strategies which played a vital part in sentencing decision making in City court are identified: simple schemata and offender characterisations. The use of information about the involvement of alcohol in an offence to enhance these simplifying strategies is explored. In addition, the utility of offender characterisations, not only for explaining offences but also for formulating and justifying responses, is shown.

THE RESORT TO SIMPLIFICATION

Fitzmaurice and Pease (1986) identify four considerations in the judgement of responsibility: the act; the actor; the target or victim; and the environment in which the act occurs. However, the potential quantity of information which these four elements may yield is vast. The difficulty of processing this mass of information is exacerbated by features of courtroom procedure – for example: the quality of the information itself may be poor (Hogarth 1971); the formal sequence of its presentation disrupts efficient processing (Hogarth 1971; Shapland 1987); and there is pressure of time (Pennington and Lloyd-Bostock 1987). In this context, decision makers develop 'simplifying choice heuristics in an effort to reduce cognitive strain' (Carroll and Payne 1976, p. 24; also Eiser and Van Der Pligt 1988; Lawrence and Homel 1986; Van Duyne 1987).

This is not a phenomenon peculiar to magisterial decision making. Psychological theories which depict human judgement as an exercise in logical, scientific and mathematical reasoning based on the rigorous accumulation and assimilation of available information (e.g. Kelley 1967) have attracted increasing criticism (Abelson 1976; Carroll and

Payne 1976; Eiser and Van Der Pligt 1988; Hewstone 1983; Ickes and Layden 1978; Jaspars 1983; Langer 1978; Mandler 1984; Nisbett and Wilson 1977; Palmerino, Langer and McGillis 1984; Semin and Manstead 1983; Sillars 1982; Tversky and Kahneman 1974). Critics point to the fact that 'the highly influential views of information-processing psychology argue that human rationality is seriously limited by biological constraints' (Carroll and Weaver 1986, p. 20). In so far as individuals may be capable of processing information in such highly rational ways, the likelihood of their doing so is inhibited by pressures of time, the difficulty of such reasoning processes and the huge amounts of information in the environment which would need to be processed to achieve results (Abelson 1976; Hewstone 1983; Mandler 1984; Sillars 1982). In these circumstances, the notion that the sentencing decision is reached through a logical, mathematical weighting of discrete items of mitigating and aggravating information, as advice to sentencers suggests it should be, is highly suspect (Fitzmaurice and Pease 1986).

The difficulty of the information-processing task confronting magistrates in individual cases, when cues to assist rapid interpretation were slight or absent, may be illustrated.

Example 6.1 Two defendants, aged 17 and 18, were jointly charged with theft of a motorcycle.

> CPS: The loser of the motorcycle, at 7.30 p.m. on 29 April, put it in his shed at his home, but didn't lock it. He noticed it missing at 10.45 a.m. the next day. The cycle had already been spotted by an observant passer-by, driving along, when he saw two youths near a cycle, lying down in the grass. He stopped and saw them go back to it and start taking parts off it. He took the number of one of the cycles they were riding. Next day he again passed the lay-by and noticed that someone was continuing to strip the cycle. He contacted the police, who located the owner, to identify it. The owner estimated the value of the cycle at about £900, but the insurance company have paid him and there is no claim for compensation today. The defendants were traced through the number taken of the cycle.

This oblique approach to describing the offence commission, through a discussion of the behaviour of non-offending parties rather than that of the defendants, was quite common in more serious, and complex, cases. Magistrates exposed to information in such a manner would have to work hard to form a judgement of defendants' personal blameworthiness.

In this context, an observation may be made about the use of SERs in complex cases. Not infrequently, magistrates were given SERs to read prior to the formal commencement of the sentencing court. Occasionally this also happened during a normal court session, when there were interruptions and delays in the processing of cases. The intention behind this practice, innocently enough, was to save time. The manner in which this purpose was achieved, however, might have surprised probation officers, or given court personnel cause for concern about the protection of due process, had they considered it. In a post-sentence interview a magistrate remarked appreciatively:

> The report told us about the background, but also about the incident. It's a good thing that reports do that more these days. We had the reports before the court and this saved everyone a lot of time. It makes for more efficiency with such complicated information. We didn't have to rely on a recital of facts and it wasn't slanted in any way. It was a straightforward account of what happened.

In the absence of clear guidance from solicitors or probation officers, magistrates had to find their own explanations for criminal conduct.

Example 6.2 The defendant, aged 28, admitted causing an affray. The prosecution solicitor told the magistrates that the incident escalated out of 'a rather ludicrous row', over the allegation that a coin had been stolen from the defendant's son by a neighbour's child. This defendant had some prior convictions, which did not include serious violence, and of which the most recent had occurred eight years previously. While recounting in detail somewhat conflicting versions of the offence, neither the prosecution nor the defence solicitor offered a persuasive explanation as to why the defendant had armed himself with an axe for the conduct of this neighbourly dispute, and had lost his temper in an unnerving manner out of all proportion to his grievance.

The defendant was black, wore his hair in dreadlocks, and, being legally represented, did not speak during the proceedings. It appeared that the magistrate had found an explanation for his disproportionate aggression, when imposing a fine of £100 with the unwarranted advice: 'There is no need in this country to go round armed with an axe and deal with situations in this way.'

SIMPLE SCHEMATA

Alternative theories of information processing explicitly recognise that 'people fail to behave consistently with normative rationality, but instead make simplifications and shortcuts that are reasonable but may produce inferior outcomes' (Carroll and Weaver 1986, p. 20). These theoretical perspectives on decision making outlined above have even stimulated social psychologists to confront 'the question of whether humans analyse social cues *at all* in their day-to-day social interactions' (Hewstone 1983, p. 10). The answer has increasingly been couched in terms of the 'mindlessness of ostensibly thoughtful action' (Langer 1978, p. 38). The consequent theoretical perspective has centred on the learning and utilisation of basic intellectual frameworks for selecting and interpreting information in the environment in order to make rapid judgements about the nature of specific situations and the appropriate action within them. Such frameworks have been called 'cognitive scripts' (Abelson 1976; Hewstone 1983; Langer 1978) or 'cognitive schemata' (Crocker, Fiske and Taylor 1984; Eiser and Van Der Pligt 1988; Holstein 1985; Mandler 1984; Sillars 1982). Cognitive scripts or schemata enable individuals to ignore substantial quantities of information in the environment and yet to respond rapidly, by prescribing basic cues for the identification of, and appropriate response to, specific situations.

Crocker, Fiske and Taylor explain the advantages of utilising cognitive schemata.

> Social schemas are very useful to perceivers: They help us to structure, organise, and interpret new information; they facilitate encoding, storage, and retrieval of relevant information; they can affect the time it takes to process information, and the speed with which problems can be solved. Schemas also serve interpretive and inferential functions. (1984, p. 197)

Decision-making research suggests that 'schemata' (Holstein 1985; Mandler 1984) are established early, as information emerges, providing 'initial characterisation' (Fiske and Neuberg 1989), or 'working hypotheses' (Lloyd-Bostock 1988), to guide the selection and organisation of subsequent data (similarly Carroll and Payne 1976; Hawkins 1983b; Scheff 1966).

In City court, in cases which were relatively non-serious and unproblematic for sentencing, the prosecution solicitor sometimes opened with the reassurance: 'This is a straightforward case', or 'The defendant has no previous convictions'.

Alternatively, magistrates could be offered cues to suitable schemata by the prosecution solicitor's opening remarks. These cues suggested obvious explanations of the offence under consideration which simplified the information-processing task for magistrates. No other item of information could rival the success of intoxication in the provision of these simple schemata. Indeed, in a search of 50 sober cases, only 2 simple schemata could be identified. In a case involving 4 shamefaced youths who had climbed up flagpoles to appropriate the flags while out for a drive, the prosecution solicitor announced: 'This appears to be a jaunt'. This diagnosis was confirmed by the defence solicitor's reference to 'a jolly night out'. Of criminal damage to a car perpetrated by a 43-year-old first offender, the prosecution solicitor remarked that it was 'a revenge attack' aimed at his ex-wife's new boyfriend.

These simple schemata were derived from information specific to the offences and offenders. Although readily understood as explanations for these particular offences, they are not applicable to a generality of cases. Intoxication, however, is widely available as a simple, intuitively obvious explanation for offending because of the range of behaviours and moods with which it is associated in lay theory. Moreover, this information rapidly conjures a vivid picture, conveying the moral flavour of the case in question. These illustrations of opening remarks by prosecution solicitors quite literally 'speak for themselves':

At about midnight, the defendants were going in a group to a party, already having been drinking. They were high-spirited, and they decided to run across the roofs of cars for some reason.

This arose from an argument between the landlord at the [pub] and the defendant, who didn't want to give up his drink at closing time.

The defendant was walking past the window of [a department store] at 5 to 1 a.m., with friends. They had been drinking and the defendant described himself as 'merry'. For some reason he picked up a bin and threw it through the window.

This case can be dealt with very simply by using the defendant's own words: 'I was in a pub and bought them. They were nicked.'

At mid-day the defendant was found asleep beside an empty beer can by a police constable.

The defendant is charged with theft of handbags. He was seen by a shop manager in the shopping centre, who saw a drunk sitting there. He opened his coat to a female drunk, showing her four handbags.

Occasionally the prosecution solicitor would open with oblique references to intoxication, which were nonetheless intuitively obvious to the listener. A brief indication of the moral flavour of the offence, often aided by pointed references to its timing, would suffice to prepare the audience for the emergent picture of intoxicated disinhibition.

At 9 p.m., in the city centre, a police officer saw the defendant lying propped against a pillar. He heard him say to two young ladies: 'What are you fucking looking at?'

It seems appropriate to start with the comments of [one defendant], who said to the police after the event: 'I was walking down [the] street with my mum and there were insults shouted at us and things got out of hand.' It was 11.30 p.m. on a Friday night. Things got so out of hand that eight police officers and a dog handler were called to the scene.

To begin by an explanation, really an apology, that I am going to have to use certain abusive language, which is really what brought this to court. At a quarter to one in the morning...

In cases such as these, the defence solicitor often confirmed and reinforced the simple schemata suggested by the prosecution.

This was two young men, the worse for drink, swearing themselves into arrest. They were warned and they continued, because of the drink.

An opening announcement by the defence solicitor of the fact of intoxication could immediately impose a vivid schema upon information blandly recited in the prosecution address, even for such relatively serious offences as burglary.

My client describes this offence as 'plain stupidity', and his two co-defendants agree wholeheartedly with that view. All had been out that night drinking – and drinking heavily.

The utility of statements about intoxication for constructing simple schemata becomes even more evident when compared with mental disorder as an explanation for offences. References to defendants' psychiatric problems were severely constrained by the delicacy of the subject, which demanded a tact and diplomacy quite unnecessary in the treatment of intoxicated offenders.

Example 6.3   The defendant, aged 22, admitted two thefts from a bookshop and asked for a similar offence to be taken into consideration. He had no previous convictions.

> CPS: This is not quite the typical theft of books...What happened was that he went into [the shop] with some books and swopped them for books on the shelves. In interview he explained he had come to [City] to go to the library and also to exchange some books he had with him for books of a similar value in [the bookshop]. He was effectively using [the shop] as a library. He also admitted to a theft from another bookshop that day and two books from [the same shop] previously, which is the offence to be taken into consideration.

The prosecuting solicitor's opening remark alerted magistrates to unusual features of a common offence without providing an explanation. The defence solicitor explained that the defendant, finding that he had earlier bought study books which he did not need, 'could not bring himself to go into the shop and approach an assistant and actually barter for the exchange'. However, letters from the defendant's doctor and psychiatrist, passed without verbal commentary to the bench by the solicitor, revealed a chronic physical complaint which had provoked severe depression, now being treated through psychotherapy. The defendant was conditionally discharged with an expression of magisterial sympathy.

References to a defendant's mental disorder, notwithstanding the potential vastly to simplify a case, could be politely oblique to the point of virtual obscurity.

Example 6.4   The defendant, aged 38, was charged with three shoplifting offences, with three more to be taken into consideration.

Guilty pleas were taken with some difficulty, with many interruptions by the defendant who eventually threw up his hands and cried: 'Oh! I've just had so much!' He bowed to the bench: 'I'm sorry, it's your court, there'll be no more.' He then sat quietly through most of the hearing.

> CPS: The defendant is a noticeable man. He was seen in [a chemist's shop], and next day he was approached by a police officer, who said he believed he had taken some pills. The defendant gave him some pills, saying: 'I took them for experimenting on myself.' He also said: 'I've taken some books too.' The books were found at his house –
>
> Def (*interrupting*): I showed them where they were.
>
> CPS (*resuming patiently*): I think you all know this defendant has a habit of stealing books, and has had that habit for years...

The defence solicitor similarly appealed to magistrates' long familiarity with the defendant.

> His problems are well known to the bench. Because of his problems he is a persistent offender, but they are more nuisance offences, at the lower end of the scale. He did co-operate with the police. You know his problems. He has his ups and downs...

The magistrates decided upon financial penalties while the defendant held up his hands in a prayer-like attitude.

This defendant liked the more outrageous fashions. He was missing an eye as a result of self-mutilation during an extreme psychosis some years earlier. His recurrent mania was exacerbated by chronic substance abuse. His interest in the occult informed his choice of misappropriated literature. Yet, had these magistrates been unfamiliar with the defendant, these veiled references to his 'noticeability' and 'ups and downs' might have been unintelligible. They glanced frequently in his direction as they listened, as if to confirm the implications of some of the solicitors' remarks. Today, however, the defendant was soberly dressed in a grey jersey and jeans. His dark glasses, though inappropriate to the occasion, concealed his disfigurement. His demeanour during most of the hearing was submissive. Only his early interruptions, his prayer-like posture as sentence was considered and later protestations about the size of his unpaid fines provided clues to his capacity for bizarre behaviour. These actions, however, were ambiguous: they could have been taken for mockery of the court.

The unrivalled power of intoxication schemata, by contrast, derived from free and explicit use, unrestricted by the rules of decency and social restraint which constrained references to tragic facts about defendants' mental disorder.

OFFENDER CHARACTERISATIONS

Processes of characterisation are central to human judgements about the world, and are at the heart of decisions made in the criminal process from the policeman on the street onwards. Characterisation is a means of endowing individuals with attributes to make sense of them and to place them; it creates and organises expectations since it embodies a description and a prediction. (Hawkins 1983a, p. 119)

Thus, sentencers utilise lay conceptualisations of deviance in ways which simplify the particular task of processing cases (Lloyd-Bostock 1988; Tajfel and Forgas 1981). While these lay conceptualisations involve commonsense notions with wide familiarity, different courts may favour different lay theories. For example, Parker, Casburn and Turnbull (1981) found that magistrates in a punitive juvenile court appealed frequently to the concept of 'criminal families' in their explanations of juvenile delinquency. Such a theory of deviance is widely understood in everyday life, and, indeed, has received a measure of academic attention. It is unlikely that City magistrates were unaware of this commonsense theory, but it was not one upon which they appeared to be reliant in their case characterisations.

Similarly, the basic offender characterisations which enabled City court to process complex cases appeal to recognisable commonsense notions of deviance. Characterisations which had particular relevance to the use of information about intoxication or alcoholism could be identified: those concerning young adult offenders aged 17 to 20; those concerning young men aged between 21 and 25; the category of 'tragic' offenders; and the category of 'sick' offenders.

Young Adult Offenders: the Vulnerable and the Undisciplined

The widespread ambivalence in conceptualisations of, and attitudes towards, youthful crime is reflected in criminal justice policy itself

(Rumgay 1990). For example, the co-existence of rehabilitative borstal training and punitive detention centre regimes characterised British responses to young offenders for more than 30 years. While there may be general agreement that young offenders 'may be at a turning point which decides whether they will become recidivists or responsible citizens' (Home Office 1980), opinion fluctuates as to the means to achieving the latter outcome.

At the heart of this dilemma lies the question whether youthful crime is a symptom of maturational vulnerability or of indiscipline. In City court, however, both of these explanations were true. There was no need for a choice in the theoretical abstract between the competing explanations for youthful crime. The choice between them was made at the level of assessments of individual offenders.

Example 6.5 The defendant, aged 18, admitted offences of burglary, taking a vehicle without consent, theft of petrol, and allowing himself to be carried in a stolen vehicle. He had been hitch-hiking from Scotland to London with a friend. They were offered a lift by two youths who, it transpired, were juvenile runaways driving a stolen car. This gradually dawned upon the defendant, as the prosecution solicitor observed, 'yet his wish to get to London over-rode his scruples'. Indeed, after a while, 'it seems his wish to get to London had rather faded', as he became involved in further offences. He had one previous conviction for assault.

The defence solicitor produced the conviction records of the juveniles, 'as it is part of my mitigation that one of them is a sophisticated car thief'. The offences were portrayed as the response of a naive youth to the persuasions of a unique set of circumstances.

The defendant was unsophisticated, in a situation where they couldn't get lifts, and were picked up by two sophisticated car thieves, albeit young ones. He has hitch-hiked regularly, but only in these circumstances was he encouraged on this path.

The defendant was 'a sensitive, articulate young man, with a bad start'. His potential strength of character was suggested by his conscientious compliance with the court proceedings.

He has had to appear in court on four or five occasions and, coming from Edinburgh, has always been here punctually. That says a lot about him when you know some young people in [City] find difficulty in getting to court on time.

The SER substantiated this characterisation of a youth without criminal intentions falling prey to the vicissitudes of an unstable life-style. The defendant's adolescence had been disrupted by the death of his mother, rejection by his stepfather and educational failure. Poor accommodation and employment opportunities encouraged repeated, but always unsuccessful, forays to England to try to improve his prospects. In this context, his acquaintance with his co-defendants 'was the result of ill-luck and even worse judgement'.

His unsettled, rootless background has obviously developed con-siderable self-reliance, but he is aware of a need for adult advice and guidance to help him settle into a more responsible lifestyle. Despite his chequered career, he is clearly not an habitual offender and is extremely anxious to make a new start.

Example 6.6   The defendant, aged 18, admitted wounding, theft and failure to surrender to his bail. He had three previous convictions for dishonesty. The assault was the result of a grievance against the male victim who had stolen and damaged his bicycle. Encountering the victim by chance, the defendant demanded money in compensation and punched him, breaking his nose. The thefts involved the persua-sion of a female shop assistant by the defendant and another male to pass them some clothing.

The defence solicitor argued that the suggestion to the shop assist-ant had initially been intended as a joke: 'They were in fact quite taken aback when she complied.' For the assault, however, it was acknowledged that little mitigation was possible, although 'it was a culmination of the frustration he felt as to how he had been robbed'. The breach of bail had arisen because the defendant had been ordered to appear on different, but consecutive, days for the different offences. He missed the first appearance while looking for employ-ment, volunteered this information to the court next day and was told a warrant had been issued for his arrest. The defence solicitor coun-tered a complaint in the SER that the defendant had missed an appointment with the probation officer with the claim that he had informed the probation service of a prior arrangement to play football in Holland.

The writer of the SER recounted that the defendant had been expelled from school, and cautioned by police, for striking another pupil. This appeared to be the basis for the subsequent observation that 'he has a history of violent acts when he perceives he has been wronged'. The defendant had left various jobs through stealing, boredom and disputes with supervisors. The probation officer remarked:

> [The defendant] presents as a casual young man. This is reflected in his failure to surrender to bail and perhaps in his first missed appointment with me. His attitude is further reflected by his opening a bank account... after leaving school and issued (*sic*) cheques which could not be honoured... [T]he bank recovered the money from his mother... It is perhaps this attitude which led [him] to act in such an ill-considered way on these occasions, with little thought for the consequences.

Compensation to the victim of the assault was recommended, because, since the defendant considered 'he had some justification in his actions such an award would have a salutary effect'. In addition, a probation order, with a condition of attendance at a groupwork programme, would 'address the issues central to [his] offending'. The magistrates followed the recommendation on the grounds, explained in a post-sentence interview, that this would be 'a greater punishment' for 'this horrible young man' than custody.

Both of these defendants were placed on probation. This may owe much, in the latter case, to City magistrates' preference for the non-custodial options and to a mitigation address which succeeded in moderating some of the moral inferences in the SER without undermining the credibility of the recommendation.

These two cases illustrate the kinds of information upon which the assessment of young adult offenders was based. Notably, the ambivalence between views of this group as either vulnerable or undisciplined is reflected in the ambiguity of the information deemed pertinent to the assessment. The characterisation of young adults as vulnerable or undisciplined relied upon essentially similar information in each case. The information itself appealed to three commonsense beliefs about the causes and nature of youthful crime:

1. Impulsivity

The notion of the impulsivity of youth is most strongly invoked in Example 6.6, in which the defendant acted upon feelings of grievance evoked by a chance encounter. Mitigation addresses frequently appealed to this theme.

> This seems to have been a flash of temper, the over-reaction of an immature young man.

We are under a duty to co-operate with the police, however unreasonable their behaviour may be. But you can understand that you are a young man, perhaps not as imbued with law-abiding instincts as others. You are stopped in what you think is an unreasonable manner and you react.

SERs also invoked this notion:

[Probation] will aim to promote the defendant into thinking more carefully about his behaviour and to try and act in a more responsible and mature fashion.

One magistrate graphically described the impulsivity of youth in a post-sentence interview:

None of this was done with any criminal intent. He acted out of impulse, not planning to bash her face or drive the car at her.

2. Contamination

The notion that young people are susceptible to the evil influences of others is heavily invoked in Example 6.5. Defence solicitors used this theme as a means of imputing blame to others without the connotations of evasion of personal responsibility by the offender himself which such a strategy could have.

The defendant has no previous convictions ... Certain items ... were deposited in his room by others and he was told not to touch them.

During the early part of this year, my client appeared to get into a bad lot. He was in a group of youths who were in trouble, and may still be. He has since left that group ...

SERs, as in Example 6.5, could contextualise offending within a problematic period in the defendant's life which rendered him especially susceptible to the promptings of others.

[The defendant] had argued with his girlfriend, and feels he was in such a state of mind that he was easily led astray.

Since coming to [City] he has not been particularly selective about the company he has kept and recognises that he needs to choose his friends more carefully.

Magistrates, in post-sentence interviews, expressed their views on contamination in the following ways:

He seemed to be easily led, but on the other hand he must have known something about crime because he had a cousin who had all those other offences...He's from a culture where taking cars is a way of life. To him it probably isn't a terrible thing to do at all.

Our thoughts were directed at whether he was involved in the drugs scene, because people of that age wouldn't need to arm themselves [with a carving knife].

3. Turbulence

Adolescent turbulence was an extraordinarily useful concept in the explanation of youthful crime. Firstly, young adults were still sufficiently close to their childhood for the effects of early trauma to be perceived in their present plight. Example 6.5 illustrates this approach. One magistrate, in a post-sentence interview, expressed this theory in the following remarks:

He'd had a most unfortunate early life...I think immaturity is an important word here...His age and lack of guidance. He's lacked that most of his life. Very immature, due in part to a very disrupted life from the age of two.

Secondly, a turbulent phase in a defendant's personal circumstances could explain his susceptibility to criminal temptation or contamination. This was a common theme in mitigation addresses.

The offences were committed at a time when he had to leave his parents and was living rough.

He was short of money. Perhaps, at a deeper level, the offences were committed at a phase when he was leading an unsettled life. Particularly, he was in difficulties with his family and particularly his step-father, which persuaded him to leave home and adopt this unsettled way of life in [City].

In an SER, a probation officer identified turbulence in a manner which reflected well on the defendant's sense of personal responsibility:

He offered no excuses nor (*sic*) reason for his behaviour, and only when I pushed the point did he say that all the offences had occurred after he had been asked to leave his mother's home.

These concepts of impulsivity, contamination and turbulence, often in combination, richly informed the characterisation of young adult offenders. Yet objectively similar information could evoke different responses and moral judgements in individual cases. In respect of young adult offenders, the moral ambiguity of even well-developed and complex theories of criminality was striking.

The age-related patterns of heavy drinking and offending might encourage expectation of very frequent invocation of the intoxication excuse in this age group. However, about half of the young adult defendants in the study were classified as 'sober' offenders: there was no reference to alcohol in the proceedings. This even balance could reflect the complex and well-developed theories of youthful criminality on which characterisations were founded, reducing potential reliance on explanatory information about defendants' use of alcohol. Certainly, it seemed that in many of the alcohol-related cases, this information was less important than social information pertinent to the identification of impulsivity, contamination and turbulence. Direct reference to intoxication thus often took the form of a minimal statement which, by implication, illuminated the claim that an offence was impulsive, a response to peer influence, or part of a turbulent phase. Thus, SERs contained information such as the following:

> Following an argument with his father he left home and whilst in a distraught state committed an offence of criminal damage. I understand that [he] had consumed a considerable amount of alcohol.

> He advised me that he met his co-accused through a friend of a friend. He suggested that they had been drinking and simply went around car parks in [City], breaking into cars and stealing the contents...There are two particular areas of concern – being offending behaviour and family and relationships, that [he] could well do with looking at in some depth. I am also concerned for one so young to be rootless and without any guidance.

Information about defendants' alcohol use could on occasion contribute heavily to characterisation. However, the contradictory lay beliefs about motivations for drinking and alcohol's effects could exacerbate the ambiguities inherent in the characterisations themselves.

Example 6.7 The defendant, aged 19, was sentenced for offences of theft, handling, breach of the peace and two offences of criminal damage. He had served a custodial sentence for his first, sexual, offence, and had been twice subsequently convicted for less serious offences.

The SER noted the onset of heavy drinking following the defendant's release from custody, when 'he was shunned by the local community and all of his friends bar one'. Later, a long relationship with a girlfriend broke down, after which 'his alcohol consumption rose again and he committed the offences currently before the court'. Against this background, the SER detailed the offences.

One offence of criminal damage was committed while the defendant was 'light headed' after drinking, and was 'rather bored and still angry about his recent breakup with his girlfriend'. The defendant fell asleep in his car beside the wall on which he had spray painted graffiti: 'He did not own up to the offence as he thought that he could get away with it.' The second criminal damage offence involved throwing a beer mug through a car windscreen. This followed a drinking session with other youths during which 'conversation deteriorated and eventually verbal abuse was exchanged', culminating in the driving of a car into the defendant's path by another of the group. The public order offence also followed a drinking session, when the defendant slapped his drunken sister 'to bring her to her senses', and punched a man who remonstrated. Dishonesty offences involved stage passes and a crate of beer stolen at a music festival.

These detailed accounts of drunken loutishness overwhelmed the original suggestion that drinking reflected unhappiness and rejection. The writer concluded that the defendant was easily influenced by peers and 'lacked the self control and the sound judgement to deal with situations more appropriately especially having consumed a lot of alcohol'. Despite the lengthy attention to the detail of the offences, including the number of pints consumed on each occasion, the writer thought the defendant had not been 'entirely honest' during interviews for the report. Accordingly, it was argued that 'he would neither respond to the exacting supervised structure of a Probation Order, nor would he positively address his previous offending behaviour individually or in a group setting'.

This conclusion as to the defendant's unreliability was curiously at odds with the information also provided that he had held stable employment for two years, had nearly cleared a £400 fine, had become almost teetotal in deference to a new girlfriend, and 'expressed feelings of guilt and embarrassment about his offending'. He was fined £750, and told: 'You really are in deep trouble.'

Alternatively, skilful use of information about a young defendant's drinking could enhance a clear characterisation.

Example 6.8   The defendant, aged 20, was jointly charged with an older man with telephoning police with a hoax warning of a bomb at a local factory. His only previous conviction, for burglary, had occurred four years earlier.

The writer of the SER reported that the defendant was 'at a complete loss' to explain the offence, the more so since he had spoiled a chance of employment at the factory. Having been drinking beforehand, the defendant had little recall of the offence. This observation led to an examination of his drinking habits, which raised 'the possibility that he may already be doing himself some permanent health damage'. The probation officer then contextualised this drinking pattern in the lifestyle of 'a young man who has somewhat lost his way in the world', who 'appears rather aimless and depressed' and who 'regards the regular and excessive consumption of alcohol as a means of identifying with his friends'. Recommending a probation order to give the defendant 'a much needed "push" in the right direction', the probation officer explained:

> [The defendant], like many of his contemporaries, has come to view the time spent in a public house as being the only interesting or enjoyable part of his day. Motivation towards finding employment or stretching himself in any more constructive way would appear lacking. In such circumstances a loss of self-respect and a deterministic view of one's fate becomes something of an inevitability.

21–25-year olds: the Independent and the Needy

There was no ambiguity in the deep personal problems or serious offending histories, sometimes in combination, of this older group of young men. It was quite common for defence solicitors representing such young men to juxtapose their age and criminal record. This technique stressed their alarming predicament and the urgent necessity for action to halt the slide into chronic recidivism.

> The defendant is 22 and now on his third page of previous convictions... There is a frightening pattern of offending now emerging.

He is aged 24, with an appalling record...Sentences passed have spanned the whole range of options including a 13-month custodial sentence.

The defendant is just 21 and has chalked up a number of convictions, some quite serious for his age.

Age was also connected with the intensity of personal problems to heighten the sense of urgency.

My client has an appalling record... All of the offences arose when he was not only heavily drunk. He was very drunk indeed. He was associating with the alcoholics in [the city centre]. I repeat: he is 21.

He is 23. There you have the real problems and the stark reality of his age... The relationship (with his girlfriend) will go if he is imprisoned, there is no doubt about that and that raises the possibility of him being itinerant at about 24-years-of-age.

Against such a background, the court could be urged to seize a last opportunity to avert irretrievable deterioration.

You might look at the past failure. But all I can say is that it is a positive sentence, not a negative one. This would obviously be the last chance to him of the devotion of such funds to treatment.

I ask you to say you will give him a chance and defer sentence ...This would enable him to continue, as he is now desperately trying to do, to take the right steps.

The [day-centre] option is perhaps the only choice open to you. Custody, or probation with a [day-centre] order. That may at least give him some real direction to pursue for the rest of his life.

In this context, 'the turning point' was often a key concept in the argument.

But he does realise, perhaps for the first time, that it is up to him to change. And he has been making an effort with help from others to take the first steps along the road.

The ingredients of stability – a home, a relationship – which were previously lacking, are now present. I invite you to defer sentence to see if what he promises is true. By sending him to prison you may be destroying the only chance he has for the future, because, for once, it's all there waiting for him.

Within these general parameters for mitigation, complex cases in this age range were understood in terms of two broad characterisations: the independent and the needy. Because of the preponderance of alcohol-related cases any attempt to distinguish these characterisations in terms of sober offenders would be misleading.

Example 6.9 The defendant, aged 22, admitted burglary, three shoplifting offences and breach of bail. He had three previous convictions, the last being three years earlier.

The burglary involved smashing the window of a leather goods shop to take a jacket. On arrest, the defendant disclosed earlier thefts of clothes. It was explained that he was a Glaswegian, who had come to City to live with relations, attracted by the prospect of work. Whilst he was unemployed, his girlfriend became pregnant and he committed the offences to raise money to support her. After his arrest, his girlfriend returned to her parents in a distant city, and he went back to Glasgow to help with a crisis in his own family. Thus pre-occupied, he lost track of the court proceedings.

The SER outlined a history of parental alcoholism, cruelty and institutional care. His recent offending, in a state of panic, 'was not rational behaviour, but the product of an unstable young man the worse for drink'. The probation officer offered the following assessment:

> The present offences seem to represent an isolated episode of madness in a young man whose unstable history suggests he could have turned out much worse. [The defendant] impresses as a likeable and otherwise intelligent individual of considerable energy. He talks so much and so fast that it is at times hard to keep track of him. He seemed very determined, and I had the impression that if he set his mind to something, he would either succeed one thousand per cent or fail utterly.

With this in mind, the probation officer recommended financial penalties, observing:

> Whilst I could see some benefit in the Probation Service monitoring and encouraging his progress, I would not consider him an ideal candidate for Probation as he stated his determination not to reoffend and I consider he may well manage this...

The defendant was ordered to pay compensation totalling £775, and placed on community service, although the probation officer had questioned the realism of such an order given his geographically scattered commitments.

The probation officer's remarks in this case illustrate the point at issue. Independence, in these judgements, did not necessarily entail either the absence of personal problems or the ability to solve them in a laudable manner. Rather, it concerned a defendant's will to deal with his problems in his own way, for better or worse. Thus, SERs contained the following assessments:

> [The defendant] is an independent young man who has encountered some problems in his use of alcohol and its effects. He appears to have recognised this and states that he has consciously reduced his drinking considerably. [He] does not, however, wish for specific help with this. Whilst [his] circumstances have clearly been chaotic in the past he has recently made efforts to find secure employment and independent accommodation reflecting a more responsible attitude to his situation than the Court maybe (*sic*) aware of, given his failure to appear in Court.

> [The defendant] is a young man who appears to have the potential and the ability to make something of his life rather than to continue committing offences. In the past he has been unable to capitalise on his assets and the serious current offences appear to arise from him taking a fairly easy option in obtaining money without regard to the consequences.

This capacity for self-determination could evoke some annoyance with offenders who chose the less respectable routes through life. One magistrate in a post-sentence interview remarked: 'He's an irritating young man, with qualifications but going nowhere.'

Example 6.10 The defendant, aged 25, was charged with assaulting a police officer, criminal damage and a public order offence, all arising from a single incident when police intervened in a domestic dispute. The defendant, 'unsteady on his feet and smelling of drink', kneed an officer in the groin and tore another's jacket. He had 14 previous convictions, mostly for burglary, but including arson and assault.

The defendant's probation officer attended court, explaining: 'I realise this report is lengthy, but, having known the defendant for seven years, I have tried to point out the circumstances behind his offending and the influence of the various sentences he has had passed on him.' The detailed account of a miserable life was summarised in the SER in the following way:

> [The defendant] is a reasonable young man who desperately wishes to avoid further trouble. He grew up in a home where excessive drinking occurred and there was little opportunity to develop secure relationships, hence his inability to do now. He had no particular skills at school either academic or sporting which would have provided some self-esteem and he has developed into an anxious man. When his anxiety levels became high he turned to drink and drugs as the quickest way of alleviating these anxieties. Unfortunately it served merely to compound his difficulties... [He] has served four lengthy periods of imprisonment and it holds neither fear nor confrontation for him as the regular routine of prison life shelters him from anxieties. Indeed it has only been in institutions that he has been able to sustain any growth.

The magistrates dispensed with the defence solicitor's services by signalling their intention to follow the recommendation for a probation order including requirements that the defendant attend a groupwork programme and 'undertake whatever treatment the probation service should direct for [his] alcohol problem'.

Despite the persistence, and often unpleasantness, of these needy defendants' offending, their plight was frequently illustrated by the intractability of their problems and a pathetic reliance on other individuals or institutions. SERs contained observations to this effect:

> [The defendant] is a man of considerable, but not necessarily disabling, intellectual and social limitations. He has been well, possibly too well, supported in the past by his mother, and probably lacks the capacity to exercise much self-discipline. His life lacks structure, and has become increasingly focused on the consumption of alcoholic drink, probably limited only by his lack of means. Drinking is the root of his offending.

> In such cases results cannot hope to be achieved instantaneously but will require instead sustained intervention over time. The major task until now has been to attempt to minimise the seriousness of the defendant's offending; thus avoiding the damaging effects of custody; whilst awaiting the level of his emotional maturity to catch up with his chronological age.

[D]uring his first period on remand...he looked visibly ill through worry about the experience. Now he seems relaxed and confident in the cells which have regrettably become like a second home for him...When in custody, he is always full of regret for his actions and of good intentions for the future, and I believe these are all genuine at the time...The question remains...how long can he maintain this progress?

Defence solicitors and probation officers thus appealed directly to magistrates' humanitarian instincts and antipathy to imprisonment as unconstructive. As one defence solicitor despondently concluded: 'It's an uphill struggle, I don't pretend that it's much more than a case of one step forward and six back.' Magistrates' remarks in post-sentence interviews expressed their sympathetic despair.

I somehow didn't want to be fierce to him. I just looked at him and wondered: '*Why* are you offending like this? *Why* can't you pull yourself together?' It stuck in my mind that he's a good worker. I felt he would like to overcome this and become a good member of society. At his age he's either going to do it or not.

He's thoroughly inadequate. He doesn't work. He doesn't do any-thing. He was at [special school]. No-one's managed to make any-thing of him. In the old days he would have been in what we used to call 'colonies', but nowadays it's all community care...He needs someone to organise his activities, take him out, see he is occupied.

'Tragic' Cases

This was a group of 11 cases involving 3 defendants in their 30s and 8 in their 40s. They had usually been successful earlier in life; they had lost all close relationships; in several cases their criminal histories began relatively late; and they were addicted, 2 to drugs and 9 to alcohol. Essentially, the picture in each case was of a life ruined by drink or drugs, a downward spiral of disappointment, followed by substance abuse, precipitating further disappointment. The incomprehensibility of this apparently inexorable progress into physical and material ruin was blatant. No 'right-thinking' person, equipped with the capacity to do otherwise, could conceivably elect for this life of decay.

Example 6.11   The defendant, aged 42, had admitted six shoplifting offences, extraction of electricity, two breaches of bail and breach of a community service order. These offences dated back 11 months. Sentence had been deferred 6 months earlier in the expectation that the defendant would get treatment for his alcoholism, 'make efforts to work' and pay his extensive fines.

Before relating the individual offences, the prosecution solicitor helpfully eased the information processing burden for magistrates with the preface: 'All (stolen) items were either bottles of alcohol or foodstuffs... It's right to say that in respect of every matter before the court the defendant was under the influence of alcohol'.

The defendant had pursued a successful naval career, followed by skilled work in the Middle East. Then his wife and children left him, his career ended and his substantial criminal record began. The SER concluded:

> [The defendant] has been unable to fulfil the objectives set by the Court during the period of deferment and appears to be someone who is on a course of self-destruction. He has talked of suicide... [H]e would find any financial penalty almost impossible to pay... He is considered unsuitable for Community Service because of his poor health and his performance on a previous work placement. [He] has been placed on Probation a number of times ... However, he remains a vulnerable individual and if the Court feels able to make a non-custodial disposal today, I would ask the Justices to consider imposing a six-month Probation Order on [him].

After reading this, the magistrate addressed the defence solicitor: 'We've got to approach this realistically and my colleagues and I really think that the recommendation... is the way we ought to deal with this, unless you have other representations'.

The alacrity with which these magistrates reached their decision was striking. It illustrates the power of compassion to obscure considerations of offence seriousness and persistence. The clerk, who encouraged the magistrates to make a probation order for 12 instead of 6 months, subsequently commented:

> Six months is really too short. Even [City] probation service can't cure someone like that in only six months!... With someone like that, even if he seems better in six months, problems recur, don't they? He was very lucky not to go down today, or even upstairs [to Crown court], with a record like that. OK, he's a sick man, but look at his record.

The drug addict of example 5.2, who was placed on community service whilst in breach of a conditional discharge, a probation order and a suspended sentence, provides a further illustration of this phenomenon. Another case concerned a 45-year-old alcoholic charged with drunk and disqualified driving. He had numerous previous convictions and was in breach both of a suspended sentence imposed at Crown court for serious assaults and of a probation order made subsequently. The magistrates adjourned the case for enquiries into placement at a therapeutic community: 'No-one wants to put anyone – particularly an intelligent man – away if there's another way out.'

One magistrate, in a post-sentence interview in one such case, remarked:

> It's very hard to put yourself apart from the social aspects of things and not be swayed by the emotion of it, but it's nice when you *can* take a more benevolent view.

'Sick' Offenders

The ubiquity of 'sickness' as a metaphor in lay life for alien, frightening or distasteful phenomena was considered earlier. During the course of the study, the word 'sick' was applied to certain offenders by magistrates in interviews, and by clerks and solicitors in informal exchanges. The category of sick offenders cut across age distinctions among defendants over 21, although most were middle aged and alcoholic. Notably, no young adults fell into this category. Since there was no logical impossibility preventing a young adult from being 'sick', their absence from the category possibly reflects the less-entrenched appearance of their problems. Turbulence, impulsivity and vulnerability to contamination were qualities of a transient maturational phase. Sickness, by contrast, was an intractable condition.

There was more to sickness, however, than intractability. The superficially gross notion of sickness involved a nuance which underpinned a serious sentencing dilemma. Something in the inner experience of sick offenders defied both comprehension and rational response. Although they were capable of criminal responsibility, they appeared incapable of exercising responsibility on their own behalves. Their behaviour was not only socially inappropriate; it was self-destructive. They seemed to lack the basic self-interest which should inform rational behaviour and upon which the available responses of the court relied. This characteristic went deeper than defiance or excessive neediness. Sick offenders simply did not appear to grasp the advantages to be had from co-operating with the courtroom process. It was this absence of, in a quite literal sense, 'personal responsibility' which lay at the core of the concept of sickness. The responses of City magistrates to sick offenders must be understood in terms of the acute difficulty this posed them in sentencing.

Two basic groups of sick offenders could be identified: sick young men and hopeless cases.

1. Sick Young Men

As has been seen, the categories of independent and needy young men were capable of embracing deep personal and social problems and relatively serious offending. They therefore sufficed for the vast majority of offenders aged from 21 to 25. A few defendants, however, could not be accommodated within these categories. These defendants differed from the majority in that some aspect or aspects of their behaviour appeared bizarre. However, although they appeared to need psychiatric treatment, they thwarted all attempts to provide it.

Example 6.12 The defendant, aged 23, admitted offences of driving a stolen vehicle with excess alcohol, whilst disqualified and without insurance. His criminal history included offences of taking a vehicle without authority, drunk driving, drugs possession and criminal damage. Reports were requested from services in an adjacent county, where the defendant had moved to be near his parents. A SER and a report from a drug-counselling agency described abuse of cannabis, amphetamines and hallucinogens. At the suggestion of the writers of these reports that the defendant should seek treatment at a therapeutic community for drug dependent people, magistrates deferred sentence to review his progress. The defendant, however, was asked to leave the community after six weeks, for persistently breaking the rules, although he did abstain from drugs. He was returned to court, where the defence solicitor asked the magistrates to order SERs again, with a view to making a probation order. The clerk asked the magistrates to consider how much further forward this would take them. Initially, the magistrates declined to order SERs, but after hearing from a mature relation of the defendant that he did not cope well when he did not feel safe and that he needed support, possibly psychiatric, to deal with his problems, they changed their minds.

There was some confusion about the defendant's whereabouts, since he was constantly moving between City and his parents' locality. Eventually, a new SER was prepared by a City probation officer who had known the defendant over several years. This officer professed to be 'shocked at his deterioration': 'he behaved in a bizarre and uncommunicative fashion, making meaningful discussion impossible'. Unable to determine whether this behaviour reflected drug intoxication or psychosis, the probation officer suggested psychiatric assessment. However, the officer cautioned: 'a fresh Probation Order would serve very little purpose, since he seems unaware of the necessity for change, or of the commitment that such an Order would demand'. The magistrates requested a psychiatric assessment.

An outpatient psychiatric assessment was inconclusive, but indicated possible schizophrenia. The magistrates followed the suggestion to use their powers under mental health legislation to order inpatient assessment. The subsequent report indicated that the defendant had behaved normally throughout the four weeks in hospital. The defence solicitor continued to favour a probation order, in the face of resistance from the probation service on the grounds that the defendant was constantly on the move, making supervision impossible. The magistrates imposed fines totalling £500 and disqualified the defendant from driving for three years.

This case took a total of eight months to process, with a final result which was hardly different from that which would have been dictated by a 'just deserts' approach in the first instance. The magistrates repeatedly pursued information relating to the defendant's drug abuse and mental condition, although such information could not alter the issues which determined sentence and which were known from an early stage: the defendant was rootless, was not amenable to supervision in the community, and could not be coerced into treatment. Notably, among the volume of information amassed over these months there was no attention paid to the real nature of this defendant's offences, which were neither drug induced nor the product of a psychosis, but alcohol-related driving matters similar to those of previous convictions.

Magistrates' fruitless pursuit of information over a period of several months in this case was symptomatic of the manner in which these defendants paralysed sentencing decision making. This was not the fault of the magistrates alone. Another case took nine months to process, impeded partly by the defendant's failure to respond to bail on several occasions, partly by his changes of address and partly by the quest for medical, psychiatric and social information. Even at the final hearing, the defence solicitor urged the magistrates to seek a new psychiatric report, despite the fact that 'the SER recommends community service and that will be my submission at the end of the day'. This curious advice illustrates the dilemma. It seemed doubtful that anyone really believed that the sentencing options would alter in consequence of yet more information in these cases. The problem was the unease aroused by the prospect of imposing any 'real-world' sentence on a defendant, when, as one magistrate remarked in a post-sentence interview, 'you wonder if he's in touch with the same world as us'.

The result, in each case, was procrastination, in which all court personnel, to some degree, conspired, although it was the magistrates who were ultimately held responsible for these delays. The following exchanges occurred in one already protracted case, as the defence solicitor pre-empted the prosecution address:

DS (*hesitantly*): I'm wondering whether I should make an application here. Just after he appeared last, he was committed to custody for breaking a [civil court] injunction. He spent his time in custody in the hospital. There is a SER which outlines a poor response to supervision. I wouldn't normally ask for a further report, but...his circumstances have changed...Because there isn't a favourable report you will be considering custody and should have all the information. He has an appointment with [a forensic psychiatrist].

M (*to PO*): Anything to add?

PO: He's in breach of his probation order by these further offences, failing to notify change of address and he consistently fails to keep appointments. In my view he finds supervision more of a burden than a help and his problems are not amenable to probation supervision. Possibly [the psychiatrist] may have something to offer, but it's a matter for you whether you want that information or not.

Clerk: A SER might assist you in your sentencing, to give you the up-to-date circumstances.

M: Psychiatric reports?

DS: I asked [the psychiatrist] if he was willing, but I can't order reports... It's for you if you feel it would be helpful.

M: Well, we feel it would be helpful. Yes.

In the post-sentence interview, these magistrates were not optimistic that the psychiatric report would have much to suggest, 'unless he's *very* sick, but that might make sentencing even more of a problem'.

He's a sick man, obviously, although some of his behaviour may have been for our benefit. We need as much information as we can get, but then what can we do at the end of the day?

These sick young men were all alcohol-related offenders, but the significance attached to this fact varied. It was ignored in Example 6.12. In another case, the 'chronic alcohol abuse' identified by the probation officer was thought by a magistrate to reflect the defendant's escape into fantasy.

Is it a dependency, a prop because he can't cope with life, or is it an escape route for someone who likes a binge? It's not the same when someone is trying to blot out problems... We would take a different view of someone who just enjoyed it.

In a third case the defence solicitor laid great emphasis on alcoholism, combined with epilepsy, as the key to understanding the bizarre offences which included accompanying firemen to a blaze started by the defendant himself, and demanding money from strangers on the pretence of being a detective: 'He was driven by an insatiable urge to consume alcohol.'

2. Hopeless Cases

The numbers of destitute alcoholics appearing before City magistrates for drunkenness offences had fallen in recent years, since the introduction of a cautioning scheme. Court personnel, however, were familiar with the 'regulars': the core of deteriorated, destitute alcoholics who inhabited the city centre by day. Their petty thefts and public order offences still brought them into court, where their appearances were viewed with some foreboding by the clerks, upon whom fell the burden of dealing with their unpredictable behaviour.

The compassionate treatment of tragic defendants was inspired by recognition of their fall from respectability. The hopeless cases, however, appealed to no such tragic history. Indeed, they had shed their histories, living and being judged entirely in the present. They seemed never to have been otherwise than they were now: vagrant, dirty, physically ruined and temperamentally uncertain. It was rarely necessary to enquire into the backgrounds of these men to establish their hopelessness. It was simply obvious.

This alien condition inspired a mixture of distaste, impatience, embarrassment, humour and patronisation, in concentrations which varied according to the behaviour of the defendants in the courtroom, which in turn altered with their degree of intoxication, impatience to resume drinking, sense of grievance and general irritability or tranquillity. When such defendants, alone or with supportive company, entered the courtroom to sit at the rear awaiting their turn in the dock, their restiveness could become distracting. At these times, the police officer would walk over and stand beside them, occasionally leaning to whisper advice to remain calm. Thus, there was a generally low-key, non-confrontational approach to control in the courtroom.

Not always successfully. Once, when this routine signally failed to maintain disturbance at a tolerably muted level, the clerk, losing patience, asked the police officer to take the man downstairs to the cells. The police officer led the protesting man to the dock and through the door, assisted by the usher who instructed him, like a bothersome child: 'Off you go now.' The man slept off the worst of his intoxication and was produced in the afternoon, when, for theft of a bottle of wine, he was sentenced to spend one day in police custody, thus to be released at the close of court business.

The prosecution solicitor, exchanging some humour about the manner of this defendant's removal, nevertheless observed: 'But what was the basis really for taking him into custody? Contempt of court? I know he was a problem, but as a matter of civil liberties, it's not too good, is it?'

One answer to this question may be simply that swift removal was the easiest way to preserve social control in the courthouse, given the inflamed responses of the defendant to mild attempts at reason. However, a further element in this response derived from the fundamental belief that such people were incapable of regulating their own behaviour, coupled with the paternalistic notion that responsible decisions should therefore be taken on their behalf. Patronisation also sprang from this source.

Example 6.13 It was nearly Christmas. The obese 41-year-old defendant was apparently sweating, despite the season. He clutched a handkerchief, with which he mopped his face.

Clerk: You're charged with theft of a bottle of alcohol –

Def: I didn't mean to –

DS (*raising hand*): Shhh.

   ...

Clerk: Do you plead guilty or not guilty?

Def: Guilty. I'm sorry I did it –

Clerk: Yes, your solicitor will explain for you later.

CPS: The proprietor [of a guest house] heard someone walking out, went to investigate and found the defendant with a bottle of whisky...He said that he had often walked past and saw it was a cosy place with plenty of drinks available and he thought he would go in and get himself a nightcap.

The defendant's previous convictions spanned 9 pages and 25 years. He was in breach of a suspended sentence, and had already been reconvicted once since its imposition, for similar 'walk-in' burglaries.

DS: Each time he comes to court he says this will be the last time, and looking at his previous convictions I think I can say he has been trying very hard. I have counted up his previous convictions and they have been lessening...due very much to the help and support of the [homeless person's hostel], where he has been living after many years of living rough.

The defendant wrung his handkerchief while the magistrates and clerk conferred.

M: We've got quite a difficult problem, because you've got a suspended sentence for burglary almost a year ago, you've been to court during the period of suspension but it wasn't activated, and here you are again. We're going to impose one day's imprisonment for the suspended sentence and we're going to impose one day for this offence, concurrent. So you'll be kept in custody till the close of business today.

Def (*puzzled*): Till the close of business?

M: Yes.

Def (*holding up one finger*): One day?

M: Yes.

Def (*beaming*): Oh, thank you very much. Merry Christmas!

M: Yes, we hope you have a merry Christmas, and an honourable one. Now go with the officer.

Def (*cheerfully to waiting police officer*): How are you? All right?

(*Smiles exchanged among those left in court.*)

CONCLUSION

Simplification by characterisation is not necessarily dysfunctional or unjust. Decision makers may learn over time that, in the context of the situation within which they operate, certain gross cues constitute fairly reliable guides to more complex distinctions. Characterisation thus provides usable information at relatively little cost in cognitive effort or time (Fiske and Neuberg 1989). For example, Mileski (1969), studying a minor American court, found that black and white defendants in intoxication cases differed in several key respects: white defendants tended to be skid-row drunks, in late middle age, destitute, and arrested in states of intoxicated incapability; black defendants were generally younger, reasonably solvent, and arrested for causing a disturbance. Although the occasional 'misclassification' revealed the extent of sentencers' reliance on colour cues, this gross characterisation nevertheless usually served to distinguish appropriately between cases. Characterisation techniques, therefore, can provide

> a way of maintaining smooth-running operation of the court, without gross violation of either the court's concepts of punishment, on the one hand, or the defendant's rights, on the other. (Scheff 1966, p. 140)

The basic offender characterisations identified in this chapter do not cover the entire range of defendants. Most notably, defendants aged between 26 and 30 are absent. One reason for this may be that these apparently uncategorisable offenders could have been accommodated under the broad headings of independent and needy on the basis of SER assessments. They are not, however, included here in those categories because of a striking change in mitigation addresses. The emotive juxtaposition of age, criminal record and personal problems, and the concept of the turning point abruptly disappeared from defence solicitors' speeches on behalf of defendants older than 25. Perhaps, as one magistrate remarked, 'once you get into your mid–late 20s, hopes are beginning to fade'. Nevertheless, in complex cases, the independent and needy characterisations were perhaps sufficiently flexible to embrace these few defendants.

It is perhaps not surprising if City court's basic characterisations did not cover the entire range of defendants. The majority group was that of the young adult offenders. Hence, for this group, concepts of the nature of their criminality, and characterisation, were richly developed. Defendants in the age range from 26 to 30 years were comparatively scarce. There is no need for well-articulated 'simplifying choice heuristics' for comparatively rare events, particularly when there is a serviceable alternative.

Thus, much of City court's sentencing decision making could be understood in terms of a few gross characterisations. This should perhaps not be surprising. Decisions in lay magistrates' courts are a collective exercise. Categories, therefore, must be such that most people can subscribe to them quite easily. Numerous categories, categories involving crucial fine distinctions, or esoteric categories not generally intuitively accessible, would incapacitate collective decision making. Small wonder, perhaps, that magistrates ascribe great importance to 'like-mindedness' in recruitment to a bench (Burney 1979). Particularly bearing in mind City magistrates' penchant for debate, discussion of individually idiosyncratic characterisations, or of fine distinctions, could have protracted decision making almost interminably.

Nor do magistrates function in isolation, constructing idiosyncratic interpretations inaccessible to other courtroom personnel. All contributors to the decision-making process must be able to participate in the characterisation process for most of the time. They could not otherwise contribute effectively. This is perhaps particularly important in the operation of a democratic court such as City. Indeed, magistrates were clearly susceptible to the inferences of information givers. In this respect, as will be argued later, the non-participation of probation officers in the concept of 'sickness' could be significant.

The 'broad brush' with which characterisations were drawn enabled individuals with differing perspectives nevertheless to agree as to outcome. But this is not to suggest that the characterisations themselves did not matter: they conveyed important information or held particular meanings. An inappropriate characterisation by one party would be discernible to others. Thus, to a defendant of whom the defence solicitor said that he was 'terribly unhappy' as a child, was 'too frightened to refuse' to commit the offences, and had not had 'the right person to turn to up to now to confide in', the magistrate caustically remarked: 'You're 27, and there's no problem about sending you to prison if we're so minded. Understand?'

7 Making the Most of the Intoxication Excuse

This chapter turns from the broad strategies and characterisations employed at City court to interpret case material, to a close study of the intoxication excuse advanced in mitigation. It examines firstly the styles of impression management adopted by alcohol-related offenders at court. It then considers variations in mitigation based on intoxication or alcoholism according to types of offence and offender.

IMPRESSION MANAGEMENT

Offenders who drew the court's attention to their alcohol problems could successfully enhance the process of characterisation described in the previous chapter. For some defendants, however, the potential attractions of this technique for reducing punishment were counterbalanced by their ambivalence about the deviant identity which it conferred on them.

Enhancement of Identity

Occasionally, defendants appeared to contribute to their characterisation more by accident than by design.

Example 7.1 A 24-year-old defendant in a sober case was recommended for a 'last chance' on probation with a condition of day-centre attendance. He was an 'independent' young man whose sustained offending prompted the defence solicitor to observe: 'No-one could criticise you for imposing a custodial sentence today, but nevertheless I ask what it would achieve. Nothing, save to get him out of everyone's hair for a while.'

The hearing took place in one of the juvenile courts, in which the defendant sat directly in front of the bench at a few feet distant, and at the same head height. The magistrates thus had an unimpeded close-up view of his remarkable looks: angelic features in a cloud of red curls. In a post-sentence interview, explaining their decision to accept the recommendation, the magistrates commented with satisfaction:

> His demeanour influenced me and the thought he would respond to the sentence...I'm fairly optimistic...His reception of the sentence seemed appropriate – relief – positive – he was taking it seriously. That confirmed the idea that custody was wrong at this point, because he wouldn't have responded in that way. It seemed as if it was the right sentence at the right time.

Example 7.2   A 22-year-old defendant was charged with further offences whilst already the subject of a probation order, a suspended sentence and a community service order. This defendant's neediness was summed up in the SER: 'This is a disturbed, vulnerable and physically sick young man who does seem to be making a supreme effort at the present time.'

The colourful portrayal in the SER and mitigation address of a pathetic young man in need of long-term support was rather at odds with his large, square, burly physique, with close-cropped hair, which conveyed an appearance of thuggishness. As the hearing progressed, however, the defendant grew increasingly blotchy faced, and he produced a handkerchief with which surreptitiously to wipe his reddening eyes. He was openly weeping by the time the magistrates announced a further community service order.

Other defendants played a more obviously active part in their characterisation. Of particular interest, here, is the enhancement of identity through drunkenness at court. If young defendants had been drinking before their appearance, they did not advertise the fact in the courtroom. To do so would probably have been received as defiance; certainly, the boisterousness of young adults was likely to be regarded in the courtroom as evidence of their indiscipline. For older defendants, however, drunkenness could be an advantage. These defendants often advertised their alcoholic status by referring to themselves as 'registered' (or in one case 'qualified') alcoholics. This claim invoked medical authority on their condition by borrowing from the bureaucratic terminology of drug addiction.

Tragic defendants were frequently drunk in court. In this condition they were miserable and repentant. They were sometimes also voluble, in an apparent attempt at explanation. Magistrates showed considerable patience with the rambling interruptions of these defendants.

Example 7.3

DS: I would point out that he is in work and also has come to the realisation that he is an alcoholic. He has joined Alcoholics Anonymous and been with them for the past month.

M: The indication from the probation service is that they think there is something positive here.

Def (*belatedly*): There's a meeting tonight.

M: Do you think you're getting help?

Def (*swaying to feet*): I missed probation that I had previously, and [my new probation officer] seems a good person. I used to go to see [my other probation officer] at the drop-in.

M: Well, you'll get as much help from [this probation officer] as [the other one]. Now, we want to make a probation order... and you know what means. You've got to stay out of trouble.

Def: Well, that shop across the road, I used to go and buy drink – they won't let me in.

Example 7.4

DS: He attends a weekly group where he takes a central role and he feels optimistic, despite the setbacks, that he can overcome his difficulties –

Def: Can I say something?

The defendant leaned confidentially towards the defence solicitor and began speaking incoherently but loudly.

DS (*desperately*): Perhaps he'd like to tell you himself.

Def: I went to the consultant at the drugs clinic and he said: 'We've got to come to an agreement, you've got to cut down on drink or we'll cut your script'. I said: 'That's blackmail!' – But – we both took it in – you know – so I accept that's what I've got to do, but it's difficult with [my lodger] being there because he drinks more than I do. But I've just got to try harder –

M (*encouragingly but rapidly*): That's quite right.

The behaviour of hopeless defendants, drunk or sober, was quite different. The degree of self-expression permitted in City court was often increased for these defendants by virtue of their lack of legal representation. These men belonged squarely in the realm of 'ineligibility' (Macandrew and Edgerton 1969), noted in Chapter 4. 'Sick' beyond all hope of repair, they enjoyed a state of 'non-responsibility' in which there were no real boundaries to their behaviour, except in the negative sense that they were not expected to observe the normal rules of courtroom propriety.

The hopeless defendants, particularly well-known 'regulars', rarely disappointed this expectation. The resultant theatre of their appearances, foiled by the discomfiture of struggling clerks and magistrates, inspired overt amusement among spectators.

Observing these performances, it was increasingly difficult to believe that these men were, as they seemed, oblivious of this ridicule. Rather, one began to suspect that they were pleased to share what, for them, was a perpetual experience of their lives, with people who usually enjoyed immunity from it.

Alcoholic defendants commonly became increasingly impatient as the morning drily wore on. They were, however, low on the court's list of priorities, particularly since their time spent waiting did not add to the legal aid bill for the day's work. There was always a possibility, as a result, that they would not return to the afternoon hearing, or would arrive drunk. Whatever their condition, it was usually impossible to record more than a sample of their generous contributions to the proceedings.

Example 7.5 The two defendants, in their 50s, were jointly charged with a public order offence. Several times during the morning, one poked his head round the courtroom door and was sent away by the police officer. Eventually he entered and sat down. When the police officer remonstrated, he announced loudly: 'I want to be tried *now*.' The clerk granted his wish.

Clerk: Do you plead guilty or not guilty?

1st Def: Guilty.

2nd Def: Guilty. I was drunk.

CPS (*speaking over indistinct mumblings from dock*): The two defendants were in the [shopping centre]. A police constable saw them on the seats. One was grabbing food from another person. The

constable warned him. The other defendant intervened, he pro-
tested and used abusive language. His friend became involved.
Both defendants were extremely drunk at the time.

2nd Def: This man wouldn't harm anybody. I'm sure I wouldn't
either.

Clerk: Well, what would you like to say?

1st Def: Someone gave me drink. I'm ever so sorry for causing all
this trouble to the court.

2nd Def: I'm sorry from the bottom of my heart. I was drunk and I
was in a bad mood.

M: You will each be fined £20. I'm just going to tell you, you've
apologised to the court, but you should apologise to the people of
[City] whom you have caused distress. Just you remember that,
next time you go out and get drunk.

2nd Def (*inflamed*): You've no heart. You've no understanding.

The defendants were ushered, grumbling, from the court.

Example 7.6   When all other business was completed, the 53-year-old
defendant was brought up from the cells, to which he had been
removed as he and his supporters grew steadily more noisy in the
waiting area. The clerk began putting the two charges of public order
offences to him.

Def (*interrupting*): I want to tell you, I think it's a bit wrong. I take
tablets, I've lost half my lung, I don't use words like that. I've
been in the war, I lost my brother in the war, but I've never
insulted a woman in my life –

M: Is that a not guilty plea?

Def: If you say so. I've paid my fines –

The defendant continued talking as the magistrates and clerk conferred.

M: We don't want this to go on unnecessarily.

Clerk: I'll try, but if he says he didn't, then it's a not guilty plea.

The clerk began again to put the charge.

Def: If *you'd* done two years in the hospital and took tablets *you* wouldn't remember. *I* don't remember, but I've studied the law –

Clerk (*raising a hand*): In that case, if you've studied the law, you won't have any trouble grasping this. If you say you don't remember –

Def: I don't.

Clerk: But still you accept that you did do it –

Def: Well, yes.

Clerk: Then a guilty plea is acceptable.

The clerk put the second charge.

Def: Well, I don't agree there. There's a lot of people use my name. Someone's been using my name.

Clerk: That has to be a not guilty plea.

The magistrates and clerk conferred, leaving the defendant to resume his declamation. He took his glasses on and off and waved his arms expansively as he addressed the whole court.

Def: Who broke into my house and stole all my things? Did you catch *him*? He took my cooker, my money – I knew who it was actually, but *I* don't go to the police. I'm homeless, I've been in hospital, my rent is £15 a week –

Clerk: This will be adjourned to 6 April, when you're already due for trial on another charge.

Def: Will you give me a piece of paper? I might not remember.

Conflict of Identity

The academic discussion of 'deviance avowal' was considered in Chapter Four. Some of this literature tends to portray the embracement of a 'sick' or alcoholic identity in order to reduce criminal culpability as an 'easy option', in the same way that, as seen in Chapter 2, the criminal or alcoholic lifestyle is simplistically seen as an easy alternative to the rigours of respectability for the undersocialised. That the issue is more complex, however, was suggested by the discussions of the relationships between rationalisation, mitigation and self-image.

Observation of defendants in City court who grappled with the choice between sick or alcoholic and criminal identities revealed the difficulty of deviance avowal. The ambivalence of these men was abundantly clear. The immediate attractions of reduced punishment were offset, and in many cases outweighed, by the prospect of having a purported pathology professionally confirmed and treated.

Example 7.7 The defendant, aged 24, was charged with theft and criminal damage. He had a number of previous convictions, had appeared in court already several times during the observation period, and had been placed on probation two months previously. At that time, the SER writer had despondently concluded:

> I am not convinced that a Probation Order would have much impact on [the defendant's] offending behaviour however (*sic*) if the Court were to consider such a course appropriate, the supervision would focus on his drinking habits and employment prospects. If the Court considers that a Probation Order is an appropriate disposal today, a period of six months would allow for some focused work and is in my opinion this is (*sic*) the maximum length that [he] could realistically sustain.

On this occasion, I got into conversation with the defendant in the waiting area. He looked seedier and shabbier than when I had last seen him, and was nursing a recently disabled arm. He rehearsed his problems with an apparent unconcern for privacy which often seemed to characterise those who had become accustomed to living out their lives in public.

> I'm getting it adjourned. I'm going to see a psychiatrist. My brain box has gone. I went to ask my doctor for valium, but he wouldn't give me any. He said I'd never get off them. That's what this is all about – I've been very depressed. I've lost the use of my hand as well – I put my arm through a window when I was drunk and cut the artery. It doesn't hurt so much now it's warmer, they've given me exercises to do. I can't work. I've been sleeping rough for four days – my brother's just moved into a new house with his wife and baby and they say they want their privacy. I've lost my wife as well, but I'm glad now. She kept on at me and didn't give me time to think. She was taking drugs in front of my son – that's why we split up because I objected to that. But I've been very depressed and I suffer with my nerves.

This defendant may genuinely have feared for his sanity. With so many problems piling up, this might be an understandable anxiety. It is, however, one thing to wonder whether one is going out of one's mind, but quite another to have it confirmed by a psychiatrist. This was the first of several occasions on which this defendant arrived at court having made an appointment with a psychiatrist which he subsequently failed to keep. Meanwhile, his condition apparently deteriorated. A month later, while a further adjournment for psychiatric assessment was debated, he sat in court hunched over himself with an odd, faintly smiling expression, as if puzzling over the situation. This 'sick young man's' ambivalence about his condition in turn helped to stifle the sentencing process for a considerable period.

Example 7.8   The defendant, aged 45, had committed offences of drunk and disqualified driving. He had several previous convictions, was in breach of a suspended sentence and a probation order, and, in his probation officer's view, would 'never be free from further offending or fulful (*sic*) his potential even in part, until such time as he seeks effective treatment for his alcohol and underlying psychological problems'.

The probation officer described this 'tragic' defendant's ambivalence about treatment in the following way:

[The defendant] is an intelligent man who shows some insight into his situation. He yearns stability and the intimacy of a close relationship but has proved quite unable to sustain one; fearing as he does that people will get too close and begin making demands of him that he is unable or unwilling to meet. Such a fundamental area of difficulty underlies his drink problem and has not, thus far, been addressed by the various contacts that [he] has had over the years with the [drinking problem service]. He is clearly resentful of any intervention that might seek to explore this side of his personality too deeply and as a consequence such professional treatment has only ever been of limited value.

The defence solicitor challenged this aspersion on the defendant's integrity:

He felt at that time that he could not face what was in his background. He was not resentful but scared of facing up to things...He realises now that he must delve into his background, but feels that he needs the support of a therapeutic community to do that.

While the magistrates were in retirement, the defendant spoke to the defence solicitor: 'I'm not really sure about this idea, I think I might rather get a prison sentence over with than keep this hanging on.' Nevertheless, on the magistrates' return, the defence solicitor again pressed for an adjournment for enquiries into therapeutic community opportunities. The magistrates complied.

In a subsequent written application to the court for the discharge of the probation order as being of no further advantage, the probation officer explained:

> [The defendant] struggled with the notion of spending twelve months or so in rehabilitation and [sic] when he could, as he saw it, simply choose to go to prison for six months – a sentence which he did not regard as onerous... In the event [he] chose the 'safer' of the two options; appearing in court on his adjourned date drunk, thereby disqualifying himself from eligibility at the rehabilitation unit where he was due the next day, and giving the Magistrates little alternative but to activate the suspended sentence.

VARIATION BY TYPE OF OFFENCE

Certain systematic differences in the appeal to intoxication were related to the type of offence in question. Essentially, these differences turned on the issue of self-control. Intoxicated loss of control was advanced as mitigation for some types of offences, but was apparently deemed inapplicable to others. The differences may be examined under the broad headings of excess alcohol, violence and dishonesty.

Excess Alcohol

This heading is used generically to include offences of drinking and driving, being drunk in charge of a vehicle and failing to provide specimens for alcohol testing. Mitigation speeches in these cases were starkly contrary to those in all other types of alcohol-related offences, which relied in varying degrees on an appeal to intoxicated loss of control. Such a condition would be acknowledged only in extreme cases of drunken driving, when only an appeal to mercy was realistically available to the defendant. Defence solicitors went to considerable lengths to demonstrate that the technical intoxication of their clients did not reflect upon their competence as drivers. There were several basic techniques, often utilised in combinations, for making this point.

Firstly, it could be pointed out that the police had initially approached the defendant engaged in an innocuous activity such as tending a broken-down vehicle or sitting in a parked one. Occasionally it was claimed that the defendant, while driving safely, was the victim of a malicious report to the police by someone with a grudge against him.

Secondly, it could be observed that the discovery of the excess alcohol offence was a by-product of apprehension for a minor transgression such as having a defective light or failing to display a tax disc. Even for a defendant stopped after speeding or driving through traffic lights at amber, it could be claimed that 'there is no suggestion that his driving caused danger at any time'.

Thirdly, it could be argued that the defendant was a careful drinker who had unwittingly exceeded the alcohol limit despite his best efforts to avoid it. This was apparently achieved by surprising numbers of defendants, who had drunk a responsibly small quantity, forgetting that they had not eaten all day, believing that the effects of last night's binge or lunch time's sherry had worn off, or unaware of the now obvious inadvisability of mixing alcohol with their medication.

Fourthly, it could be claimed that the defendant had no intention of driving at the time of his drinking, but some unforeseen necessity, such as the wife going into labour, arose. In some of these cases, driving was portrayed as the responsible act of a comparatively sober defendant, taking over the wheel from his intended chauffeur who had become irresponsibly drunk.

As long as scope for such arguments remained, affirmations of defendants' competence as drivers would persist even in the face of extraordinarily high alcohol readings or chronic alcoholism.

Example 7.9 The defendant, aged 45, admitted driving with excess alcohol, whilst disqualified and without insurance. The circumstances were unusual in that he had driven to the police station, announced that he been drinking and driving, handed in his car keys and asked to be locked up for safety. He was four times over the permitted level of breath alcohol. This was his second excess alcohol conviction. He had a history of alcoholism which was fully documented in the SER.

In the face of this defendant's evident disbelief in his own fitness as a driver, the defence solicitor advised the magistrates:

> He knows he is an alcoholic in some ways. A man who drinks a lot is able to cope a little better in some ways. On the last occasion of drinking and driving he was actually parked on the side of the road looking under the bonnet to investigate a funny noise. He was not stopped for anything he did driving.

Loss of self-control, in excess alcohol cases, was rarely, if ever, attributed to intoxication. For example, a defendant who drove erratically at high speed through a housing estate when signalled to stop by the police, and who assaulted one of the arresting officers, had panicked because, in the words of the SER, he 'felt some vulnerability as an Irishman'. In several cases, the decision to drive was portrayed as an impulsive reaction to stress, such as a family argument provoking a desire to escape. Such impulsivity, however, was never causally linked to the defendant's intoxication.

Example 7.10   The defendant, aged 23, admitted failing to provide specimens of breath and criminal damage. Police, encountering him staggering at the roadside with a motorcycle, had asked him to take a breath test.

> CPS: At [this] the defendant became extremely abusive and went into a complete rage. At the police station he became verbally abusive and wouldn't quieten down. At one point, sitting in a room being spoken to by the sergeant, his rage was such that he began to punch the wall boards, apparently unaware of the damage he would do to himself as he kept punching and punching the wall.

The defence solicitor explained that the defendant had lost his licence for driving with excess alcohol several years previously.

> On this occasion, he was at a party, and remembering well the consequences for his licence of drinking and driving, he pushed his bike down [the] road ... believing there was nothing wrong with this ... He honestly and sincerely thought that as long as he was pushing his bike he was within the law. You may take it as an indication of the firmness with which he held that view that he behaved with such vehemence afterwards, to the extent of not noticing the injury he may have done to his own hand.

Violence

This heading includes assaults and offences of criminal damage. Two types of excuse underpinned the differential use of information about defendants' drinking: the appeals to provocation and to misjudgement.

1. Appeal to Provocation
Where strong provocation was offered in mitigation for an act of violence, intoxication would be denied. The offender's declared sobriety underlined the reasonableness of his response to the unreasonable behaviour of another.

> He had, in his view, unjustifiably been thrown out of [the nightclub] and was venting his spleen. He wasn't drunk.

> My client had been out with a friend in perfectly orderly fashion.

> The defendant has lived with the victim's family for about nine years, and is his sister's boyfriend. And it's plain the victim is not a particularly popular person in that family. He throws his weight about. In these circumstances, when the victim started throwing his weight about [in the pub], and involving the defendant's girlfriend, it became too much. And when the victim said, 'Go on, I dare you', when he saw the defendant squaring up to him, that was the final incentive to strike.

> He is clear that the victim struck him first. There was a degree of provocation, the victim might have been in court himself on a similar charge, but the defendant did not consider the matter that serious...He asks me to make clear that he wasn't drunk and was not acting under the influence of drink. He knew perfectly well what he was doing.

A level of violence beyond that which could be entirely explained by provocation could, however, be attributed to the defendant's loss of restraint through intoxication.

> Alcohol is the factor in this offence. A further factor is the defendant's frustration and aggression, feeling he had been put down by members of the other group. He went to give them a piece of his mind and at that point he lost control.

This appeal to the disinhibition of violence through intoxication against a background of provocation was quite common in cases of assaults on female partners.

The ABH relates to a long standing relationship. The victim is also a heavy drinker and during drinking sessions tempers became frayed and violence occurred on both sides. On this occasion he perhaps went a little beyond what was reasonable in self-defence.

The assault happened in a nightclub on the night after they broke up. The defendant was in the club, and who turns up but his girlfriend with two friends? Why was she there? It wasn't her usual stomping ground. The defendant took the view that she was provoking him. Words passed. He went to throw a drink in her face and the glass unfortunately touched her.

Anticipation of this line of argument apparently prompted the prosecution solicitor in one case to remark pointedly:

It might be said that striking is an appropriate way to deal with a hysterical woman, but the prosecution say that the defendant punched her whilst she was on the floor.

In cases in which no provocation was discernible at all, mitigation might then appeal to extreme intoxication to the point of irrationality or the indiscriminate discharge of emotions usually constrained by sobriety.

It was because they were Irish. He was substantially in drink and wasn't behaving himself.

This particular behaviour is out of all character to him and we must go back into his history to understand them... On this occasion, he went to the fair and consumed a very large quantity of alcohol. These offences represent the release of long pent-up emotions.

In one case, even this resort was ruled out by the probation officer's observation:

He realises now that what he did was totally wrong and that to hit somebody because he perceives that they are 'eyeing him' is totally unacceptable behaviour. It was pointed out very strongly to him that his victim did not, in any way, retaliate and therefore not only was his reasoning no excuse for his actions but it also appears to have no validity. From his own admission he had only drunk some two pints of alcohol that evening so it seems unlikely that that was a strong factor.

The defence solicitor remarked sourly: 'It is unfortunate that the report should refer to the events surrounding the assault in quite the way it does.'

2. Appeal to Misjudgement
The term 'misjudgement' is preferred here to 'accident' or 'mistake', in order to identify more clearly the issue at stake: confused intoxicated reasoning, leading to an unfortunate outcome.

> The defendant had quite a bit to drink. He went over to a house where an old friend lived. What he didn't know was that his friend had died. The new occupant didn't know him at all. There followed an altercation and the window was broken in recklessness as he was quite distressed.

Intoxicated misjudgement could explain why a defendant would attack an unprovocative third party. It was a popular mitigation for assaults on females against whom provocation could not be alleged. Such females were less likely to be involved in relationships with the defendant. Quite often they were intervening in a confrontation between the defendant and another victim or potential victim.

> The offences were committed under the influence of drink and at a time when he was emotionally very upset. It's not an intentional, direct assault, but took place when he was on the floor being restrained... The blow was one which unfortunately caught the woman police constable on the nose.

The faulty reasoning of the intoxicated offender could result in the inappropriate use of force as a means to problem solving.

> This criminal damage was again committed in drink. He had gone to get his belongings back from where he had been staying with a friend. Had he not been clouded with drink he would have gone away when he realised his friend was not there.

> He was sitting [in the car] when the police came. He said he was messing about with the lock. I think in my own mind he was looking for a place to sleep, but he was drunk.

Paradoxically, sobriety was strongly pressed in mitigation in a case involving a disastrous misjudgement in a crucially heated moment against a background of stress.

It seems that each of these problems, none of them that important in itself, came to a head together. I wish to stress on his behalf that the defendant was not under the influence of drink. This is not a case of a young man getting drunk and behaving violently as a result. The defendant himself says: 'There's no point in hitting your own brother. I wouldn't have had the bat if I hadn't been kicked out [of home].' He was not under the influence of drink and it was a background of family difficulties which erupted into the street. Firstly, then, I ask you to bear in mind that he has no previous convictions. Secondly, it was not a question of drink and senseless violence. Thirdly, it was not a direct attack on the police officer, but invective directed at his brother, not at the police. Fourthly, also, these offences occurred against a background of family difficulties, which don't excuse his behaviour but do explain it.

Dishonesty

The intoxication of a burglar or thief was advanced as a cause of impulsive, and often incompetent, crime. Thus denying premeditation or professionalism, this technique relied on the assumption that the precursors to dishonest crime were directly reflected in its disappointing outcome. Failure to recall the offence was frequently advanced in support of this argument, although memory dysfunction appears to be unrelated to intentionality (Mitchell 1988). Indeed, during their intoxicated bouts of amnesic activity, alcoholics showed a remarkable sense of purpose in their misappropriation of alcohol from the array of available goods. Motivelessness was also a useful claim, although even 'common sense', applied to the data, would suggest that in many cases the most mundane motivations lay behind intoxicated offending. Of an offender with a university education and a career in academic research, a defence solicitor observed in all seriousness: 'Most of the time he steals books. He doesn't know why.' A number of examples from mitigation addresses are given, to illustrate the sometimes complex nature of these impulsive intoxicated aberrations.

My client would describe this as a drunken escapade... He told the police: 'I knew we were pratting around, I knew it was wrong, but I wasn't in a straight state of mind, I had drunk so much'... None of the four co-defendants had any need or plans to use the items taken. They were simply taking items during the drunken time they were on the premises.

The defendant was deeply hurt about his dismissal and whilst in drink he decided to teach his employer a lesson by showing that he could circumvent the security system.

My client says: 'I was pissed out of my mind'...He got drunk and, as he says in his statement: 'I just picked it up, walked out with it. No reason, just drunk. I said to my friend: "I'll give it back tomorrow"'. So even though he was drunk he did realise he had done wrong. He is extremely angry with himself to have taken something of no use to him and which he would have to take back.

This was a lapse by the defendant, who had met friends who had just got their giro cheques and offered him drink. He can't remember much about the offence and was very vague when I questioned him, because of the amount he had had to drink.

This offence was committed while the defendant was much the worse for wear for drink and out with a friend. He was armed with a screwdriver and determined to take the bike, and, I emphasise again, because of the drink, when they couldn't start it they threw it in the river.

In this context, thefts by employees provide a useful illustration of the boundaries to the availability of the intoxication excuse. In six of the eight cases involving thefts by employees which arose during the observation period, it might have been possible to generate an explanation invoking an alcohol problem. This did not happen. Indeed, defence solicitors made no reference to their clients' use of alcohol. SERs, however, provided information of two kinds, sometimes in combination: the defendant spent part of the proceeds of his thefts on alcohol; or the defendant had a history of alcohol abuse. Evidence supporting the possibility of a drinking problem could usually be found in these cases in the form of factors associated with alcohol-related harm, such as were earlier noted in Chapter 2: for example, severe debt, absenteeism from employment, employment in the licensing trade or prior alcohol-related convictions. These offences were more often than not described as impulsive, at least in their origin, incompetent and lacking a satisfactory motivational explanation. Nevertheless, alcohol addiction was not postulated in any of these reports.

It appears that particularly heavy drinking was a factor in [the defendant's] previous offending. His parents were pub landlords and this may have led to an alarmingly high alcohol consumption at an early age. He told me, however, that he has cut his drinking right down, mainly due to the long hours he works [as a barman]... The present offence has a rather odd and devious quality... [The defendant], however, claims that he is experiencing no real difficulties at present... [He] has a tendency to minimise his guilt in that he sought to justify his actions as to some extent reasonable given the circumstances.

[The defendant] has told me that he enjoyed a comfortable lifestyle as a child and that he enjoyed spending money and having an ambundance (*sic*) of clothes and material items. It appears that mainly through the use of credit cards he accrued considerable debts and when he was faced with the opportunity at work of obtaining cash he took it. The defendant says that (*sic*) it was his intention to use the money to pay off debts but instead he used it for leisure purposes... [T]his offence clearly represents the serious lack of self-discipline and greed.

[The defendant] committed this offence knowing he was certain to be caught. He was under financial strain and although he had approached his father for help had received none. Thus he took the money as what he perceived to be an easy way out of his financial difficulties in the short term, paid £180 rent arrears and frittered £170 away in four days in what he describes as a binge, buying drinks for himself and friends... [H]e has a chronic problem managing finances... Also of concern is his dismissal for absenteeism on two occasions, which may be a reflection of the attitude which led to the current offence.

[The defendant] was in the Merchant Navy... [T]here followed a series of seven catering jobs... His relationship with his father... broke down because of a drink problem for which he has received treatment... in the past. He tells me he is now a controlled drinker, although he admits to drinking between 10 and 20 pints of beer per week... [He] cannot give an exact account of what he spent the money on except to say it was on drunk (*sic*), rent and food, nor can he offer an adequate explanation as to why he should commit his first offence at this stage of life.

In these cases, it appeared that neither defence solicitors nor probation officers conceived of the possible utility of motivational explanations based on alcohol addiction, even in the absence of identifiable alternatives. While systematic dishonesty may commonly be regarded as symptomatic of drug dependency (Miller and Welte 1986), such notions of 'feeding an addiction' were not applied to alcohol use. Alcohol-related dishonesty generally concerned impulsive crime committed in a state of acute intoxication. Thefts by employees were thus perceived as a form of 'sober' crime.

VARIATION BY TYPE OF OFFENDER

Systematic differences in the use of information about defendants' alcohol consumption derived from the selective advancement of the most persuasive representation of their characters or problems.

The Character Reference

Social and moral judgements about individuals and groups are often conveyed in assertions about their drinking habits (Archard 1979; Bahr and Caplow 1974; Cook 1975; Gusfield 1963; Harford 1983; Harford, Wechsler and Rothman 1983; Hauge and Irgens-Jensen 1987; Mars 1987; Phillimore 1979; Rubington 1958; Stone 1962; Wilsnack and Wilsnack 1979). In the previous chapter, the process of characterisation described the portrayal of wholistic case typologies. Some observations about defendants' use of alcohol, however, were apparently intended to make specific points about their characters and offending. These points may be described as 'character references': the sober character; the lapse; the reformed character; and the new leaf.

1.   The Sober Character
As in mitigation addresses the assertion of sobriety could establish a point about the nature of an offence, so, in SERs, comments about a defendant's abstemiousness could form part of a complimentary character reference.

> An apparently fit young man, the defendant doesn't smoke and drinks little. He sees his girlfriend pretty well every evening, including those on which he attends karate classes. He is on good terms with his mother and brother, and says he has no problems outside of his unemployment and the present matter.

[The defendant] enjoys good health. His interests are fishing, sailing, and listening to music. He says that he does not abuse alcohol or drugs and the offence relating to the possession of cannabis reflects an infrequent indulgence in this drug.

[The defendant] has a regular girlfriend who he has known for two years. He spends every weekend at her parent's home, and one night during the week. He rarely goes out with friends, and he and his girlfriend visit pubs or discos for entertainment. He does not appear to be a heavy drinker.

In one case, involving damage totalling £15 500 caused by squirting a fire extinguisher onto computer equipment, the defence solicitor sought to distinguish between the defendant's lamentable behaviour and real loutishness.

You have heard there was drinking – that is a slightly emotive expression – it is both quantitative and qualitative in its interpretation. Yes, they had been drinking, but the defendant had only had one lager and was not in any sense intoxicated. This was a very pleasant evening for six or seven young men before Christmas, which unfortunately due to the defendant's exuberance became very unpleasant.

2. The Lapse

For first offenders, or those without recent convictions, an offence could be portrayed as an isolated, regrettable lapse from customary good conduct inspired by intoxication. Defendants in such cases were often said to be aghast when sober at the discovery of their intoxicated transgressions.

These offences were clearly committed under the influence of drink and my client can remember very little of the events. He has been shown statements and evidence to the effect that it was he who did these things and no-one else and therefore he accepts that this must be so. This particular behaviour is out of all character to him...

My client had gone to the pub for a social drink. He is a respectable married man with children. The incident happened after closing time, when he had had too much to drink and his recollection is clouded as to what happened.

3. The reformed character

SERs often offered comparisons between defendants' previous and current offences. A switch from alcohol-related to sober crime, particularly after a gap between earlier and present convictions, was generally seen as a change for the better, reflecting greater maturity.

> [The defendant] says that much of his offending in the past was related to his heavy drinking and his involvement with other young men who were committing offences. He tells me that since his marriage he has stopped drinking and now occupies his time by working during the week and dirt-track racing at weekends.

> The defendant's offending was clearly related to alcohol abuse on that occasion and [he] says that he had developed an increasing dependence on alcohol during the preceding years. [He] acknowledges that he had a drink problem that he has since overcome.

4. The New Leaf

Recent changes in a defendant's drinking pattern could be advanced as evidence that he had been brought to his senses, often by the fact of the offence and conviction, sparking a new resolve. Influential relationships featured largely in this kind of argument. In particular, female partners, who earlier were said to provoke offences, were seen in this context to control defendants' excesses.

> He feels his alcohol problem is now under control and is aware that this must continue if his relationship is to survive. Drinking and offending are not acceptable to his partner. He has a strong incentive to prevent the problem from re-emerging.

> Quite recently he has formed a relationship with a young lady and ... they are now living together. This will curtail his drinking activities and be a support to him in trying to overcome this problem and avoid this kind of drinking binge with other young men.

> Things seem to have improved substantially, with the support of his family and a new relationship with a girlfriend, and in particular the alcohol abuse has ceased and he is able to look forward to employment and a stable relationship.

> Alcohol and bad company all played its part. Since the offence he has formed a long-standing relationship with a girlfriend who is in

court taking an interest in these proceedings and in him, and keeps a grip on his activities.

SERs also offered these appraisals.

[The defendant], thankfully, does now appear to be making efforts to tackle the serious drink problem that he has had for many years and which underlies the present offences and all his previous convictions. He has sought help of his own initiative and I gained the impression he was sincere in his desire to stop drinking.

[The defendant] impresses as a likeable man of apparent satisfactory upbringing and probable good ability, to whom independence in early adulthood led to him forming apparently undesirable associations and to his becoming involved in damagingly heavy drinking, leading to his offending. With the onset of possible greater maturity, he may now be freeing himself from his destructive dependence on alcohol, and to be on course once more for the achievement of conventional goals, in terms of employment, home and marriage.

Persuasive Problems

A major attraction of the intoxication excuse, indicated in the foregoing section, is that it readily establishes a means by which an offender can demonstrate repentance and reform: to reduce his alcohol consumption. This act of contrition appeals to the 'malevolence assumption', noted in Chapter 2, in which the involvement of alcohol in an offence is equated with causality. A drinking problem, in this respect, could be something of an asset for an offender prepared to participate in some form of treatment, notwithstanding the real ambivalence experienced by defendants about such an undertaking. It offers both an explanation of his offending and a solution to the problem of demonstrating remorse and reform (Shapland 1981). It did not, however, follow from this that alcohol-related offenders' drinking habits would receive attention in all cases. In particular, there were two types of offender whose drinking problems were routinely disregarded on discovery of another difficulty: the mentally disordered and the drug addicted.

1. The Mentally Disordered Offender
On one occasion, surveying the court list, I noted the name of a defendant whose case had already been adjourned several times for

different psychiatric assessments and whose numerous problems had given rise to considerable debate. I remarked to the probation officer that drinking at least appeared to be absent from this defendant's list of troubles. I was told, with surprise, that the defendant drank 'like a fish'.

Mental disorder was much more powerful than intoxication in attracting the court's attention and concern. Unfortunately, it was a problem for which the court had no readily identifiable solution, although it appeared to be willing to devote weeks or months to the search. Indeed, this has already been seen in the case of the sick young man in Example 6.12.

At a simplistic level, in alcohol-related cases, the relationship of defendants' drinking to their offending was far more direct and obvious than that of their mental disorder. They offended while intoxicated, they stole alcohol, or they were self-confessed alcoholics, and they often combined these qualities. Had the court processed these defendants on the basis of these cues, it might be hypothesised that it could have dealt with them rapidly as straightforward cases using simple schemata invoking intoxication, or as hopeless cases. Instead, the court's attention focused on defendants' mental disorder, generating a search for the fullest information and for suitable treatment.

There may have been some feeling that mundane motivations for criminality could not confidently be attributed to the mentally disordered. In a post-sentence interview concerning a schizophrenic who broke an off-licence window to take a bottle of alcohol, a magistrate said:

> He didn't have an alcohol problem, he's not a habitual drinker. He didn't have any number of drinking offences. I don't think he commits drink offences so much as mental lapse offences. Something triggers him off mentally.

Perhaps, more strongly, basic humanity and concern were the motivating factors in these decisions. The well-intentioned quest for treatment, however, could result in remands, often lengthy and in custody, at the end of which it was established only that the psychiatric services either were already providing or held little prospect of providing it. At this stage, any suggestion of a treatment provision offered a way out of an impasse for the court rather than real improvement in the defendant's situation. Thus, the suggestion that a manic-depressive defendant be placed on probation with a condition of psychiatric treatment was viewed without enthusiasm, but with resignation, by the reporting probation officer.

> [The psychiatrist] takes the view that a Probation Order with a condition to attend for treatment as an out-patient and take his medication would give an added incentive to [the defendant] to co-operate in the administration of prescribed drugs. However, I am of the opinion that supervising [him] under the conditions of such an order would prove extremely difficult and I anticipate that there would be problems regarding reporting, keeping out-patient appointments and taking his medication. Should the Court consider that a Probation Order is an appropriate disposal today I would ask the Court to stress upon [him] the importance of complying with the condition, as outlined... Alternatively the Court may take the view that [his] period of remand, that was equivalent to four months imprisonment, was adequate for these offences.

Example 7.11   The defendant of Example 6.4, who stole books about the occult, continued to appear in court at intervals during the study. Alarmed by his deepening slide into fantasy, the magistrates eventually remanded him in custody, apparently in the hope of precipitating his hospitalisation. There followed several weeks during which the probation officer experienced difficulties of access to him and there were delays and confusions over the production of reports by both prison and community psychiatric services. The eventual emergent professional opinion, however, was quite emphatic: the defendant's psychosis was increasingly resistant to medication and possibly irreversible; nevertheless, he probably still knew that it was wrong to steal; he was an unco-operative, disruptive patient, for whom no suggestions for bettering his condition presented themselves.

Astonished by this implied refusal of treatment to an unpopular, but admittedly mentally ill, man, the magistrates again remanded the defendant in custody. The clerk wrote to the Health Authority requesting clarification of the position on the provision of care. The placatory response explained that there had been no intention to deny the defendant treatment, but only to acknowledge the difficulties and pessimistic prognosis.

Defeated, the magistrates discharged the defendant.

2.   The Drug Addict

Probation officers occasionally appeared puzzled when I mentioned that I had an interest in one of their clients, and helpfully sought to correct me by explaining that the offender was a drug addict, not a drinker. This diagnosis routinely overlooked the obvious relationships between these drug-addicted defendants' drinking and offending: usually acute intoxication coinciding with criminal behaviour, sometimes theft of alcohol. Their drug addiction, by contrast, was often a chronic background condition. Indeed, the regular receipt of prescribed drugs was likely to be advanced as evidence of increased stability, reducing the likelihood of criminality. In this context, intoxication by alcohol was deemed to precipitate the occasional unfortunate lapse. Thus, defence solicitors observed:

> He is serving the life sentence of a drug addict. In times of stress he tends to abuse alcohol.

> He gets depressed and drinks on top of the drugs... On this occasion he had been to my office to discuss divorce proceedings and he became so depressed he drank a bottle of vodka and committed the [theft of whisky].

> [This] is a hiccup along the long road to rehabilitation... His drug problem is on the mend because he has managed to get a prescription. On this occasion he was drinking because he had mismanaged his methadone.

> He has been able to organise his drug intake through having a prescription so that he doesn't do any drinking whatsoever... He is very pleased he's not drinking any more and that's probably why he's not committing so many offences.

The argument that drug addiction represented a distinct improvement on defendants' former alcohol abuse appeared quite frequently in SERs. Indeed, it was so highly developed in some cases that drug abuse appeared to achieve the status of socially responsible behaviour, weighed against the evils unleashed by alcohol.

> I understand from [the defendant] that much of his offending in the past has been related to alcohol abuse. He tells me he no longer uses alcohol as when in drink he can be violent. He states he has replaced alcohol with drugs which enable him to survive without resorting to violence.

> Before he began to use heroin or its substitutes he drank heavily, up to a bottle and a half of spirits per day. This alcohol abuse decreased and he now rarely drinks... It is clear from this pattern

that [he] has attempted to find the drug which proved most satisfactory for him, substituting and changing his use of various drugs until developing a regular reliance on opiates...[He] would seem to have made the assessment that the gains from drug use outweigh any disadvantages.

He says that he used cannabis as an alternative to alcohol for recreational purposes, and that he prefers its effect in that it does not create the same undesirable after-effects as alcohol and that as a drug it does not increase one's level of aggression or unpleasantness...[He] has said that he smoked cannabis despite the fact that it was illegal, but this would not seem to be an act of deliberate defiance. Rather [he] regards the use of cannabis as preferable to the use of alcohol and is prepared to accept the consequences that this may have on him should he be arrested.

Although probation officers did acknowledge in some reports that defendants liberally abused both drugs and alcohol, the former tended to command their greatest attention. At times, this focus appeared to obscure recognition of the involvement of alcohol in the offence. Thus, of a defendant who committed a 'walk-in' burglary, taking a crate of beer, and who also stole from a friend while 'quite drunk', according to his solicitor, the probation officer wrote:

[His] offending history is inextricably linked with his use of drugs...The current offences are a continuation of a pattern of offending established since 1971. [The defendant] has entered premises when under the influence of drugs or to obtain money for drugs.

Of another chronically drug-dependent offender, the probation officer reported, with no apparent irony:

[He] maintains that he entered the shop intending to purchase a tin of cat food. Whilst there, he realised that he would be unable to feed his cat for the forthcoming week and decided to steal the bottle of whisky for resale in order to buy food for his pet.

This 'alcohol blindness', reminiscent of that revealed in some academic research which was noted in Chapter 2, cannot simply be explained as a deliberate ordering of priorities or argument, although these factors may have influenced presentation in some cases. So often did my interest in alcohol-related defendants meet with the confident assertion that these were 'drugs, not drink' cases, that I returned to an examination of my notes to check whether I was mistaken. One probation officer, presenting a report on a defendant who had obtained tranquillisers by deception over a substantial period, ruefully told me the following tale:

> When he came up to my office for the interview, when he came in, I thought I smelled alcohol on his breath. But, you know when you're in a closed room, you get so you can't smell it so much. And I asked him about his use of alcohol and he denied it totally. He said he didn't like it. Well, I wasn't entirely convinced, but I let it go. And then after I saw him out – I went outside with him – I went back into my room and it *stank* – it absolutely *stank* of stale alcohol!

The phenomenon whereby multiple substance abuse is identified as *either* a drug problem *or* a drink problem has been noted in other studies of professional decision making in clinical (Plant 1976; Sokolow, Welte, Hynes and Lyons 1981) and criminal justice settings (Abram 1990; Miller and Welte 1986). This same research questions the real utility in professional practice of single-addiction attributions in multiple-abuse cases, finding differences in the nature and severity of the problems, including criminality, associated with multiple- and single-abuse. Nevertheless, this predominance of drug addiction in the perception of multiple-substance abusers appeared to be more than a professional idiosyncrasy of probation officers. The relegation by defence solicitors of alcohol intoxication to secondary status as an episodic lapse within the chronic, 'real' problem of drug addiction has already been noted. In post-sentence interviews, magistrates offered these observations of alcohol-related, drug-addicted offenders:

> I had more the impression he was a drug addict who took to alcohol sometimes as well. But the occasions he said he couldn't remember seemed to be the ones when he was drunk. It seems as if drink was the adjunct, not the main thing. He didn't look as if he drank that much.

> I don't think any references to alcohol really influenced us. He took an occasional drink. In fact I imagine he didn't want alcohol as long as the drugs kept coming. He's not a great alcohol user or offender as far as we could see.

> Most drug addicts have alcohol as well. It's a general emotional instability.

It is not clear, but might be hypothesised, that the focus on drug addiction is prompted by the alien experience of the drug user, in comparison with the familiar one of alcohol consumption. Common sense, however, prevailed over professional wisdom in the reaction to one case.

I didn't really swallow that story about stealing the bottle to sell to get cat food! Why didn't he steal more cat food? It must have been for himself.

CONCLUSION

Studies of courtroom processes can be remarkably reticent on the subject of the defendants themselves (e.g. Parker, Casburn and Turner 1981; Parker, Sumner and Jarvis 1989). Of alcoholics it is often claimed that they deliberately keep a low profile in court (Cook 1975; Mileski 1969). It is sometimes alleged that courtroom procedures embrace a conspiracy to mute the hapless defendant (Carlen 1976). Bottoms and McClean's (1976) exploratory study of self-presentational styles in the courtroom is a comparatively rare attempt to consider the active participation of defendants in the decision-making process.

The comparative latitude for self-expression enjoyed by defendants in City magistrates' court facilitated, and even necessitated, their inclusion as actors in this analysis. This study, then, extends our understanding of the styles of impression management available to defendants in pursuit of mitigation, and the extent to which these styles complement or conflict with their personal self-images. Of greatest interest here was the courtroom behaviour of alcoholics who advertised their condition by overt drunkenness but who varied in the degree of their ambivalence about or embracement of this public identity.

To observers, the extreme inappropriateness of the courtroom displays of the 'hopeless' cases signified irrationality, thereby confirming their pathology, or 'sickness'. Such a perspective, however, assumes that the rewards on offer in the courtroom, which serve as incentives for decorum, apply equally to all defendants. These incentives are to do with the prospect of ameliorating the potential damage to be sustained from an appearance in court: material or financial loss, reduced social status and public humiliation. But these incentives had no relevance to these destitute men. Materially, financially and socially they had already lost whatever advantages they had once possessed. They lived out their lives in a state of public humiliation. Physically, they could even gain from brief incarceration.

These defendants derived quite different rewards from their court appearances. Amongst the most significant, apparently, was the satisfaction of seeing the chaos and embarrassment of their world impinge upon the protected existence of others. At the end of the day, there was little court personnel could have done to prevent this. The limits of the court's sanctions for such behaviour were fairly narrow, and nothing within the courtroom could alter the perverted system of rewards and punishments of the alcoholic's world. But these men were also behaving as they were expected to behave. It was part of their 'sickness' to contradict the rules of propriety which governed courtroom activity.

The examination of this chapter has vividly revealed the extraordinary flexibility of the appeal to intoxication in explaining and mitigating criminal behaviour. The earlier theoretical discussions indicated that lay theories about the relationship between alcohol and criminality involved a network of factually inaccurate and mutually contradictory assumptions selectively applied to different situations. The analysis here demonstrates the practical reality of this phenomenon.

The process of analysis reveals the inaccuracies of and contradictions between the various assumptions about alcohol which underpinned mitigation. The result is that the arguments proffered in the courtroom appear somewhat ludicrous, impossible to take seriously. This effect, however, is the product of analysis. It does not reflect the impact of these arguments in the courtroom itself. Even to an observer paying concentrated attention to references to alcohol, these shifts in presentation of the relationship between alcohol and offending did not begin to emerge for some considerable time. The most probable reason for this is the readiness of the listener to suspend scepticism based on general, abstract 'truths', and to focus on the concrete, situationally specific 'schema' or 'script' constructed for each case. This is the seductiveness of lay theorising. Case by case, these explanations 'made sense'.

The key to an analysis freed from case-specific, commonsense reasoning was the recognition of the stark contrast between mitigation for excess alcohol offences and the broad thrust of arguments in respect of all others. Court personnel, to whom I mentioned this observation, usually appeared puzzled by my interest. When I drew magistrates' attention to the contrast during a talk about my research to a bench meeting, a senior magistrate remarked: 'Well, I never noticed that before.' Another magistrate, to whom I mentioned it during an interview, demurred: 'I don't think defence solicitors would say that about drunk driving these days. I should go back to my notes on that one if I were you.'

These responses reveal, not magisterial inattention, but the situationally specific 'sense' which appeals to quite different assumptions about alcohol could make, rendering them unremarkable. Moreover, these appeals addressed themselves directly to the crucial question of culpability at the heart of the sentencing decision. Precisely because of their direct concern with defendants' capacities for moral self-control in particular situations, they could not be disregarded as extraneous pieces of information.

To speak of 'the intoxication excuse' in mitigation is, therefore, misleading. There is no single intoxication excuse, crudely applied to all alcohol-related offences and offenders. Rather, there is a plurality of intoxication excuses, capitalising on the plurality of lay beliefs about alcohol, selectively and powerfully applied to explain and attribute responsibility for different kinds of criminality. The reach of these lay beliefs, and their moral connotations, is such that even the absence of alcohol from the circumstances of an offence is worthy of mention. This appears to be a unique adaptation of an excuse in mitigation; it is hard to find another single quality of an offence or offender the absence of which is so regularly and forcefully remarked upon.

Earlier theoretical chapters considered the availability of excuses in rationalisation and mitigation. Here, it can be seen that 'availability' means more than presence. The presence of intoxication, or even alcoholism, in the 'facts' of a case had little import if it was not available as an explanation to the perceiver. Thus, since intoxication and alcoholism were conceptually associated with impulsive dishonesty, they were not utilised in mitigation for the sustained and pre-meditated thefts committed by employees, even when other motivational explanations were unidentifiable and despite a plethora of opportunities which in different cases would be seized.

Availability was also related to an implicit hierarchy of social problems. Within this hierarchy, the persuasiveness of a problem related to its emotive appeal rather than to practical utility in the formation of a response. Mental disorder was more persuasive than either acute intoxication or chronic alcoholism, even though sentencing was paralysed by the inaccessibility of treatment. Drug addiction was also more persuasive, possibly because of the seemingly alien nature of the condition when compared to the stockpile of 'common knowledge' and everyday experience of alcohol.

8 The Professional Theorist: Probation Officers at Court

It has been noted on several occasions in the preceding chapters that probation officers were influential in the sentencing process at City court. It is therefore pertinent to explore their perspectives more closely. This chapter explores aspects of the theories held by magistrates and probation officers of intoxicated deviance, responsibility and the probation service's professional role in provision of SERs and probation supervision. These issues are considered for their potential influence on sentencing decision making. The chapter also examines tensions in probation officers' professional theories and experience, and the implications of these tensions for their professional identity.

THE IMPORTANCE OF PROFESSIONAL THEORISING

Professional theories are geared to the interpretation of and response to real-world examples of phenomena such as alcoholism and crime, and are informed by professionals' exposure to this reality. However, this concern with real-world instances does not in itself demonstrate the objective 'truth' of professional theories. For example, Scott argues:

> One of the connotations associated with the notion of a professional ideology is that the conceptions of stigma embodied in them are empirically true, or at least truer than the conceptions which laymen hold. The claim of expertise implies that the claimant has a comprehensive understanding of the nature of stigma and its impact on human behaviour – an understanding firmly rooted in scientific knowledge ... [T]his connotation is partly inaccurate if only because the meaning of a stigma to different experts is often quite different and in some cases even contradictory. (1970, p. 269)

Professional practice requires the application, in real-world instances, of general theories about the nature of a social phenomenon and the appropriate response to it (Curnock and Hardiker 1979). Studies of professional practice suggest that this is achieved through typification: the construction of general case typologies, or diagnostic categories, and their application to individual cases, cued by information from personal contact, case records and discussion with third parties (Drass and Spencer 1987; Giller and Morris 1981; Hawkins 1983a; McCleary 1978; Pfuhl 1980; Sudnow 1965). Typologies provide both explanations of individual character and behaviour, and prescriptions for the appropriate professional response.

Professional practice is also shaped by the goals and resources of the organisation in which it is located. Thus, professional typologies are not simply generalisations about an organisation's clientele, but concern the services which it provides.

> Since the typologies which agents use are provided by the organizations within which they work, the typologies are heavily influenced by the organization. In particular, typologies and their use reflect and are sensitive to organizational goals and functions, particularly in reference to the organization's place in some larger social structure. They also reflect the goals and viewpoints of the agents themselves within these organizational arrangements. (Drass and Spencer 1987, p. 279)

THEORIES OF INTOXICATED CRIME AND RESPONSIBILITY

Magistrates and probation officers were asked whether there were real or hypothetical cases in which they believed that an alcohol-related offender should not be held responsible for his crime, or in which they perceived alcohol to be a mitigating or aggravating factor. They were also asked questions about hypothetical instances of alcohol-related crime.

Principles of Intoxicated Responsibility

Only six magistrates (30 per cent) responded with an unequivocal negative to the question whether there were real or hypothetical cases in which they thought that an alcohol-related offender should not be held responsible for what he had done. Six (30 per cent) identified the 'spiked drink', or involuntary intoxication, as an occasion for absolving an offender from criminal responsibility.

If it could be proved that he'd been spiked...That would be the only one because all the others are self-inflicted wounds. Whether it be one drink or whether it be ten, you should know what it can do. You should know what your reaction is.

Only if somebody else had doctored his drink...People should be responsible for what they drink...In today's world, when we're trying to teach everybody about drink, people should know that their responsibility is not to drink so that they can't control whatever it is that they're doing.

Thus, in principle, intoxication was a self-induced condition, in which the drinker courted loss of control. Nevertheless, eight magistrates (40 per cent) acknowledged further occasions when these judgements were problematic. One magistrate conceded that driving might become unexpectedly necessary after drinking. Two magistrates acknowledged a problem in general terms.

I do find this a problem sometimes. I know it's no defence that they were drunk, but there have been times when I've thought: 'This person wouldn't have done it if they weren't drunk.' I really have thought that.

Three magistrates thought that alcoholism, as a disease or illness, diminished responsibility.

Some people are much more culpably drunk than others...If it's got to the stage where it's an actual disease, that's a different kettle of fish altogether. And I certainly [wouldn't] regard [that] as culpably drunk, because I feel that it's just a disease.

Somebody who is an alcoholic may well not be responsible for his actions...It's like a drug addict. It's an illness.

Two magistrates thought that responsibility was diminished when drinking was a response to personal trauma.

There are obviously times when somebody's gone through an enormous personal trauma...If somebody's wife had just died or something and maybe because of that the person had drunk too much and that had led perhaps to an offence. Yes, personal tragedies of that sort, certainly would be taken into account.

When people drink through despair and are at their wits end, and one hears about extremely distressing family circumstances, you think to yourself: 'Well, no wonder they've been drinking!'

Finally, one magistrate described a case in which alcohol consumption played a vital part in a defendant's livelihood.

That was a chap who was a steel fitter, working up on massive places, sky high... He could not do his job unless he'd got a drink inside him. Every[body] on that site who was a steel fitter had alcohol – *always* had alcohol... He said: 'You tell me somebody else who'd be 130 feet up in the sky with no safety harness, walking across a piece of steel'... It's a Catch 22 situation... You either lose your job or you lose your licence.

Magistrates also equivocated on the subject of mitigation. Six (30 per cent) rejected the intoxication excuse here.

I'm hard on that. I just feel that it's self-induced and no excuses. And as long as you're aware of what you're up to, well then you've no need to get into trouble with it. I can understand those who are weak and who like it. I know of those who are shy and can't do anything till they've got their sherry down. I can understand that. But... when it comes to criminality, I would give it very little weight in mitigation.

The remainder (70 per cent) offered a variety of instances in which intoxication was potentially mitigating. Four mentioned alcoholism.

Somebody who doesn't know what they're doing and is perpetually in an alcoholic state. I still say there *was* a responsibility, but they have become so debilitated that they are – not *in*capable of responsibility – but much less able to make a conscious decision.

Five observed that intoxication could mitigate when they sympathised with a person's motivations for drinking.

There are times of crisis in a person's life when a resort to the bottle seems to be the only thing. Personal grief, personal sorrows, or a series of disasters. When drinking oneself into oblivion does seem to be the only way out, perhaps. But it's rather at variance with my former assertion that I do believe that one has a sense of personal responsibility which should take over-riding preference. I can well foresee that with some people this would be submerged into their own requirements at the time.

Some magistrates pointed to unusual features of an intoxicated offence, such as accident or emergency, and uncharacteristic or incompetent behaviour. Here, the issue seemed to be the absence of prior expectation of offending.

> If it's a very young person, yes. People have got to learn. If somebody has never come across alcohol before and ends up going to a party and therefore that leads to an offence.

> There are certain situations that...backfire on you. He was probably in the wrong place at the wrong time and drinking the wrong alcohol. If it had been somebody else he might have been able to cope with it and walk away and deal with it another way.

Eighteen magistrates (90 per cent) identified circumstances in which alcohol was an aggravating factor. Seven mentioned driving offences involving alcohol. Here, the seriousness of such offences was linked to the risk of severe harm, and to a perceived element of deliberation in the offence.

> Drink-driving...Because there's so much publicity about...the dangers of drinking and driving. When you're in a car having drunk so much that you are actually going along with this weapon, you can cause people so much harm. And it's the fact that they do it knowingly. They actually *must* know.

> There was one very bad one where a chap...ended up driving into the front of somebody's house. He was well gone...His actions were irresponsible from beginning to end, because he went out, with the knowledge that he was going to drink, and didn't take any steps to stop himself from driving...His whole attitude was wrong.

Six magistrates (30 per cent) mentioned violence, and one commented on the quality of 'noise and terror'. Alcohol was thought to unleash excessive savagery in an attack. In some of these responses, it was suggested that alcohol was used intentionally to engender aggression.

> Street violence...If somebody has been drinking they're probably going to be far more violent towards the other person than they would be if they were sober.

> Attacks on publicans...People who habitually go to certain kinds of pubs which have a reputation for violence, or where nobody's

particularly surprised when violence breaks out... There's a whole culture of aggressive drinking.

The notion that alcohol might be consumed intentionally to facilitate offending was taken up by five magistrates (25 per cent), for whom this quality of drinking was the aggravating factor rather than the type of offence.

> When you have deliberately got yourself into a drunk condition so that you will lose your inhibitions and then commit a crime. To me that makes it worse. If there's absolutely no question of disease, you know perfectly well what you're doing.

One magistrate considered the rejection of treatment while persistently offending to be an aggravating factor.

Thus, judgements of responsibility were problematic for magistrates because of their belief in loss of control through intoxication or alcoholism. The assessment of motivations for drinking weighed heavily in judgements of culpability for subsequent offending. Loss of control over drinking itself, drinking in response to personal trauma or drinking without prior expectation of offending reduced culpability. 'Provocative' drinking, whereby offending was deliberately or recklessly facilitated through intoxication, increased culpability.

Probation officers were considerably more confident and uniform in their responses. Out of the 15 officers 14 (93 per cent) gave an abrupt negative to the question whether there were cases in which an alcohol-related offender should not be held responsible for his crime. In clarifying this unequivocal response, they became eloquent on the topic of personal responsibility.

> It would be very dangerous to start making exceptions, saying because they were drunk therefore they had no knowledge or control. That's a very slippery slope... I'd be very worried because ultimately people *have* to be responsible for their own behaviour... If people don't take responsibility for themselves, we're into a very patronising way of viewing the world.

> For many people it's a lot easier to... blame the alcohol, instead of blaming themselves for drinking... But because people have always got the choice about their drinking they've got the choice of doing something about it. I don't think people are unaware of the effects of their drinking. They may choose not to see it that way. They may choose to ignore it.

The officer who said that 'the only exception would be if somebody had spiked a drink of somebody, who knew that they reacted to alcohol...and therefore deliberately avoided it', also subscribed to this fundamental perspective.

Several officers explained their firmness by reference to their professional role.

> Part of my job is about saying to people that they do have self-determination and that they can control their own behaviour.

> I don't see myself being in the job anyway to excuse people. I respect clients for what they are. I care about what happens to them. But I'm not in the business of excusing them. That's a totally different thing.

Only two officers (13 per cent) identified circumstances in which they would consider intoxication to be a mitigating factor in an offence. Like magistrates, they were concerned with the motivational background to the drinking.

> Circumstances of considerable stress. Bereavement, for example. A break up of a relationship, loss of a job. Stress, I guess.

> If it's a youngster who doesn't realise just how strong alcohol can be. And he's with a group...and he's perhaps encouraged or gets carried along.

Three probation officers (20 per cent) conceded the possibility of mitigation through intoxication, but with strong reservations.

> The only difference it makes is that I might say this person has a drink problem, and therefore could do with some help to address it, rather than this person has no problems at all and is just thoroughly nasty. So I suppose we do accept it as mitigation.

Seven probation officers (47 per cent) rejected mitigation through intoxication. These officers were often concerned to clarify their professional role. Indeed, some appeared quite affronted by their inference that they should concern themselves with questions of mitigation.

> But I'm not in the business of mitigating! Mitigation is for solicitors and barristers...I'm there to give an assessment of a person's situation and some understanding to that situation. Which is not to mitigate. Mitigation is providing excuses and I don't think I'm from the Ministry of Excuses.

I don't see my role as mitigating at all. That's a solicitor's role. In the court setting I see my role as explaining the offence and saying this offence is inextricably linked with abuse of alcohol...And maybe using that to say rather than just look at the offence, what we've got to look at is the drinking, to stop further offending. That's not mitigation. That's explaining the offences. No, I'm quite clear about that.

The hesitant concessions to mitigation were perhaps also linked to this distinction which probation officers drew between mitigation and explanation. Explanation was a legitimate role for probation officers. It was linked to the construction of sentencing recommendations and concern for offenders' problems.

Where I come in, as a probation officer, is looking at how to avoid offending in future, which is where alcohol may well come in. In terms of whether it makes the offence more or less serious, I don't concern myself with that.

Paradoxically, probation officers were much less professionally self-conscious on the subject of aggravation. Only one officer re-iterated the view that these issues were not legitimate professional concerns. Two officers inclined to the view that alcohol *per se* was essentially a neutral factor in an offence.

If you beat somebody over the head with an iron bar, I don't really think that it should make it worse or better if you'd been drinking beforehand. The fact that you've done it should be the issue...Otherwise, one falls into the trap of making alcohol into some kind of a determinant of behaviour, and we should start from the assumption that it isn't.

Eleven probation officers (73 per cent) gave examples of aggravation through intoxication. Nine (60 per cent) cited driving offences. Often the tone of probation officers' remarks conveyed personal abhorrence of such offences.

There *has* to be an aggravating factor, particularly in things like death through reckless driving...If somebody's deliberately putting other people's lives at risk and in fact takes somebody's life...then that seems to have been, in a sense, planned, in that they didn't take the necessary precautions or didn't think it was important enough to protect other people.

Reckless driving combined with drinking. It's an additional offence. I personally don't have much time for drink drivers. There's so much publicity about drinking and driving that even relatively irresponsible people ought to be sufficiently aware to control their drinking if they're going to drive.

Three probation officers (20 per cent) mentioned violent offences. For two officers this was linked to the belief that intoxicated disinhibition would increase the severity of an attack. The third combined personal antipathy with a sociological explanation of alcohol-related violence.

I don't like violence. Violence with weapons in particular... Those sorts of offences as a probation officer and as a citizen make me uncomfortable... I don't like being in pubs when fights start, I don't like seeing fights... Inner cities in this country seem to me to have started to become the exclusive property, almost, of the 18–30 year olds... My fear is that the more [other] people are excluded from the city centre, the more likely that sort of violence is on the bubble... People feeling afraid to go certain places. Drunken, loud, violent people.

One probation officer regarded the invocation of the intoxication excuse itself as aggravating.

I don't think drinking necessarily makes the offence worse... When you see somebody who's actually excusing their behaviour through drink, that makes it worse. It's almost as if they're licensing themselves to offend.

Probation officers did not struggle with the notion of intoxicated responsibility as magistrates did, nor concern themselves greatly with prior motivations for drinking, except when considering aggravation. Personal abhorrence, particularly concerning intoxicated driving, intervened to disrupt the dispassionate professionalism upon which they had previously insisted. The topic of aggravation thus began to reveal the tensions between professional theorising and personal attitudes.

Theories of Alcohol-related Crime

During questions about hypothetical instances of intoxicated deviance, two questions produced markedly different responses from probation officers and magistrates: one concerning City's crime problems; and one concerning personal success in avoiding trouble through drink. Further questions explored explanations of types of alcohol-related crime, revealing differences in perspectives.

1. City's Crime Problems

Magistrates generally did not think that City suffered from any particular problems with alcohol-related crime. One magistrate summed up this sanguine view.

> When you come here and you sit in the court building and these people are ranged up and the lists are long, you think: 'By Jove! [City] is a shocking place to be and crime is rampant and the police have absolutely got it out of control!' But that isn't the case at all... We're pretty law-abiding, by and large.

Six magistrates (30 per cent) mentioned City's alcoholics. Magistrates here were identifying a social problem rather than a crime problem.

> We've got the habitual drunks, but I imagine that probably every community has these days. In fact, I'm quite sad that they've taken away those seats in the [shopping precinct]... The more you isolate people with problems like drinking, it's not going to help.

Nine probation officers (60 per cent) identified violence as a particular crime problem. Some officers wondered if their perception of the phenomenon was distorted by the type of work they predominantly undertook.

> Most of my impressions would be from people serving custodial sentences, in which case I've probably got a skewed view anyway, because they tend to be... more serious offences.

However, five officers compared City unfavourably with places in which they had previously worked. Notably, all these officers had prior experience in bigger metropolitan and inner city areas. Moreover, these officers in particular tended to remark on the viciousness of City's violence.

> The thing that surprised me coming to [City] was the amount of offenders we have on our books for violent crime... That struck me as soon as I came to [City]. And it's always seemed that way to me here. It seems to get a lot of gratuitous violence and unsuspecting victims.

2. *Personal Success in Avoiding Trouble Through Drink*

Fourteen magistrates (70 per cent) attributed their success in avoiding trouble through drink to the fact that they drank little or nothing. Their collective abstemiousness was impressive.

> I don't drink very much, simply because I'm a nervous sort of person...and I find drink just exaggerates it...I don't think I've ever even remotely approached being drunk!

> Easy! I just can't take drink. That's it. End of story...I've never ever been drunk. Never.

Nine magistrates (45 per cent) identified a sense of personal responsibility or self-discipline, which influenced their conduct in all areas of their lives, including, by implication, alcohol consumption.

> It's a frame of mind, isn't it?...My youth wasn't that easy. I had it quite difficult. Because I left home when I was barely 17...and I used to get drunk every night. But I got out of that...I had to make certain decisions...That's what people have to do for themselves.

> Discipline, in a word, probably self-discipline. My discipline was that I wasn't going to struggle in the way I saw my mother struggle. And therefore I'd got to make something of my life.

Seven magistrates (35 per cent) identified their upbringing as a key element in the development of adulthood abstemiousness.

> I'm fairly puritanical about it...I was brought up in a teetotal household.

> I always consider spending money on drink excessively a complete waste. Perhaps I'm a bit of a puritan! My tradition, my upbringing. Alcohol didn't feature very largely.

Two magistrates considered the possible significance of the drinking environment.

> We would drink at home, but not outside...Maybe that's what it is. In certain types of family you drink at home, so if you're going to do anything obnoxious you do it in the house. Whereas the youngsters that drink in the pub, their opportunity for criminal damage is on the way home...So maybe that's what it is. It's where you do your drinking.

When I was an undergraduate we went to our fair share of parties, and I've no doubt that we all occasionally overindulged, but in those days we didn't have cars at all. Colleges do mop up an awful lot of drink problems among students.

Only one magistrate, however, explicitly acknowledged personal fallibility.

It's not planned. It's the unplanned set of circumstances which leads somebody to do something which they haven't thought about...I can think of all sorts of circumstances when I might, or no doubt have – however much I deplore or normally avoid it.

These lay theories of personal success in avoiding trouble through drink belong predominantly in the arena of dispositional perspectives, considered in their academic formulations in Chapter 2. The heavy reliance on abstention as a primary explanation implies a strong belief in the potential for pharmacologically induced loss of control. Nevertheless, magistrates' explanations of their abstemiousness itself drew predominantly on beliefs about personal responsibility and self-discipline, inculcated through upbringing.

Probation officers displayed a keen awareness of their own potential fallibility. Five officers (33 per cent) explicitly said that they were moderate or non-drinkers. A sixth concentrated on the aversiveness of intoxication.

A. I think I know what it does to me. B. I don't like what it does to me. C. I don't like being that out of control of myself....So I'm aware of its effects at all levels: physically, emotionally and psychologically.

For other probation officers, it seemed that moderation was not the only available solution to potential trouble through drink.

I'm a bit of a coward! When I've had a few beers, I'm still cautious enough not to pick a fight with a bloke in a T-shirt at the bar. I am very conscious about drinking and driving, which means that I nowadays very rarely drink in [City], but I drink at home in the village and just walk backwards and forwards from the pub.

Being cagey, probably!...I could never put my hand on my heart and say I've never drunk and driven. But I'm aware enough to know what the implications would be for me if I did get caught for drinking and driving. So quite often I'm aware of where the police

traps are, and I wouldn't drink and drive if I know I'm going
through those areas. I've got to say, over the last five years or so
I've got more responsible in that way. Certainly, now, I wouldn't do
it ... Because the trouble with me is I do like a drink. And one pint
is not enough!

Only one probation officer mentioned upbringing, and none talked
about personal responsibility or self-discipline in the manner of
magistrates, as a stable disposition. Probation officers did not seem
to see their drinking behaviour as originating in the same self-will
which had brought them to their present status in life. Rather, as
suggested in the last officer's comments, their present status provided
the incentives to control their drinking or its effects.

[When] people are in perfectly satisfactory relationships and good
jobs, the incentives aren't there. Or the incentives are there for *not*
offending. You have something to lose.

It seems to me that most of the people I see who get into trouble
through drink have got not a lot in their lives other than drinking
with their mates, having a good time. Very short term goals. Maybe
it's the case that the longer term your goals are – the more you've
got to lose – the less likely you are to get into trouble.

For two more officers, their professional experience in itself altered
their drinking behaviour.

If you're talking about drinking and driving, so often they're people
my age and [with a] similar background ... But it's having worked
with people and learned more about its effects. That's the difference. It's so much a part of our everyday working life.

Probation officers predominantly attributed their success in avoiding trouble through drink to the context in which their drinking
occurred. Ten officers (67 per cent) made this point. The social and
environmental context of their drinking dominated most officers'
responses. Seven officers explained the point by contrasting current
and previous drinking patterns. This recognition of change in their
personal attitudes and behaviour distinguished probation officers
from magistrates. Only two magistrates reported a shift in drinking
pattern between youth and maturity. The candid acknowledgement of
a change in their view of drinking and driving was one aspect of this
for two probation officers.

There was the odd time when I was younger when I drank and drove. I did not say that with pride because I'm very against drinking and driving. But when I was about 17 and I'd just passed my test, I was rather irresponsible in a lot of ways.

Recollections of studenthood prompted recognition of the merciful protectiveness of certain drinking environments, together with sociological observations of class and culture.

In some ways it's a matter of chance. I know from my own experience that at university there are a fair amount of people who get into trouble through drink and are never prosecuted. They're dealt with informally. The higher up the social scale you go the more likely you are to be weeded out from the whole prosecution process.

I was at university...where I used to drink a lot. That was partly about being in a culture where it's expected. One expects rugby players to be drunk on Saturday nights!...A group of similarly aged people in the street are more likely to attract police attention. That would be a class thing.

For two officers, the environment and culture of drinking was also a matter of gender.

Dare I say being a woman?...First of all, if there's a group of you in the street, the police will tend to go for the men...It tends to be the blokes who are prominent in any kind of disturbance. And if...in my domestic circumstances, I hit the bottle, I'd probably just lounge around the house and get depressed. Which is a typically female response...I'd just languish around the house, be a trouble to myself, but not society.

For the six magistrates who said that they did not visit pubs, this information appeared largely to be supportive evidence of their abstemiousness. For probation officers, this was usually part of their explanations of the circumstances in which they did currently drink. Once again, the significant issue was the protective physical and social context of drinking.

Luck, number one, in my younger years. Number two, rarely drinking, now, outside of the house. Number three – which is probably related to number two – domestic responsibilities. They keep me at home and make me generally exhausted and I (haven't) got the energy to go out drinking and breaching the peace. A bottle of wine with supper and I fall asleep.

Most of the drinking I do will take place at home. It's to do with preparing meals for friends... I don't tend to drink a lot in pubs ... It was about people who worked together and had interests in common... a drinking circle that was about providing entertainment for each other. Quite an introspective sort of thing.

Concerning their success in avoiding trouble through drink, therefore, most probation officers were situational theorists. Although they believed in pharmacological disinhibition, in this context the quantity of consumption was largely beside the point. Thus, some probation officers talked about 'luck', referring to the happy coincidence of social situational factors which protected them from the potential risks engendered by alcohol consumption. Nevertheless, probation officers did not link their personal fallibility within situationally inspired temptation to an abdication of personal responsibility. In this respect, their professional belief in 'explanation, not mitigation' of offenders' behaviour was consistent with their personal moral standards.

3. Types of Intoxicated Crime
Theoretical perspectives shifted in response to a sequence of questions asking for explanations of types of intoxicated deviance. Of primary interest is the shifting reliance on intoxication itself. Disinhibition was invoked most often by both magistrates and probation officers in the explanation of pub violence. Sixteen magistrates (80 per cent) mentioned this.

It must be alcohol! You're in a pub, you're going to drink, you're going to get excited, you're going to be elated. The alcohol's going to make the adrenalin flow, and you're in a different world... However, they react differently when they've got this alcohol inside them.

Eleven probation officers (73 per cent) also invoked disinhibition.

Too much drink! People drink too much, lose control, lose their faculties... They lose the inbuilt things they have that stop them doing things normally. Alcohol is a depressant, and depressed people may fight!

Only three magistrates (15 per cent), but eight probation officers (53 per cent) cited disinhibition in the explanation of marital disputes. Officers here seemed to be trying to relate disinhibition to a more complex function of drinking within a close relationship.

Because the physical effect of alcohol is to suppress your inhibitions, and maybe all the feelings that you've had pent up...come bubbling up to the surface. It's a bit like why do [marital disputes] always happen at Christmas? Expectations that things should be nice and suddenly they're not...When the inhibitions are gone, people express the disappointments that they have in each other, which are probably perfectly healthy and normal – to be disappointed in your partner – but it suddenly reaches tremendous proportions.

It's an easy way of exerting power...It's a weapon which is used because it's very powerful. If one party's drinking that completely disarms the other, because you can't be rational, you can't attempt to address problems logically through discussion. You can only deal with the symptoms you're being presented with...That's why it's such a pernicious weapon.

Only one magistrate and two probation officers postulated intoxication, through judgement impairment, as a cause of drinking and driving. As the magistrate put it:

You've got to decide before you have a drink whether you're going to drive. It's too late once you've had a drink...Your brain's affected.

Intoxication *per se* was not mentioned by magistrates at all in relation to chronic alcoholics. Two probation officers remarked on its incapacitating effects.

One of the reasons that people with chronic drink problems appear to commit a lot of crime or get caught for a lot of crime is that when they're drunk they're not very good at it.

There was, in fact, a wide difference between magistrates and probation officers in their explanations of the offending of chronic alcoholics. Two themes dominated magistrates' responses. Firstly, chronic alcoholics could not help themselves.

Because they're almost continually under the influence of alcohol and are not aware of their actions...They are just not aware. Their minds are never clear enough to reach any form of clear decisions about their actions.

Because they can't do anything. They've got no control over their actions. They are so committed to alcohol that there is no way that they can be other than they are.

Secondly, chronic alcoholics were sick.

Because they're sick. That's very disturbing. I hate to see [them] being brought and brought into court... Because they are – they're *sick*. They're as sick as somebody who's got a mental illness.

The drink takes over from them. I guess they don't realise what they're doing. It's an illness and not a crime.

These two theories appeared in the responses of 15 magistrates (75 per cent), vividly demonstrating their belief in the power of alcoholism to strip individuals of their capacity for personal responsibility. Magistrates were fully aware of the structural problems in the lives of chronic alcoholics. However, they tended to remark on their offensiveness, rather than their offending.

They're *dirty*, they're a *nuisance*, they *frighten* people – they're quite frightening! – they demand money. Most people try to avoid them. [But] when you see people so far down the road to oblivion and degradation, I do feel sorry for them... You can't just sweep offensive people out of sight.

Only three probation officers (20 per cent) unambiguously referred to loss of control through alcoholism.

[Some of them] probably break the law because they lack control... I would suspect that some of them... are not responsible for their actions, once they get beyond a certain point.

The majority of probation officers took a sociological perspective on this question. Nine (60 per cent) offered theories of the alienated or anomic condition of the chronic alcoholic, or of social control.

Because... they [don't] feel they are part of society, or the rules of society apply to them. But it goes deeper than that. They probably deep down feel such outsiders that the rest of the world has very little to do with them, and they have very little to do with the world.

Chronic alcoholism is defined by a number of factors which are social, which would include unemployment, difficulties with accommodation, difficulty with finance, difficulty with relationships, that tend to push people towards the margins of their society. And the margins of society are controlled and patrolled by agents of social control, which is what brings them into conflict with the law, quite often.

In this context, loss of control was as much to do with social disempowerment as with physical and mental debility.

They are in such an impossible situation, because they are in the grips of an addiction that is so overwhelming and resources are just not there to help them. [So] in some senses they would perceive themselves as having no choice about their actions. *I* think they *do* have a choice, but the difficulty is that *they* don't believe [it]. So life is a conspiracy, and it's very difficult for them to behave in a way which is within the law.

On other topics, the differences between magistrates and probation officers were more emphatic than theoretical. Both saw the involvement of alcohol in marital disputes in terms of the quality of a relationship, in which drinking might be a cause or a product of dissatisfaction. They commented equally on the exacerbating effects of deteriorating finances and the potential for violence. Magistrates, however, were more likely to assume that the drinker would be the male partner. One magistrate expressed the problem vividly:

It's one of the saddest things if the person sees his or her marriage partner dwindle away into chronic alcoholism. It's terrible. Because it really means you've lost them, and they won't come back for your sake, either. They won't try to change their ways because it's impossible. So you've lost your influence. Therefore, they've lost your respect, yes, and you've lost your relationship.

Magistrates and probation officers largely agreed that pub violence was perpetrated by young males in groups. Magistrates were perhaps rather inclined to see this phenomenon from a dispositional perspective. Probation officers' theories of pub violence utilised rather more complex perspectives. Seven magistrates (35 per cent) and four probation officers (27 per cent) thought that the perpetrators were undisciplined or looking for trouble. Six officers (40 per cent) and one magistrate (5 per cent) invoked sociological theories of the alienation of working-class youth. Seven officers (47 per cent) and four magistrates (20 per cent) referred to features of the drinking environment, and these officers tended to mention more situational factors than the magistrates who did so.

> With lots of milling around, violence is much more likely to be around because of people being in close proximity to each other, liable to bump into each other, to knock over each other's drink. Also quite a lot of violence happens outside the pub, which to me is to do with how pubs are located near each other, where there aren't dispersal points or alternative things to draw people away. So...it's not just about individual choice. There are things which affect people's individual choice to get into violence.

The three probation officers who mentioned publicans did so unfavourably, while the references by five magistrates were sympathetic.

> PO: Pubs probably don't take their responsibilities seriously enough. They're quite happy to go on serving people beyond any point which could be regarded as sensible.

> M: I admire publicans tremendously, because they have a very difficult job to do...The good ones deserve our support.

Drinking and driving was regarded as the personal fault of the offender by 15 magistrates (75 per cent) and 7 probation officers (47 per cent). Probation officers here compensated for their fewer numbers by the force of their remarks. Eight officers (53 per cent) offered a sociological perspective on this topic, often in combination with individual condemnation.

> They're pig ignorant! It's true! People have this inflated idea of what civil liberties is all about. 'I must have my car, I will drive, I don't have responsibilities to other people.' They drink and drive because other people do, and because magistrates do, and because solicitors have done it. They think it's more socially respectable.

Magistrates tended to comment on the challenge and machismo of drinking and driving. Seven (35 per cent) offered a sociological perspective.

> A far quicker route to sanity on the roads...is a complete bar to drinking and driving. So that one cannot be tempted to have this extra glass or two, thinking that you are still below the limit...With parties and entertainments removed from housing, with public

transport getting worse because society is running more cars, it's an ever increasing problem.

It was noted in the previous chapter that alcohol provides a key reference point for social observation. Here, both magistrates and probation officers were able to provide rapid 'top of the head' explanations of instances of alcohol-related crime by associating them with particular types of offender, social situations and intoxicated behaviours. Within these hypothetical 'schemata', particular motivations could be imputed to offenders, with consequential implications for judgements of their culpability. Probation officers produced more complex and more varied theories of intoxicated deviance than magistrates, yet retained a stronger sense of personal responsibility. In particular, they did not subscribe to theories of 'sickness'.

SOCIAL ENQUIRY REPORTS

Magistrates' enthusiasm for information was amply demonstrated in their stated reasons for requesting SERs. They sometimes seemed to attach significance to the lack of information *per se*.

> If there was something... about the defendant which was a bit of a puzzle, and they weren't prepared to say... The information that we really sought about background wasn't forthcoming. Therefore, in spite of them, we want to know more about them... It [may] not be fair, even though somebody is deliberately putting themselves in the position where we'd be quite justified in going ahead.

The need for information, cited by nine magistrates, was closely linked to explanation, which was given as a reason by 10 magistrates. In all, 15 magistrates mentioned either or both information and explanation.

> When you really don't understand why the person has done something and there isn't the information readily to hand... The exploration of the background can make something incomprehensible perfectly comprehensible.

The popularity of information and explanation as reasons for requesting SERs suggests that in many cases magistrates suspended judgements of culpability prior to their receipt. Magistrates apparently expected their judgements to *emerge* from perusal of SERs. They did not appear to approach SERs with the suspicion noted in other research (Parker, Sumner and Jarvis 1989).

> I see [probation officers] as mediators, in a way that I don't see the solicitor, because I see them as honest brokers... There's no skin off the probation officer's nose... It doesn't matter to them if you don't follow their advice. But with a solicitor, it's his professional reputation.

While magistrates regarded the information provided by probation officers as neutral, they saw their recommendations as heavily biased towards the defendant's interests. Magistrates thought that by their recommendations probation officers were trying to keep defendants out of custody (four), to achieve 'the best possible solution in the interests of the defendant' (four), or to rehabilitate or reform him (eight). Magistrates generally seemed to accept these motives as professionally appropriate.

> Most probation officers have a very strong aversion to penal institutions. A *very* strong aversion.

> Probation officers believe they can do a better job than prison. They *have* to believe that. That's why they're probation officers. You wouldn't want them *not* to feel that, really. They've got to believe in what they're doing.

In probation officers' statements of their goals in making recommendations two themes appeared most frequently. Six officers said that they were trying to divert offenders from custody, to keep them down tariff, or to preserve probation recommendations for high-tariff cases.

> County policy would say diverting people from custody! I would agree with that. Ensuring that those who aren't at risk of custody are kept as low-down tariff as possible.

> If I think people are likely to reoffend one of the agendas for me is to keep them down tariff. So I'll use conditional discharge recommendations as long as I think I can get away with it... If I'm looking towards a probation recommendation I'm trying to make sure that they're fairly high tariff.

Eight officers answered in terms of preventing or reducing reoffending, although explicit references to rehabilitation, reform or welfare were absent from probation officers' stated aims.

To affect his offending. To offer the court my assessment of his offending and to use the lowest possible thing on the tariff to change that.

I'm trying to provide the courts with credible alternatives to custody. I'm also trying to make them understand that those alternatives are not soft options... So the recommendations should positively address the issues that I've identified as underlying the offending.

The alcohol factor in an offence was a useful tool in the construction of proposals for reducing offending, just as it was useful for offenders in demonstrating remorse and reform. The utility of an alcohol factor as an organising principle around which to construct offender characterisations and recommendations has already been demonstrated. Organising principles such as this were utilised in the interests of cognitive economy under pressure of time. That SERs do not reflect the total sum of probation officers' professional knowledge and theory is illustrated by their responses to a question asking about the differences between drink and drug problems. This was asked in an attempt to clarify the apparent 'alcohol blindness' of report writers in cases concerning drug users. However, not only were probation officers' responses considerably more varied than those of magistrates, but they sometimes appeared to assume that the question reflected *my* ignorance of alcohol's toxicity. They seemed quite unaware of the discrepancy between their judgements in individual cases and the complexity of their more leisured abstract theorising.

Magistrates generally thought that drug problems were more serious, harder to overcome and arose from personality disturbances in the addicts. Their responses supported the hypothesis of the previous chapter that concentration on drug rather than alcohol abuse stemmed from the alien experience of the user.

The destruction of the body... Somebody who's got a healthy body who then pollutes it. That's the thing about drugs I find very difficult to take... Alcohol also abuses the body, but you get away with it for much longer.

I've seen all these people on amphetamines and the cannabis business. They all look pretty sad sorts of people. But what it's all about internally I'm not aware... What effects they have, what they feel, what their cravings are I don't know.

Probation officers, however, disagreed among themselves about the comparative seriousness of drink and drug problems. Some felt strongly that drink problems were more dangerous, or harder to overcome. Only two thought that more disturbed personalities succumbed to drug addiction. Once again, probation officers utilised more sociological perspectives.

> Drink is freely and legally available. So by drinking one isn't automatically entering into a subculture...Leisure activities, especially for the young, are inextricably linked with the use of alcohol...So not only is it freely available, it's expected that people will drink...There is a more direct link between drink and offending than between drug use and offending, apart from the fact that drug use is an offence in itself.

> Alcohol can have a very wide social effect...[With drug abuse], you've got it underground, you've got the suppliers of drugs and people being drawn into the net...Drugs seem more insidious. Whereas [with] the excessive use of alcohol, you get vast numbers, like in football or riots, it seems more open. Maybe alcohol is more visible. Maybe that's the only difference.

Thus, probation officers did not distinguish as clearly as magistrates between the information and recommendations in SERs. They saw their reports more wholistically in terms of their objectives. In the exercise of constructing rationales for their recommendations, probation officers focused on an organising principle, of which alcohol was one of the most available and utilisable.

PROBATION

Relationships between City magistrates and the probation service were generally considered to be good by both sides. However, probation officers complained that magistrates did not understand or accept their contemporary professional role.

> One of the big issues with the court is patrolling the welfare boundary. They want to assign us a welfare role which is increasingly incompatible with what we're trying to do.

> In [City] magistrates' court, there is a genuine concern for some of the people that appear before them, that they do have very difficult lives with lots of problems. They genuinely want them to be linked

up with an agency that's going to help them sort those out. They've looked traditionally to the probation service to be that agency and have had some confidence in us to do so. Now they're facing us saying we are not the agency to work with these people. That would be OK if we could tell them who was. But it's leaving a gap in community provision to help people with myriad problems – debt, housing and so on – but we're saying they haven't got offending problems and therefore are not our target group.

Magistrates, in fact, quite often expressed support for the notion of probation as an alternative to custody, which would be expected in the light of their personal antipathy to it. However, they did not see it as unproblematic, for themselves or for the probation service.

As I understand it, a probation order was about befriending. If that's the ethos...then they've got to have a dramatic change of thinking in the probation service if they're now going to be an alternative to custody...There's no reason why they can't do that, but they've got to recognise that it is going to be a total change of their reason for being.

Probation is something on its own. Community service is something we use instead of custody. I would hate to see us having a juggling act over the same thing...So if you put somebody on probation, what do you do if the probation doesn't work? Do they then go inside? No, I don't like that idea...It's not helping anybody...Probation should be used for its own sake. It shouldn't be weighed off against anything else.

Magistrates and probation officers conceptualised suitability of alcohol-related offenders for probation in very different terms. Magistrates invariably produced a concrete 'schema' of a type of person they considered suitable. Also invariably, this schema invoked the classic 'inadequate', or undersocialised, personality, particularly the young, and often the first and petty offender.

Those with few family ties, few friends, disorganised, unemployed, alcohol addicted...The drifter with few friends or family who becomes a drinker for some form of personal comfort. The weak-willed, the easily led.

A young married man, perhaps, who's got a family and a drink problem. Because he has got responsibilities which he as yet is too immature to cope with.

Such a theory of suitability for probation was anathema to probation officers, and gave rise to some of their most overt courtroom
conflicts with the magistrates.

Example 8.1   The defendant, aged 41, had stolen four cans of lager
and a bicycle. He had numerous previous convictions, and was a
chronic drug and alcohol abuser. During the initial hearing, the
magistrates insisted on the production of SERs, despite resistance
from the probation officer on the grounds that the offences were
trivial. The magistrates were adamant that the defendant needed
'help and support'. The subsequent SER recommended nominal
fines and compensation: '[The defendant] would have some difficulty
paying these, but this would be likely to help remind him of the need
to exercise greater care and restraint in his drinking in the future.' On
this occasion, the magistrates acquiesced, and the court duty probation officer complained to me about 'the waste of time and resources
preparing reports for an outcome such as this'.

An irony in this case was the SER writer's observation: 'In interview
[the defendant] tended to be rather dismissive of the offences.' The
probation service having been publicly dismissive of his offences, the
defendant might have been forgiven for his tactical error. Instead, his
defence solicitor was obliged to counter the aspersion on his character: 'He is unhappy about the use of the word "dismissive" of the
offences. He is not dismissive. He is unhappy to be back before the
court'.

In a post-sentence interview following a protracted debate about a
'tragic' first offender who had shoplifted alcohol and admitted to a
drink problem, the magistrate declared:

We felt he was ideal for probation, but the clerk dissuaded us,
saying it wasn't appropriate because probation is now more an
alternative to custody. I said that's just political, to empty the
prisons, and he needed help... [The conditional discharge] will
hang over him at least, so if he reoffends he'll be brought
back, but even then we'll probably be told not to put him on
probation.

Probation officers defined suitability for probation in more abstract
terms. The offender's position on the tariff and pattern of offending
determined his suitability for probation. The only personal attribute of
the offender with which probation officers were concerned was his
motivation.

Motivation. That's a key determinant of when you go for a probation order. To talk about alcohol-related offenders as a whole group is not helpful, but with anyone with some alcohol dependency you've got to have a spark of motivation to do something about it... Having said that, sometimes a spark is enough, because as probation officers we'll be able to work on people's motivation and keep alongside them and seize the moment.

This concern has been noted in other research into professional decision making (Paley and Leeves 1982; Shamblin 1990). Motivation, however, was a double-edged virtue. One probation officer remarked, without a trace of irony:

> If I think that the drinking problem service can do the job better, then I'm looking to a conditional discharge with a suggestion that they go to that agency and I'll be telling the magistrates: 'If the will is there to work at it, then he'll work at it with a probation order or not. If the will isn't there, then a probation order's a waste of time.'

Even high-tariff defendants could disqualify themselves from probation by their eagerness to resolve their drinking problem.

Example 8.2   The defendant, aged 21, admitted taking a vehicle without consent and drunken driving. He had five previous convictions, including one for excess alcohol. On this occasion he had drunkenly taken his employer's van, averredly in the fuddled belief that he was required to drive it back to [City], but was delayed at more pubs *en route*. He was arrested after a near accident and a police chase.
The SER writer concluded:

> [The defendant], thankfully, does now appear to be making efforts to tackle the serious drink problem that he has had for many years and which underlies the present offences and all his previous convictions. He has sought help of his own initiative and I gained the impression he was sincere in his desire to stop drinking... Since he is already attending the drinking problem service and is therefore getting the help he needs, there would seem little point in a Probation Order as well. The drinking problem service's policy is that people should attend of their own choice, and therefore attendance there should not be a condition of any order of the court.

Thus, probation officers' theories were not invulnerable to contradiction. Their theories of probation supervision itself, their defining

activity, involved considerable tensions. This was illustrated in their
views on groupwork programmes as additional requirements of probation.

Most magistrates approved of a special programme for drunken
drivers.

> It seemed a good idea. But what was slightly puzzling was that they
> would only recommend it for the really bad cases. That I never
> quite understood...I would have thought that the first offenders
> could have done with it just as much if not more. Because the
> second offender may be past curing.

Among probation officers, however, the programme for drunken
drivers was a highly controversial topic, exacerbated at times by
officers' personal abhorrence of the offence.

> Aiming it at third-time [offenders] struck me as rather ridicu-
> lous...Should we really be giving them an opportunity to do it a
> fourth time? Once I can understand, possibly. Twice is a dreadful
> mistake. Three times is almost unforgivable...But it's something
> that should have been out of the probation service's orbit alto-
> gether. Alcohol education for drivers should be a lot more basic.
> It should be incorporated into the driving test...It was also seen by
> a lot of the courts as a let off, because it was an alternative to a fine.
> If I was given a choice of eight sessions or a £500 fine, that's a
> bargain.

> There was no tariff issue at all. It was set up to deal with the fact
> that quite a lot of people were coming through with that offence. In
> a different organisation that would have been called a crime pre-
> vention project...It just wasn't valid under the probation that's
> trying to get hardened offenders.

> We have had the luxury of getting people on probation who are
> more likely to succeed, which is very nice and rewarding. But
> perhaps we should be applying the same techniques to our main-
> stream probationers...It's a group previously untapped by proba-
> tion and I'm not sure we should be in there.

It was not only the particular offence of drunken driving which
aroused strong feelings in probation officers. Working with alcohol-
related offenders could be unpleasant, depressing and de-skilling.
Frustration, failure and hopelessness were repeated themes in officers' experience, exacerbated by other unprofessional feelings.

Whenever they attend the drinking problem service it always seems to go wrong. They always bugger it up ... That's a depressing feeling.

The hopelessness of it all ... It can be quite scary having drunken clients ... I've had clients who I have been scared of when they've come into the office, when they've been drinking.

If somebody's coming in pissed every week, then it's quite obvious that you've failed. It's brought home to you more closely. Yes, it's frustrating, because you think: 'Oh, for God's sake, just put the bottle away, won't you? It's so *easy*.' Which of course, it isn't.

I can't work with chronic alcoholics. I find that very difficult. I never like them on office duty, can't bear having to talk to them in court ... I can't cope with the filth and the aggression. It's not that I'm frightened of the aggression. It makes *me* aggressive.

These personal reactions could spill on to the pages of an SER.

Example 8.3 The defendant, aged 21, was charged with criminal damage, ABH and five offences of shoplifting. He was in breach of his probation order for the second time, and on each occasion numerous offences were involved. The probation officer wrote:

All the offences he faces today are typical of the pattern he has established over the past 18 months; all committed when drunk and he has very little recollection of any of them ... [The defendant] tells me now that throughout all this period he did not realise he was still on Probation. Certainly, his Probation Order probably seemed like an irrelevant detail at the time ... [H]e has proved exasperating in that he has offended constantly and I am at a loss to suggest what might stop him. He has reported occasionally to our Office, however, most of his failures are understandable given the sheer amount of offending, arrests and remands ... A Community Service Order proved to be a complete waste of time.

The officer's frustration was further vented on the defendant's partner.

[His girlfriend] is known to the Probation Service because of the many boyfriends ... who have unfortunately gone on to serve lengthy custodial sentences ... Now [he] tells me that he has found some stability and motivation to change through his relationship... but this is a relationship which has proved disastrous for him in the past and disastrous for several other young men.

Probation officers who derived satisfaction from working with alcohol-related offenders usually identified its sources in the methods of work available, contact with specialist agencies and intellectual stimulation. These rewards enhanced officers' sense of their professional identity.

I enjoy helping to formulate policy. There's some vanity there. I think I've got ideas that I want to put forward... It's about moving, changing and developing.

I enjoy working with other agencies. It gives me another viewpoint, I pick up more knowledge, and it gives me a feel of working in a network, rather than stuck in my own office.

There's quite a lot of literature about. When you're rummaging about for things to learn about, there is rather more about alcohol and offending than there is about what you do with people who take without consent, say... The way our society uses a most powerful and prevalent drug is of some interest.

It provides an opportunity for doing a good piece of focused work... It's a well-researched methodology for casework tools, so it means that you can implement a programme quite neatly.

CONCLUSION

This chapter reveals some issues of particular relevance to an understanding of City magistrates' sentencing practice. Firstly, the balanced perspectives of magistrates on their local crime problems may have been an important factor in their sentencing practice. The punitive results of magisterial 'crusades' against perceived epidemics of particular types of crime have been observed elsewhere (Burney 1985; Parker, Sumner and Jarvis 1989). Furthermore, since magistrates were not collectively preoccupied with particular crimes, they may have been more open to invitations to focus on offenders themselves. This, it has already been argued, is a key to successful mitigation.

The reasons for the apparent difference of opinion between magistrates and probation officers as to the dangerousness of City's streets are not clear. It should be stressed that there is no suggestion here that either the probation officers or the magistrates were 'right'. This study did not examine 'the truth' about City's crime and cannot adjudicate on the issue. There may be some validity in officers' notions of the distortions of their professional experience. Violent offenders might command a higher priority in their attention, given their greater chances of custodial sentences, and higher risk under supervision. This, however, does not explain the comparisons offered by probation officers with experience elsewhere. Yet it would appear odd for magistrates to be entirely insensitive to an unusually high level of violence in their locality, if it existed, even without great knowledge of other areas.

However, the discrepancy suggests a potential pitfall in the commonsense assumption by one group that its perceptions, being 'the truth', would be shared by another. It might not be in the overall professional interests of probation officers to air their views too loudly, thus making magistrates uncomfortably aware of a serious crime problem about which they had been apparently ignorant, and, by implication, dilatory. The professional goals of probation officers to promote non-custodial sentencing by individualising the circumstances of offenders would hardly be served by the potential, albeit unwitting, incitement to magistrates to 'stamp on' violent crime. In this context, it is interesting to note that as this part of the research data was analysed, the probation service announced, amid some local publicity, its own research into City's serious problem of violent crime. Again, it should be stressed that these comments do not depend on the objective 'truth' of City's crime problems. They arise from the *beliefs* about those problems held by magistrates and probation officers.

Secondly, the dispositional perspectives of magistrates in explaining their own success in avoiding trouble through drink could imply punitiveness, derived from the condemnation of indiscipline and the evasion of personal responsibility. However, it seemed that City magistrates generally thought that the deviant drinking of others was due to personal misfortune rather than wilful fecklessness. Commonsense versions of the academic 'undersocialisation' theory were sympathetically invoked, as were notions of personal misery.

If I were in the state that some of the people are who are here, I would drink alcohol too. Sort of oblivion seeking. Solace. Luckily I'm not in the position that I want to do it.

Most of the people who are arrested for drink-related offences tend to be...inadequate people who have other problems. So they're drinking to fill a need in the way they might be taking drugs to fill a need.

One magistrate eloquently described the tension between the condemnation inspired by a strong personal morality and the recognition of personal advantage.

People who drink out of bravado at my age, I despise them really ...If they haven't learned to master it by now then they go down in my estimation. Sounds terribly prim, doesn't it?...It sounds cataclysmically goody-goody to say you despise them. Because when you think about human beings, people have got a good reason for drinking...usually. You know what they say: 'To understand all is to forgive all'...They've taken refuge in drink, quite a lot of the ones we see. And they've had no training. It's all to do with background, isn't it? Most people I see in court...haven't had a chance! Because they've had no decent family upbringing. And if the family hasn't stood by you and given you a proper basis for your life, it's not surprising that you meet up with peer groups and start drinking.

This sympathetic distinction between themselves and others may be a key to understanding the generally humanitarian approach to defendants which has been noted throughout the observational material gathered in the courtroom.

Thirdly, the strict application of their basic principle concerning responsibility was clearly problematic for magistrates, because of their belief in intoxicated and alcoholic loss of control. In resolving this dilemma, magistrates appeared pre-occupied with the assessment of offenders' motivations for drinking prior to offending. This explains their interest in, and the power of SERs, which provided a characterisation from which to infer such motivations.

In particular, magistrates' belief in the debility of the alcoholic offender contributed heavily to the paralysis in sentencing decision making which has been noted. Here, the sociological and situational perspectives, and absence of appeals to sickness in probation officers' theories enabled them to take a more robust approach to addicted defendants. This, however, exacerbated the sentencing impasse, since magistrates frequently looked to the probation service for a resolution to the problem.

The firm stance on intoxicated responsibility adopted by probation officers was not only facilitated by their theories of deviance, but was an important aspect of their professional identity. Nevertheless, this claim to dispassionate professionalism could be disrupted by the intrusion of personal feelings. One officer candidly acknowledged the tension between professional responsibility and personal antagonism towards drunk drivers.

Drinking and driving is such a horrendous offence. I have great difficulty recommending drink-driving courses to the court...I have a gut feeling that they really ought to get locked up. It all goes back to the deserving offender doesn't it? It's there, in the back of our minds, however much we try not to say it. Who deserves our help and who doesn't? Somehow, the white-collar Sierra salesman bowling down the [road] after his business lunch doesn't evoke a lot of sympathy in me. I think: 'Why should I put my time aside for him? He doesn't deserve it! Lock the bugger up!' I recognise those feelings in me, and it ain't right, really, but that's my gut feeling that comes out occasionally. So I've got to combat that when I'm thinking about drinking and driving.

Working with alcohol-related offenders could enhance officers' sense of professional identity, through the acquisition of knowledge, skill and involvement in interdisciplinary expertise. However, it could also attack this identity. The intrusion of personal feeling into their responses did not stem only from abhorrence of some of their offences, but from the experience of professional failure. For example, the imprisoned alcoholic of Example 5.1 inspired tolerant amusement on the part of the police officer escorting him to the cells. When I commented on this to his exasperated probation officer, I was told:

Yes, they might say he's fine when he's sober, but they're only containing him. He knows the system, how to get what he wants and not to get out of line. They're not challenging his lifestyle. He thinks because he's on social security he's entitled to take what he wants from shops. And I don't really hold that view.

The 'tragic' defendant of Example 6.11 was also eventually imprisoned. His probation officer told me that after his release he went to the probation office several times in a drunken state and was 'quite obnoxious'. His offensiveness eventually resulted in a severance of relations.

I swore at him in the end. I told him to fucking well get out and not come back if he was going to talk to me like that...He's a very unhappy man, with many problems. Like so many people who rely on alcohol, he tends to dump his unhappiness on you. Over a period of time, he certainly left me feeling de-skilled and demoralised and feeling I was spending so much time and effort and nothing was changing at all.

An irony of these probation officers' experiences is that it was cases such as these that gave rise in the courtroom to some of the most moving tributes to their endeavours. In Example 7.3, as was seen, this came from the defendant himself. In Example 6.4, the defence solicitor for the psychotic book thief remarked:

Until recently he had the support of a probation officer, who he used to go to regularly, whenever he had a problem. Now [that officer] has left, and although he does have the opportunity to go to other probation officers, he feels very keenly the loss of this particular one, who was very patient with him.

A further irony for probation officers was the discrepancy between the confidence with which they argued their professional ethos against the alleged misconceptions of magistrates and the extent of their internal ambivalence. The professional identity which they publicly promoted was less easy to pursue rigorously in practice. One probation officer in interview remarked:

It's quite difficult to see sometimes where change is ever going to come from, if somebody just goes round and around and around. Very often it's round and around, down and down. So it's just being with them and holding that, trying not to make the situation worse, rather than anything else.

Talking informally to probation officers about offenders I had witnessed in court, it seemed that the plans for reducing offending, which they formulated for their SERs, lost their thrust in the messy, real worlds of their clients' lives. Indeed, I was sometimes left wondering just how far the shift in public professional identity claimed by probation officers had left their involvements with offenders' welfare privately intact. Whilst I was interviewing one senior probation officer, who was propounding the tariff and offence focus of professional philosophy with impressive vigour, the telephone rang. The request (granted) of an officer for permission to send a probation assistant daily to the home of an imprisoned offender to feed his cat was the cause of much embarrassed mirth: 'Well, that's blown my cover!' Indeed it had, and to that extent, at least, *plus ça change, plus c'est la même chose*.

The insistence by probation officers on a professional distinction between mitigation and explanation is notable. As a technical distinction, this may be tenable. Probation officers were bringing their comparatively varied and flexible range of theories of crime to bear on the explanation of individual offenders' predicaments. They did not assume that these explanations in themselves achieved particular sentencing outcomes, but rather that they expanded the range of constructive sentencing options. Nevertheless, in Chapter 4 it was argued that explanation, by attracting attention to the individuality of a case, is a crucial part of the social psychological process of mitigation. Thus, in their contributions to that social psychological process, probation officers could be masters of mitigation. Their influence on that process could also, however, be disrupted by the intrusion of personal feeling.

9 Intoxication: Our Favourite Excuse

In a special issue of *International Journal of Law and Psychiatry*, devoted to the intoxication excuse, Fingarette (1990a) declares that scientific research has established unequivocally that intoxication cannot excuse criminal behaviour. Fingarette regards continuing legal confusion, and defendants' persistent invocation of the intoxication excuse, as a product of the time lag between the scientific establishment of the 'facts' and their absorption by the general public.

> [S]cience has now rendered invalid all the familiar lines of excusatory arguments based on alcoholism. Scientific specialists in the field are of course aware of this. Unfortunately, however, most people, including most law professionals, are still unaware of it. (1990a, p. 77)

Certainly, the belief that alcohol causes disinhibition of behaviour from conventional moral standards has been challenged for nearly thirty years by the findings of academic research, since the publication of Macandrew and Edgerton's (1969) seminal review of ethnographic literature. Yet, only the year before Fingarette's declaration, Kessel and Walton confidently asserted that

> groups of people have had their passions so inflamed by alcohol that they carried out cruel, senseless, irrevocable actions from which, if the highest mental processes were functioning intact, each individual would recoil with disgust. (1989, p. 11)

Perhaps, then, it is no surprise that academic alcohol theorists themselves have been held responsible for the failure of lawyers to catch up with contemporary alcohol theory. For example, in Mitchell's (1988) view, experts offer distorted representations of research findings in order to fulfil aims beyond the pursuit of objective truth.

> Medical witnesses deny intent not from ignorance or misperception of legal definitions but in order to achieve certain results. Those results include diverting offenders to treatment, increasing psychiatric funding, publicizing therapeutic ideals, and opposing retributive practices. The duplicity here is evidenced when rehabilitationists

use the ordinary, criminal law standards of responsibility to hold their own clients accountable for behavior. Intent is only denied in a retributive context. (Mitchell 1988, p. 100)

Reviewing legal cases involving the intoxication excuse, Mitchell 'could find no genuine case where intoxication caused an automatic or involuntary act', but several in which 'odd, intoxicated behaviour was incorrectly alleged to be irrational, motiveless, and thus involuntary' (1988, p. 94). That lawyers choose not to perceive this obvious fact about their own cases must, Mitchell argues, be due to more than simple deference to the authority of another academic discipline. Mitchell offers three reasons for judicial tolerance of the intoxication excuse. A successful intoxication defence to a charge of murder, by reducing it to manslaughter, opens up the range of discretionary determinate sentences from the otherwise mandatory life sentence. Judges are attracted to this opportunity to maintain their sentencing discretion. Additionally, some judges adhere to a therapeutic ideology of legal practice. Furthermore, production of misleading testimony by defence lawyers is encouraged by the incentive to win their case.

Thus, both lawyers and academic alcohol theorists are susceptible to distortion of 'the facts' in the pursuit of their separate professional objectives. When lawyers and alcohol theorists meet in the adjudication of criminal responsibility, these objectives are pursued through a dialogue which resorts, not to the academic wisdoms of either discipline, but to appeals to the ruinous effects of alcohol on mind, mood and behaviour, despite potent arguments from both camps that intoxication is not a valid excuse for criminal conduct. It has been shown in the theoretical examination of this study that the tortuous reasoning invoked by lawyers to circumvent the intoxication defence is unnecessary in terms of the 'truth' about alcohol's effects. But it has also become very clear why this apparently superfluous debate has persisted in the face of established 'truth'. It is the power of lay theorising, or commonsense wisdom, to defy the weight of objective 'truth' and prompt interpretation of events and behaviour in terms of 'what everybody knows'.

'Common knowledge' about alcohol is deeply embedded in our ways of constructing and understanding social life, behaviour and moral character. Moral judgements, indeed, *infuse* the interpretation of situations, events and behaviour when alcohol is present. We rely upon these moral inferences to comprehend the meaning of occurrences and to adapt our responses accordingly. They are, then, impossible to ignore or discard while the judgement of legal responsibility is reached, to be reserved, neatly compartmentalised, for the subsequent consideration of punishment.

But what of that consideration of punishment? Medical conceptualisations of alcoholism have been significantly instrumental in humanising a traditionally punitive approach to drinking problems (Ajzenstadt and Burtch 1990; Heather and Robertson 1985). Nevertheless, they have been the target of sustained criticism from academics themselves that they serve the interests of those who promulgate them by misleading the public. Fingarette alleges:

> The public currently has good reason to believe (though mistakenly) that alcoholics drink uncontrollably. Physicians and health professionals of all kinds, public service groups, treatment centers, government officials – in short many kinds of seeming authorities – have for years been barraging the public with pronouncements to the effect that alcoholism is a disease, and that alcoholics are helpless victims of a compulsion to drink. (1990a, p. 82)

The promulgation of such theories is alleged to mislead even alcoholics themselves, diminishing their capacity for improvement. For example, Roman and Trice, whilst actually accepting disease theory, nevertheless question its 'double-bind' effect of consigning the alcoholic to a passive sick role which absolves him of responsibility for his condition, but simultaneously requires him actively to seek treatment and to stop drinking.

> The expectations surrounding these sick roles serve to further develop, legitimise, and in some cases even perpetuate the abnormal use of alcohol. (Roman and Trice 1968, p. 245)

Objections to medical conceptualisations of alcoholism continue (Faulkner, Sandage and Maguire 1988; Fingarette and Hasse 1979; Heather and Robertson 1985; Nusbaumer 1983). More generally, critics complain that theories of deviant behaviour which imply reduced responsibility on the part of the deviant, provide the public with ready-made excuses for their transgressions. Thus, Peele claims that 'trying to assess the combination of motives that drives people to commit crimes serves primarily to invite the more resourceful criminals to present the most saleable excuses for their misbehavior' (1990, p. 96). Similarly, Mitchell suggests that legal doctrine on intoxicated crime feeds the public with 'a false picture of the intoxicated offender as wild, dangerous, unconscious, or out of control'

(1988, p. 87), promoting belief in the excusability of intoxicated misconduct.

Discontent with the results of applying academic theory to the intoxication excuse has led several academics themselves to appeal for a return to common sense. For example, Fingarette and Hasse eloquently defend such an approach to the judgement of criminal responsibility.

> There is, unfortunately, no single, simple sign or label that identifies the condition at issue here. Only a review of the defendant's history, conduct, physical health, and general demeanour can provide an adequate picture. This is not a picture that can be read off with scientific precision, or even with science at all, though scientific data may be of help. It is a picture that can only be assembled and assessed from the perspective of practical lay judgement, the judgement of ordinary people who know how to get along in life taking practical account, as they go, of the bearing of law on their conduct. The test they apply to the defendant is a test they themselves pass every day of their lives: Is the defendant, as portrayed up to the moment of the offending act, and in the circumstances of that act, on the whole able to take into account in a practical way, in acting as he does, the criminal significance of his act? (1979, p. 193)

But the secret of the intoxication excuse's success lies in its own intrinsic attractions. Its apparent contrivance is frequently mocked by academics such as those mentioned above. Yet that contrivance flows from the appeal of the intoxication excuse to the very same commonsense, lay theories about alcohol's effects upon which we are now urged to rely. Moreover, as was seen in this study, contrivance is recognised through the systematic de-construction of the varieties of intoxication excuse proffered in the courtroom. It is not so readily apparent to the participant in the courtroom process, responding on a case-by-case basis to explanations of crime which 'make sense' within their particular, situationally specific applications.

Faith in the capacity of common sense to expose 'the truth' about intoxicated responsibility would appear to be seriously misplaced. This has been seen repeatedly in this study, during the theoretical and empirical explorations of the invocation of alcohol as a cause of morally disreputable behaviour. Disappointment in the failure of academic theory to resolve the courtroom dilemma, however, makes returning to common sense an attractive prospect for some. Peele complains:

In the area of addiction, what is purveyed as fact is usually wrong
and simply repackages popular myths as if they were the latest
scientific deductions. To be ignorant of the received opinion about
addiction is to have the best chance to say something sensible and
to have an impact on the problem. (1990, p. 101)

Closely examined, this outraged assertion makes little logical sense,
despite its intuitive appeal to distrust of academic theorising and faith
in common sense. If academic theories are truly versions of 'popular
myths', or lay beliefs, and are also usually wrong, then by implication
common sense is also usually wrong. How, then, can reliance on
simple common sense itself be expected to produce any statement
more sensible than the false wisdom of academic theory?

Offenders continue to offer the intoxication excuse in mitigation,
neither because they are seduced by academic alcohol theory, nor
because they are the last to hear of its inaccuracy, but because it
works. They appeal to common sense, not because they recognise its
superiority to academic theorising, but simply because it works.
Indeed, an offender might genuinely seize upon his intoxication as
the explanation for his misdemeanour because of its intuitive access-
ibility. Some influences on our behaviour are simply not intuitively
obvious to us as plausible causes of our actions. The presence of an
audience has been noted as an example of this. Moreover, knowledge
of 'true' influences on our behaviour does not necessarily provide us
with more persuasive mitigation for our misdeeds. 'I hit him because I
was drunk', however suggestive of moral evasion, will always sound
better than 'I hit him because no-one stopped me', or 'I hit him
because people were looking'.

From successful personal neutralisations and rationalisations for
their offending, it is a short step to public mitigation. Furthermore,
those personal neutralisations and rationalisations are not uniquely
constructed by offenders, but are available to all who seek to excuse
themselves for some departure from sober social convention. They are
rooted in the stockpile of everyday knowledge about alcohol's effects
on mind, mood and behaviour. We all share in that 'common knowledge', and the vast majority of us are practised in the art of invoking
the types of neutralisations and rationalisations which it offers. We
also have considerable experience of being offered adaptations of
those neutralisations and rationalisations in explanation of the moral
shortcomings of others. Even when we have no personal experience of
certain effects described in common knowledge, we remain confident

that they are the 'real' results of intoxication for others. The intoxication excuse, therefore, is immediately accessible, widely available, readily intelligible, and, indeed, personally meaningful as an explanation for moral infractions. The difference for offenders lies only in their more extensive practice in invoking these neutralisations and rationalisations for particular types of law-breaking activity.

Intoxication provides a platform for constructing moral judgements which might well be unrivalled for its scope, variety and power. Certainly, there was no hint of an equal in the empirical study described here. Public reference to an offender's intoxication cuts short the effort of interpreting the information about his case, is not constrained by any delicacy of the subject, evokes vivid imagery of his conduct, provides the measure of his character, offers the opportunity to demonstrate remorse and reform, and justifies both punishment and rehabilitation. There is something for everyone here. All participants in the courtroom decision-making process can benefit from the mention of intoxication. Even sober offenders can exploit it. The continuing popularity of the intoxication excuse can hardly be in doubt.

The question with which this study began was: 'How might we account for the perennial and pervasive popularity of an appeal to intoxication for our moral failings?' In answering that question, both from a theoretical and an empirical standpoint, we seem at last to have arrived at the new question: 'How would we manage without the intoxication excuse?'

To suggest that the intoxication excuse, despite its factual invalidity, will not be easily relinquished in the courtroom, because it offers important strategies for the accomplishment of the tasks with which court personnel are presented, seems, at first blush, to denigrate the pursuit of truth and justice with which they are charged. Yet the injustices which occurred at City magistrates' court did not appear to arise from inaccurate appeals to intoxication and alcoholism in themselves, but more often to situationally inspired distractions to the sentencing decision-making process (Rumgay 1995). In respect of alcohol-related offenders, this has been most vividly seen in the periodic displacement of probation officers' experiences of professional defeat onto the pages of their reports.

Contrary to popular belief, and, indeed, some of the caustic critiques of 'medical imperialism' (Heather and Robertson 1985) noted above, probation officers were more confident of individual responsibility, even under conditions of intoxication or alcoholism, than were magistrates. Probation officers' familiarity with broader, sociological explanations of alcohol-related crime did not, as is commonly supposed, dilute their belief in individual responsibility. Rather, it strengthened that belief, by reducing reliance upon narrow, deterministic conceptualisations of disinhibition, alcoholism, and particularly 'sickness'. In bringing these perspectives to bear on their assessments of offenders, probation officers proved to be masters of mitigation in practice, while in principle they sought only to explain.

Probation officers' perspectives on the topic of personal responsibility were also reinforced by an important sense of professional purpose and identity. Far from reassuring alcohol-related offenders that they could not help themselves, probation officers saw their professional task in terms of encouraging personal responsibility and the acknowledgement of culpability. However, the damage which alcohol-involved offenders were capable of inflicting upon this sense of professional identity and purpose could provoke a reaction in which personal responsibility was seen and powerfully portrayed as moral blameworthiness.

As a social psychological process of sympathetic identification with an individual offender, mitigation of punishment may be prompted by a variety of sources of information, including the mitigation address, the probation officer's report and the demeanour of the defendant himself. Mitigation of punishment is also, however, enhanced by the production of such information in conditions which are conducive to its reception. The pursuit of mitigation in City court was assisted by magistrates' collective antipathy to custody. That this did not guarantee defendants' liberty was partly because magistrates perceived that personal feeling was an inappropriate basis for the exercise of public office. The parsimonious use of the custodial sanctions in City court, as the final expression of the judgement of culpability, deserves some further consideration.

Studies of magistrates' sentencing decisions have often sought to explain why courts utilise custody (e.g. Burney 1985; Parker, Sumner and Jarvis 1989). However, as Parker, Sumner and Jarvis (1989) observe, magistrates impose custody because, hitherto, official restraints upon them have been comparatively few. Indeed, as was found in this study, magistrates see the recourse to custody as part of their public office, however personally unpleasant its imposition may be. It might be pertinent, therefore, to ask why some courts *do not* use custody as much as others.

Once the focus is shifted in this way, some of the conclusions of sentencing research seem to lose their apparent force. For example, Parker, Sumner and Jarvis (1989) suggest that a court's sentencing tradition is reinforced by the precedent of previous disposals: the visibility of a previous custodial sanction on a defendant's record, by demonstrating its failure to reform him thus far, encourages further incarceration. Such an analysis appears to offer a plausible explanation of the perpetuation of custodial sentencing. But it cannot tell us why some courts resist this 'push' towards increasing use of imprisonment. It is rather less intuitively reasonable to argue that the visibility of previous non-custodial disposals promotes their continued use, since presumably by his reconviction the defendant who has not experienced custody is also demonstrating his failure to learn his lesson.

In seeking to explain the excessive use of custody, Parker, Sumner and Jarvis overlook some potentially useful insights into its parsimonious use. In particular, they fail to examine the unusually low rate of custody shown by one of the courts in their study, concluding merely: 'The repetition of punitive decisions cannot, in the end, be disguised by the exceptions, even contradictions' (1989, p. 173). Yet, combing Parker, Sumner and Jarvis' study for possible influences on the sentencing practice of the court with a low custody rate, certain features were found which complemented the findings of this study. The courthouse was blessed with good facilities. Clerks were courteous and helpful to defendants and were influential in advising magistrates. Probation officers never recommended custody, rarely implied it, and offered persuasive alternative recommendations; their reports were strategic and coherent arguments; they engaged in a comparatively high level of dialogue with magistrates in the courtroom. Magistrates were not particularly alarmed about their local crime problems; they did not hold a simple ideology of sentencing; they took a paternalistic and consensual approach to sentencing; they were receptive to the notion of alternatives to custody.

These are observations about the decision-making environment and process. Conditions such as these promote receptiveness to the kinds of arguments which lead to mitigation of punishment, through facilitating increased attention to the plights of individual defendants. Mitigation is thus achieved by 'provoking mindfulness' (Palmerino, Langer and McGillis 1984) to case-specific detail. Yet it is also clear that the sentencing decision results from a 'trade off' between such individualised reasoning and the necessary intellectual short cuts demanded by the decision-making task in the courtroom. These cognitive economies are vital to the successful accomplishment of the court's business under pressure of time.

The intoxication excuse is extraordinarily versatile in providing strategies for resolving the tension between the attraction of case-specific reasoning and the over-riding need for simplification. It offers event schemata and personal characterisations, based on case-specific information, which appeal directly to judgements of individual culpability and suggest responses which are appropriate to those interpretations. In serving this function, at least in the decision-making environment of City magistrates' court, there was no intrinsic distortion of the pursuit of justice in invocation of the intoxication excuse, nor were the 'truths' about offenders which it revealed necessarily inappropriate to the occasion, even if the underlying assumptions about alcohol's effects were clinically inaccurate.

Susceptibility to mitigation has a price, however. This discussion of sentencing in City court should not end without acknowledging the irony of the experience of these magistrates, whose humanitarian concern for offenders was persistently thwarted by the sheer inaccessibility of treatment or help. The paralysis of the sentencing decision-making process in cases of alcoholic or mentally disordered offenders has been repeatedly observed. The failure of City magistrates' persistent efforts to secure professional help for disturbed defendants is a sad testimony to the criminal justice system's ineffectiveness as an instrument for the delivery of treatment.

Nevertheless, it does not automatically follow that defendants would have fared better under a strict 'just deserts' (Von Hirsch 1976) approach. City magistrates' paralysis in the face of profound individual distress or disturbance was an aspect of their susceptibility to mitigation. The accumulation of research into decision-making processes in general and sentencing in particular which has been reviewed and complemented by this study indicates that tolerance of deviance is enhanced by the recognition and tolerance of complexity. To seek to attenuate their sometimes laboured styles of reasoning might have made life easier for City magistrates, but there is rather little evidence that a pure just deserts approach reduces the harshness of defendants' experience of punishment (Hudson 1987). Within what proved so often to be an intractable system, the display of magisterial humanity was frequently a virtue in itself.

Bibliography

ABELSON, R. P. (1976) 'Script Processing in Attitude Formation and Decision Making', pp. 33–45, in J. S. Carroll and J. W. Payne (eds), *Cognition and Social Behavior*. Hillsdale, New Jersey: Lawrence Erlbaum Associates.

ABRAM, K. M. (1990) 'The Problem of Co-occurring Disorders among Jail Detainees: Antisocial Disorder, Alcoholism, Drug Abuse and Depression'. *Law and Human Behavior*, Vol. 14, No. 4, pp. 333–45.

ADESSO, V. J. (1985) 'Cognitive Factors in Alcohol and Drug Use', pp. 179–208, in M. Galizio and S. A. Maisto (eds), *Determinants of Substance Abuse: Biological, Psychological and Environmental Factors*. New York: Plenum Press.

AGNEW, R. and PETERS, A. A. (1986) 'The Techniques of Neutralization: An Analysis of Predisposing and Situational Factors'. *Criminal Justice and Behavior*, Vol. 13, No. 1, pp. 81–97.

AJZENSTADT, M. and BURTCH, B. E. (1990) 'Medicalization and Regulation of Alcohol and Alcoholism: The Professions and Disciplinary Measures'. *International Journal of Law and Psychiatry*, Vol. 13, Nos 1–2, pp. 127–47.

ALLEN, H. (1987) *Justice Unbalanced: Gender, Psychiatry and Judicial Decisions*. Milton Keynes: Open University Press.

ANDERSON, R. (1978) *Representation in the Juvenile Court*. London: Routledge and Kegan Paul.

ANTZE, P. (1987) 'Symbolic Action in Alcoholics Anonymous', pp. 149–81, in M. Douglas (ed.), *Constructive Drinking: Perspectives on Drink from Anthropology*. Cambridge: Cambridge University Press.

ARCHARD, P. (1979) *Vagrancy, Alcoholism and Social Control*. London: Macmillan.

ARMOR, D. J. (1980) 'The Rand Reports and the Analysis of Relapse', pp. 81–94, in G. Edwards and M. Grant (eds), *Alcoholism Treatment in Transition*. London: Croom Helm.

ASHWORTH, A. (1987) 'Disentangling Disparity', pp. 24–35, in D. C. Pennington and S. Lloyd-Bostock (eds), *Issues and Problems in the Psychology of Sentencing*. Oxford: Centre for Socio-legal Studies.

ATHENS, L. H. (1980) *Violent Criminal Acts and Actors: A Symbolic Interactionist Study*. London: Routledge and Kegan Paul.

ATHENS, L. H. (1989) *The Creation of Dangerous Violent Criminals*. London: Routledge.

AUSTIN, W., WALSTER, E. and UTNE, M. K. (1976) 'Equity and the Law: The Effect of a Harmdoer's "Suffering in the Act" on Liking and Assigned Punishment'. *Advances in Experimental Social Psychology*, Vol. 9, pp. 163–90.

BAHR, H. M. and CAPLOW, T. (1974) *Old Men Drunk and Sober*. New York: New York University Press.

BALDWIN, J. and McCONVILLE, M. (1977) *Negotiated Justice: Pressures to Plead Guilty*. London: Martin Robertson.

BALL-ROKEACH, S. J. (1973) 'Values and Violence: A Test of The Sub-
culture of Violence Thesis'. *American Sociological Review*, Vol. 38, pp. 736–
49.
BANKSTON, W. B. (1988) 'Determinants of Lethal and Non-lethal Violence:
Some Theoretical Considerations'. *Deviant Behavior*, Vol. 9, No. 1, pp. 77–
86.
BARDO, M. T. and RISNER, M. E. (1985) 'Biochemical Substrates of Drug
Abuse', pp. 65–99, in M. Galizio and S. A. Maisto (eds), *Determinants of
Substance Abuse: Biological, Psychological, and Environmental Factors*. New
York: Plenum Press.
BARRETT, R. J. (1985) 'Behavioral Approaches to Individual Differences in
Substance Abuse: Drug-taking Behavior', pp. 125–75, in M. Galizio and S.
A. Maisto (eds), *Determinants of Substance Abuse: Biological, Psychological,
and Environmental Factors*. New York: Plenum Press.
BAR-TAL, D., GRAUMANN, C. F., KRUGLANKSI, A. W. and STROEBE,
W. (eds) (1989) *Stereotyping and Prejudice: Changing Conceptions*. New
York: Springer-Verlag.
BECK, A. T., WISSMAN, A. and KOVACS, M. (1976) 'Alcoholism, Hope-
lessness and Suicidal Behaviour'. *Journal of the Study of Alcohol*, Vol. 37,
pp. 66–77.
BENNETT, T. and WRIGHT, R. (1984a) *Burglars on Burglary: Prevention and
the Offender*. Aldershot: Gower.
BENNETT, T. and WRIGHT, R. (1984b) 'The Relationship Between
Alcohol Use and Burglary'. *British Journal of Addiction*, Vol. 79, No. 4,
pp. 431–7.
BERGLAS, S. (1987) 'Self-handicapping Model', pp. 305–45, in H. T. Blane
and K. E. Leonard (eds), *Psychological Theories of Drinking and Alcoholism*.
New York: Guilford Press.
BERKOWITZ, L. (1986) 'Some Varieties of Human Agression: Criminal
Violence as Coercion, Rule-following, Impression Management and
Impulsive Behaviour', pp. 87–103, in A. Campbell and J. J. Gibbs (eds),
Violent Transactions: The Limits of Personality. Oxford: Basil Blackwell.
BEST, J. and LUCKENBILL, D. J. (1982) *Organizing Deviance*. Englewood
Cliffs: Prentice-Hall.
BLANE, H. T. (1979) 'Middle-aged Alcoholics and Young Drinkers', pp. 5–
36, in H. T. Blane and M. E. Chafetz (eds), *Youth, Alcohol, and Social
Policy*. New York: Plenum Press.
BLANE, H. T. and CHAFETZ, M. E. (eds) (1979) *Youth, Alcohol, and Social
Policy*. New York: Plenum Press.
BLANE, H. T. and LEONARD, K. E. (eds) (1987) *Psychological Theories of
Drinking and Alcoholism*. New York: Guilford Press.
BLUM, R. H. (1982) 'Violence, Alcohol, and Setting: An Unexplored Nexus',
pp. 110–42, in J. J. Collins (ed.), *Drinking and Crime: Perspectives on the
Relationships Between Alcohol Consumption and Criminal Behaviour*. Lon-
don: Tavistock.
BOND, R. A. and LEMON, N. F. (1979) 'Changes in Magistrates' Attitudes
During the First Year on the Bench', pp. 125–42, in D. P. Farrington, K.
Hawkins and S. M. Lloyd-Bostock (eds), *Psychology, Law and Legal Pro-
cesses*. London: Macmillan.

BOND, R. A. and LEMON, N. F. (1981) 'Training, Experience, and Magistrates' Sentencing Philosophies: A Longitudinal Study'. *Law and Human Behavior*, Vol. 5, Nos 2–3, pp. 123–39.

BOTTOMS, A. E. and McCLEAN, J. D. (1976) *Defendants in the Criminal Process*. London: Routledge and Kegan Paul.

BRAIN, P. F. (1986) 'Alcohol and Agression – The Nature of a Presumed Relationship', pp. 212–23, in P. F. Brain (ed.), *Alcohol and Agression*. London: Croom Helm.

BRIAR, S. and PILIAVIN, I. (1965) 'Delinquency, Situational Inducements, and Commitment to Conformity'. *Social Problems*, Vol. 13, No. 1, pp. 35–45.

BRICKMAN, P. (1978) 'Is It Real?', pp. 5–34, in J. H. Harvey, W. Ickes and R. F. Kidd (eds), *New Directions in Attribution Research*. Vol. 2. Hillsdale, New Jersey: Lawrence Erlbaum Associates.

BROWN, S. A., GOLDMAN, M. S., INN, A. and ANDERSON, L. (1980) 'Expectations of Reinforcement from Alcohol: Their Domain and Relation to Drinking Patterns'. *Journal of Consulting and Clinical Psychology*, Vol. 48, pp. 419–26.

BUCKLE, A. and FARRINGTON, D. P. (1984) 'An Observational Study of Shoplifting'. *British Journal of Criminology*, Vol. 24, No. 1, pp. 63–73.

BURNEY, E. (1979) *JP: Magistrate, Court and Community*. London: Hutchinson.

BURNEY, E. (1985) *Sentencing Young People: What Went Wrong With the Criminal Justice Act 1982*. Aldershot, Hants: Gower.

CAMERON, M. O. (1964) *The Booster and The Snitch: Department Store Shoplifting*. London: The Free Press of Glencoe.

CAMPBELL, A. (1986) 'The Streets and Violence', pp. 115–32, in A. Campbell and J. J. Gibbs (eds), *Violent Transactions: The Limits of Personality*. Oxford: Basil Blackwell.

CAMPBELL, A., BIBEL, D. and MUNCER, S. (1985) 'Predicting Our Own Aggression: Person, Subculture or Situation?' *British Journal of Social Psychology*, Vol. 24, pp. 169–80.

CAMPBELL, A. and GIBBS, J. J. (eds) (1986) *Violent Transactions: The Limits of Personality*. Oxford: Basil Blackwell.

CAPPELL, H. and GREELEY, J. (1987) 'Alcohol and Tension Reduction: An Update on Research and Theory', pp. 15–54, in H. T. Blane and K. E. Leonard (eds), *Psychological Theories of Drinking and Alcoholism*. New York: Guilford Press.

CARLEN, P. (1976) *Magistrates' Justice*. London: Martin Robertson.

CARROLL, J. S. (1982) 'Committing a Crime: The Offender's Decision', pp. 46–67, in V. J. Konecni and E. B. Ebbesen (eds), *The Criminal Justice System: A Social-Psychological Analysis*. San Francisco: W. H. Freeman & Co.

CARROLL, J. S. and PAYNE, J. W. (1976) 'The Psychology of the Parole Decision Process: A Joint Application of Attribution Theory and Information-Processing Psychology', pp. 13–32, in J. S. Carroll and J. W. Payne (eds), *Cognition and Social Behavior*. Hillsdale, New Jersey: Lawrence Erlbaum Associates.

CARROLL, J. S. and PAYNE, J. W. (1977) 'Judgements About Crime and the
   Criminal: A Model and a Method for Investigating Parole Decisions', pp.
   191–239, in B. D. Sales (ed.), *Perspectives in Law and Psychology*. New York:
   Plenum Press.
CARROLL, J. S. and WEAVER, F. (1986) 'Shoplifters' Perceptions of Crime
   Opportunities: A Process Tracing Study', pp. 19–38, in D. Cornish and R.
   Clarke (eds), *The Reasoning Criminal: Rational Choice Perspectives on
   Offending*. New York: Springer–Verlag.
CAVAN, S. (1966) *Liquor License: An Ethnography of Bar Behaviour*. Chicago:
   Aldine.
CHRISTIANSEN, B. A. and GOLDMAN, M. S. (1983) 'Alcohol Related
   Expectancies vs. Demographic/Background Variables in the Prediction of
   Adolescent Drinking'. *Journal of Consulting and Clinical Psychology*, Vol.
   51, pp. 249–57.
CLARKE, R. V. G. (1980) ' "Situational" Crime Prevention: Theory and
   Practice'. *British Journal of Criminology*, Vol. 20, No. 2, pp. 136–47.
CLARKE, R. V. G. and CORNISH, D. B. (1985) 'Modeling Offenders'
   Decisions: A Framework for Research and Policy', pp. 147–85, in M.
   Tonry and N. Morris (eds), *Crime and Justice: An Annual Review of
   Research: Vol. 6*. Chicago: University of Chicago Press.
COID, J. (1986a) 'Alcohol, Rape and Sexual Assault', pp. 161–83, in P. J.
   Brain (ed.), *Alcohol and Aggression*. London: Croom Helm.
COID, J. (1986b) 'Social-cultural Factors in Alcohol-related Aggression', pp.
   184–211, in P. J. Brain (ed.), *Alcohol and Aggression*. London: Croom Helm.
COLLINS, J. J. (1982) 'Alcohol Careers and Criminal Careers', pp. 152–206,
   in J. J. Collins (ed.), *Drinking and Crime: Perspectives on the Relationships
   Between Alcohol Consumption and Criminal Behaviour*. London: Tavistock.
COLLINS, J. J. (1986) 'The Relationship of Problem Drinking to Individual
   Offending Sequences', pp. 89–120, in A. Blumstein, J. Cohen, J. A. Roth
   and G. A. Visher (eds), *Criminal Careers and 'Career Criminals'*. Vol. 2.
   Washington D.C.: National Academy Press.
COOK, T. (1975) *Vagrant Alcoholics*. London: Routledge and Kegan Paul.
CORBETT, C. (1987) 'Magistrates' and Court Clerks' Sentencing Behaviour:
   An Experimental Study', pp. 204–16, in D. C. Pennington and S. Lloyd-
   Bostock (eds), *The Psychology of Sentencing: Approaches to Consistency and
   Disparity*. Oxford: Centre for Socio-legal Studies.
CORDILIA, A. T. (1986) 'Robbery Arising out of a Group Drinking-Context',
   pp. 167–80, in A. Campbell and J. J. Gibbs (eds), *Violent Transactions: The
   Limits of Personality*. Oxford: Basil Blackwell.
CORNISH, D. B. (1978) *Gambling: A Review of the Literature and its Implica-
   tions for Policy and Research*. London: HMSO.
CORNISH, D. B. and CLARKE, R. (1986) 'Introduction', pp. 1–16, in D. B.
   Cornish and R. V. Clarke (eds), *The Reasoning Criminal: Rational Choice
   Perspectives on Offending*. New York: Springer–Verlag.
CORNISH, D. B. and CLARKE, R. V. (1987) 'Understanding Crime Dis-
   placement: An Application of Rational Choice Theory'. *Criminology*, Vol.
   25, No. 4, pp. 933–47.
COX, W. M. (1985) 'Personality Correlates of Substance Abuse', pp. 209–46,
   in M. Galizio and S. A. Maisto (eds), *Determinants of Substance Abuse:*

Biological, Psychological, and Environmental Factors. New York: Plenum Press.

COX, W. M. (1987) 'Personality Theory and Research', pp. 55–89, in H. T. Blane and K. E. Leonard (eds), *Psychological Theories of Drinking and Alcoholism.* New York: Guilford Press.

CRIMINAL LAW REVISION COMMITTEE (1980) *Fourteenth Report: Offences Against the Person.* Cmnd 77844. London: HMSO.

CRITCHLOW, B. (1985) 'The Blame in the Bottle: Attributions about Drunken Behavior'. *Personality and Social Psychology Bulletin*, Vol. 11, No. 3, pp. 258–74.

CROCKER, J, FISKE, S. T. and TAYLOR, S. E. (1984) 'Schematic Bases of Belief Change', pp. 197–226, in J. R. Eiser (ed.), *Attitudinal Judgement.* New York: Springer–Verlag.

CURNOCK, K. and HARDIKER, P. (1979) *Towards Practice Theory: Skills and Methods in Social Assessments.* London: Routledge and Kegan Paul.

DALY, K. (1994) *Gender, Crime, and Punishment.* New Haven: Yale University Press.

DARBYSHIRE, P. (1984) *The Magistrates' Clerk.* Chichester: Barry Rose.

DENNEY, R. C. (1986) *Alcohol and Accidents.* Wilmslow, Cheshire: Sigma Press.

DIENSTBIER, R. A. (1978) 'Attribution, Socialization, and Moral Decision-making', pp. 181–206, in J. H. Harvey, W. Ickes and R. F. Kidd (eds), *New Directions in Attribution Research.* Vol. 2. Hillsdale, New Jersey: Lawrence Erlbaum Associates.

DOBASH, R. E. and DOBASH, R. P. (1984) 'The Nature and Antecedents of Violent Events'. *British Journal of Criminology*, Vol. 24, No. 3, pp. 269–88.

DORN, N. (1983) *Alcohol, Youth and the State.* London: Croom Helm.

DOUGLAS, M. (1987) 'A Distinctive Anthropological Perspective', pp. 3–15, in M. Douglas (ed.), *Constructive Drinking: Perspectives on Drink from Anthropology.* Cambridge: Cambridge University Press.

DRASS, K. A. and SPENCER, J. W. (1987) 'Accounting for Pre-sentencing Recommendations: Typologies and Probation Officers' Theory of Office'. *Social Problems*, Vol. 34, No. 3, pp. 277–93.

EATON, M. E. (1984) 'Familial Ideology and Summary Justice: Women Defendants Before a Suburban Magistrates' Court'. Ph.D. Thesis, London: London School of Economics.

EDWARDS, S. S. M. (1984) *Women on Trial: A Study of the Female Suspect, Defendant and Offender in the Criminal Law and Criminal Justice System.* Manchester: Manchester University Press.

EISER, J. R. and VAN DER PLIGT, J. (1988) *Attitudes and Decisions.* London: Routledge.

ELLSWORTH, P. C. (1978) *Attitudes Towards Capital Punishment: From Application to Theory.* Paper Presented at Society of Experimental Social Psychology Symposium on Psychology and Law: Princeton, N.J.

EVANS, C. M. (1986) 'Alcohol and Violence: Problems Relating to Methodology, Statistics and Causation', pp. 138–60, in P. F. Brain (ed.), *Alcohol and Aggression.* London: Croom Helm.

EWART, B. and PENNINGTON, D. C. (1987) 'An Attributional Approach to Explaining Sentencing Disparity', pp. 181–92, in D. C. Pennington and

S. Lloyd-Bostock (eds), *The Psychology of Sentencing: Approaches to Consistency and Disparity*. Oxford: Centre for Socio-legal Studies.

FAGAN, J. A., STEWART, D. K. and HANSEN, K. V. (1983) 'Violent Men or Violent Husbands? Background Factors and Situational Correlates', pp. 49–67, in D. Finkelhor, R. J. Gelles, G. T. Hotaling and M. A. Straus (eds), *The Dark Side of Families: Current Family Violence Research*. Beverley Hills: Sage.

FARRINGTON, D. P. (1987) 'Early Precursors of Frequent Offending', pp. 27–50, in J. Q. Wilson and G. C. Loury (eds), *From Children to Citizens*. Vol. 2: *Families, Schools, and Delinquency Prevention*. New York: Springer–Verlag.

FAULKNER, W., SANDAGE, D. and MAGUIRE, B. (1988) 'The Disease Concept of Alcoholism: The Persistence of an Outmoded Scientific Paradigm'. *Deviant Behaviour*, Vol. 9, No. 4, pp. 317–32.

FEENEY, F. (1986) 'Robbers as Decision-makers', pp. 53–71, in D. B. Cornish and R. V. Clarke (eds), *The Reasoning Criminal: Rational Choice Perspectives on Offending*. New York: Springer–Verlag.

FELKER, C. J. (1989) 'A Proposal for Considering Intoxication at Sentencing Hearings: Part I'. *Federal Probation*, Vol. 53, No. 4, pp. 3–11.

FELKER, C. J. (1990) 'A Proposal for Considering Intoxication at Sentencing Hearings: Part II'. *Federal Probation*, Vol. 54, No. 1, pp. 3–14.

FELSON, R. B., BACCAGLINI, W. and GMELCH, G. (1986) 'Bar-Room Brawls: Aggression and Violence in Irish and American Bars', pp. 153–66, in A. Campbell and J. J. Gibbs (eds), *Violent Transactions: The Limits of Personality*. Oxford: Basil Blackwell.

FELSON, R. B. and STEADMAN, H. J. (1983) 'Situational Factors in Disputes Leading to Criminal Violence'. *Criminology*, Vol. 21, No. 1, pp. 59–74.

FESTINGER, L. (1957) *A Theory of Cognitive Dissonance*. London: Tavistock.

FINGARETTE, H, (1988) *Heavy Drinking: The Myth of Alcoholism as a Disease*. Berkeley, California: University of California Press.

FINGARETTE, H. (1990a) 'Alcoholism: Can Honest Mistake About One's Capacity for Self Control be an Excuse?' *International Journal of Law and Psychiatry*, Vol. 13, Nos 1–2, pp. 77–93.

FINGARETTE, H. and HASSE, A. F. (1979) *Mental Disabilities and Criminal Responsibility*. Berkeley: University of California Press.

FISKE, S. T. and NEUBERG, S. L. (1989) 'Category-based and Individuating Processes as a Function of Information and Motivation: Evidence From Our Laboratory', pp. 83–103, in D. Bar-tal, C. F. Graumann, A. W. Kruglanski and W. Stroebe (eds), *Stereotyping and Prejudice*. New York: Springer–Verlag.

FITGERALD, M., MCLENNAN, G. and PAWSON, J. (eds) (1981) *Crime and Society: Readings in History and Theory*. London: Routledge and Kegan Paul.

FITZMAURICE, C. and PEASE, K. (1986) *The Psychology of Judicial Sentencing*. Manchester: Manchester University Press.

FORGAS, J. P. (1981) 'Affective and Emotional Influences on Episode Representations', pp. 165–80, in J. P. Forgas (ed.), *Social Cognition: Perspectives on Everyday Understanding*. London: Academic Press.

FORGAS, J. P. (1986) 'Cognitive Representations of Aggressive Situations', in A. Campbell and J. J. Gibbs (eds), *Violent Transactions: The Limits of Personality*. Oxford: Basil Blackwell.

FREIDSON, E. (1966) 'Disability as Social Deviance', pp. 71–99, in M. B. Sussman (ed.), *Sociology and Rehabilitation*. Cleveland: American Sociological Association.

FURNHAM, A. F. (1988) *Lay Theories: Everyday Understanding of Problems in the Social Sciences*. Oxford: Pergamon Press.

GALIZIO, M. and MAISTO, S. A. (1985) 'Toward a Biopsychosocial Theory of Substance Abuse', pp 425–29, in M. Galizio and S. A. Maisto (eds), *Determinants of Substance Abuse: Biological, Psychological, and Environmental Factors*. New York: Plenum Press.

GAROFALO, J. (1987) 'Reassessing the Lifestyle Model of Criminal Victimisation', pp. 23–42, in M. R. Gottfredson and T. Hirschi (eds), *Positive Criminology*. Newbury Park, California: Sage Publications.

GAYFORD, J. J. (1975) 'Wife Battering: A Preliminary Survey of 100 Cases'. *British Medical Journal*, Vol. 1, pp. 194–7.

GHODSIAN, M. and POWER, C. (1987) 'Alcohol Consumption Between the Ages of 16 and 23 in Britain: A Longitudinal Study'. *British Journal of Addiction*, Vol. 82, pp. 175–80.

GIBBS, J. J. (1986) 'Alcohol Consumption, Cognition and Context: Examining Tavern Violence', pp. 133–51, in A. Campbell and J. J. Gibbs (eds), *Violent Transactions: The Limits of Personality*. Oxford: Basil Blackwell.

GILLER, H. and MORRIS, A. (1981) *Care and Discretion: Social Workers' Decisions with Delinquents*. London: Burnett Books.

GILLIES, H. (1976) 'Homicide in the West of Scotland'. *British Journal of Psychiatry*, Vol. 128, pp. 105–27.

GOLDMAN, M. S., BROWN, S. A. and CHRISTIANSEN, B. A. (1987) 'Expectancy Theory: Thinking About Drinking', pp. 181–226, in H. T. Blane and K. E. Leonard (eds), *Psychological Theories of Drinking and Alcoholism*. New York: Guilford Press.

GOODMAN, R. A., MERCY, J. A., LOYA, F., ROSENBERG, M. L., SMITH, J. C., ALLEN, N. H., VARGAS, L. and KOLTS, R. (1986) 'Alcohol Use and Interpersonal Violence: Alcohol Detected in Homicide Victims'. *American Journal of Public Health*, Vol. 76, No. 2, pp. 144–9.

GOTTFREDSON, M. R. (1984) *Victims of Crime: The Dimensions of Risk*. London: HMSO.

GOTTFREDSON, M. R. and HIRSCHI, T. (eds) (1987) *Positive Criminology*. Newbury Park, California: Sage Publications.

GOTTFREDSON, M. R. and HIRSCHI, T. (1990) *A General Theory of Crime*. Stanford: Stanford University Press.

GREELEY, A. M., McCREADY, W. C. and THEISEN, G. (1980) *Ethnic Drinking Subcultures*. New York: Praeger.

GUSFIELD, J. R. (1963) *Symbolic Crusade: Status Politics and the American Temperance Movement*. Urbana: University of Illinois.

GUSFIELD, J. R. (1981) *The Culture of Public Problems: Drinking-Driving and the Symbolic Order*. Chicago: University Press.

GUSFIELD, J. R. (1987) 'Passage to Play: Rituals of Drinking Time in American Society', pp. 73–90, in M. Douglas (ed.), *Constructive Drinking:*

216   *Bibliography*

Perspectives on Drink from Anthropology. Cambridge: Cambridge University Press.

HAMILTON, C. J. and COLLINS, J. J. (1982) 'The Role of Alcohol in Wife Beating and Child Abuse: A Review of the Literature', pp. 253–87, in J. J. Collins (ed.), *Drinking and Crime: Perspectives on the Relationships Between Alcohol Consumption and Criminal Behaviour*. London: Tavistock.

HARFORD, T. C. (1979) 'Ecological Factors in Drinking', pp. 147–82, in H. T. Blane and M. E. Chafetz (eds), *Youth, Alcohol, and Social Policy*. New York: Plenum Press.

HARFORD, T. C. (1983) 'A Contextual Analysis of Drinking Events'. *The International Journal of the Addictions*, Vol. 18, No. 6, pp. 825–34.

HARFORD, T. C., WECHSLER, H. and ROTHMAN, M. (1983) 'The Structural Context of College Drinking'. *Journal of Studies on Alcohol*, Vol. 44, No. 4, pp. 722–32.

HARTOCOLLIS, P. (1962) 'Drunkenness and Suggestion: An Experiment with Intravenous Alcohol'. *Quarterly Journal of Studies on Alcohol*, Vol. 23, pp. 376–89.

HARVEY, J. H., ICKES, W. and KIDD, R. F. (eds) (1978) *New Directions in Attribution Research*. Vol. 2. Hillsdale, New Jersey: Lawrence Erlbaum Associates.

HAUGE, R. and IRGENS-JENSEN, O. (1987) 'Age, Alcohol Consumption and the Experiencing of Negative Consequences of Drinking in Four Scandinavian Countries'. *British Journal of Addiction*, Vol. 82, pp. 1101–10.

HAWKINS, K. (1983a) 'Assessing Evil: Decision Behaviour and Parole Board Justice'. *British Journal of Criminology*, Vol. 23, No. 2, pp. 101–27.

HAWKINS, K. (1983b) 'Thinking About Legal Decision Making', pp. 7–24, in J. Shapland (ed.), *Decision Making in the Legal System: Issues in Criminological and Legal Psychology*, No. 5. Leicester: British Psychological Society.

HEALY, J. (1988) *The Grass Arena: An Autobiography*. London: Faber and Faber.

HEATH, D. B. (1981) 'Determining the Sociocultural Context of Alcohol Use'. *Journal of Studies on Alcohol*, Supplement No. 9: *Cultural Factors in Alcohol Research and the Treatment of Drinking Problems*, pp. 9–17.

HEATHER, N. and ROBERTSON, I. (1985) *Problem Drinking*. Harmondsworth: Penguin Books.

HEIDENSOHN, F. (1985) *Women and Crime*. Basingstoke: Macmillan Education.

HEWSTONE, M. (1983) 'Attribution Theory and Common-Sense Explanations: An Introductory Overview', pp. 1–26, in M. Hewstone (ed.), *Attribution Theory: Social and Functional Extensions*. Oxford: Basil Blackwell.

HINDELANG, M. (1973) 'Causes of Delinquency: A Partial Replication and Extension'. *Social Problems*, Vol. 20, pp. 471–87.

HIRSCHI, T. (1969) *Causes of Delinquency*. Berkeley: University of California Press.

HIRSCHI, T. and GOTTFREDSON, M. (1983) 'Age and the Explanation of Crime'. *American Journal of Sociology*, Vol. 89, No. 3, pp. 552–84.

HOBBS, D. (1988) *Doing the Business: Entrepreneurship, the Working Class and Detectives in the East End of London*. Oxford: Clarendon.

HOGARTH, J. (1971) *Sentencing as a Human Process*. Toronto: University of Toronto Press.

HOLSTEIN, J. A. (1985) 'Jurors' Interpretations and Jury Decision Making'. *Law and Human Behavior*, Vol. 9, No. 1, pp. 83–100.

HOME OFFICE (1980) *Young Offenders*. Cm. 8045. London: HMSO.

HOME OFFICE, DEPARTMENT OF HEALTH AND SOCIAL SECURITY (1975), *Report of the Committee on Mentally Abnormal Offenders*. Chairman: Lord Butler. London: HMSO.

HOPE, T. (1985) *Implementing Crime Prevention Measures*. London: HMSO.

HOUGH, M. and MAYHEW, P. (1983) *The British Crime Survey: First Report*. London: HMSO.

HOUGH, M. and MAYHEW, P. (1985) *Taking Account of Crime: Key Findings from the Second British Crime Survey*. London: HMSO.

HOWARD, R. C. and CLARK, C. R. (1985) 'When Courts and Experts Disagree: Discordance Between Insanity Recommendations and Adjudications'. *Law and Human Behavior*, Vol. 9, No. 4, pp. 385–95.

HUDSON, B. (1987) *Justice Through Punishment: A Critique of the 'Justice' Model of Corrections*. Basingstoke: Macmillan Education.

ICKES, W. and LAYDEN, M. A. (1978) 'Attributional Styles', pp. 119–52, in J. H. Harvey, W. Ickes and R. F. Kidd (eds), *New Directions in Attribution Research*. Vol. 2. Hillsdale, New Jersey: Lawrence Erlbaum Associates.

IRWIN, J. (1970) *The Felon*. Englewood Cliffs, N.J.: Prentice–Hall.

JACOB, T. and SEILHAMER, R. A. (1982) 'The Impact on Spouses and How They Cope', pp. 114–27, in J. Orford and J. Harwin (eds), *Alcohol and the Family*. London: Croom Helm.

JACOBS, J. B. (1989) *Drunk Driving: An American Dilemma*. Chicago: University of Chicago Press.

JASPARS, J. (1983) 'The Process of Casual Attribution in Common Sense', pp. 28–44, in M. Hewstone (ed.), *Attribution Theory: Social and Functional Extensions*. Oxford: Basil Blackwell.

JASPARS, J., FINCHAM, F. and HEWSTONE, M. (eds) (1983) *Attribution Theory and Research: Conceptual, Developmental and Social Dimensions*. London: Academic Press.

JELLINEK, E. M. (1960) *The Disease Concept of Alcoholism*. Newhaven, Connecticut: Hill House Press.

KANTOR, G. K. and STRAUS, M. A. (1987) 'The "Drunken Bum" Theory of Wife Beating'. *Social Problems*, Vol. 34, No. 3, pp. 213–30.

KAPLAN, J. (1983) *The Hardest Drug: Heroin and Public Policy*. Chicago: University of Chicago Press.

KELLEY, H. H. (1967) 'Attribution in Social Psychology'. *Nebraska Symposium on Motivation*, Vol. 15, pp. 192–238.

KESSEL, N. and WALTON, H. (1989) *Alcoholism*. 2nd edn. London: Penguin Books.

KITTRIE, N. N. (1971) *The Right to be Different: Deviance and Enforced Therapy*. Baltimore: John Hopkins.

KONECNI, V. J. and EBBESEN, E. B. (eds) (1982) *The Criminal Justice System: A Social Psychological Analysis*. San Francisco: W. H. Freeman and Company.

218   *Bibliography*

LADOUCEUR, P. and TEMPLE, M. (1985) 'Substance Use Among Rapists: A Comparison with Other Serious Felons'. *Crime and Delinquency*, Vol. 31, No. 2, pp. 269–94.

LANG, A. R. (1981) 'Drinking and Disinhibition: Contributions from Psychological Research', pp. 48–90, in R. Room and G. Collins (eds), *Alcohol and Disinhibition: Nature and Meaning of the Link*. Rockville, Maryland: US Department of Health and Human Services.

LANG, A., SEARLES, J., LAUERMAN, R. and ADESSO, V. (1980) 'Expectancy, Alcohol, and Sex Guilt as Determinants of Interest in and Reaction to Sexual Stimuli'. *Journal of Abnormal Psychology*, Vol. 89, pp. 644–53.

LANGER, E. J. (1978) 'Re-thinking the Role of Thought in Social Interaction', pp. 35–58 in J. H. Harvey, W. Ickes and R. F. Kidd (eds), *New Directions in Attribution Research*. Vol. 2. Hillsdale, New Jersey: Lawrence Erlbaum Associates.

LANGER, E. J. (1991) *Mindfulness: Choice and Control in Everyday Life*. London: Collins–Harvill.

LATANÉ, B. and DARLEY, J. M. (1970) *The Unresponsive Bystander: Why Doesn't He Help?* New York: Appleton–Century–Crofts.

LAWRENCE, J. A. (1984) 'Magisterial Decision-making: Cognitive Perspectives and Processes Used in Courtroom Information Processing', pp. 319–31, in D. J. Muller, D. E. Blackman and A. J. Chapman (eds), *Psychology and Law: Topics from an International Conference*. Chichester: John Wiley and Sons.

LAWRENCE, J. A. and HOMEL, R. (1986) 'Sentencing in Magistrates' Courts: The Magistrate as Professional Decision-maker', pp. 151–89, in I. Potas (ed.), *Sentencing in Australia: Issues, Policy and Reform*. Canberra: Australian Institute of Criminology.

LEJEUNE, R. (1977) 'The Management of a Mugging'. *Urban Life*, Vol. 6, No. 2, pp. 123–48.

LEJEUNE, R. and ALEX, N. (1973) 'On Being Mugged: The Event and its Aftermath'. *Urban Life and Culture*, Vol. 2, No. 3, pp. 259–87.

LETKEMANN, P. (1973) *Crime as Work*. Englewood Cliffs, New Jersey: Prentice–Hall.

LLOYD-BOSTOCK, S. M. A. (1988) *Law in Practice: Applications of Psychology to Legal Decision Making and Legal Skills*. Leicester: The British Psychological Society and Routledge Ltd.

LOEBER, R. and DISHION, T. (1983) 'Early Predictors of Male Delinquency: A Review'. *Psychological Bulletin*, Vol. 94, pp. 68–99.

LUCKENBILL, D. F. (1977) 'Criminal Homicide as a Situated Transaction'. *Social Problems*, Vol. 25, pp. 176–86.

LUCKENBILL, D. F. (1980) 'Patterns of Force in Robbery'. *Deviant Behavior*, Vol. 1, Nos 3–4, pp. 361–78.

LUDWIG, A. M. (1988) *Understanding the Alcoholic's Mind: The Nature of Craving and How to Control It*. Oxford: Oxford University Press.

MACANDREW, C. and EDGERTON, R. B. (1969) *Drunken Comportment: A Social Explanation*. London: Nelson.

MACKAY, R. D. (1990) 'The Taint of Intoxication'. *International Journal of Law and Psychiatry*, Vol. 13, Nos 1–2, pp. 37–48.

MAGUIRE, M. (1982) *Burglary in a Dwelling: The Offence, the Offender and the Victim*. London: Heinman.

MANDLER, J. M. (1984) *Stories, Scripts and Scenes: Aspects of Schema Theory*. Hillsdale, N. J.: Lawrence Erlbaum Associates.

MARLATT, G., DEMMING, B. and REID, J. (1973) 'Loss of Control Drinking in Alcoholics: An Experimental Analogue'. *Journal of Abnormal Psychology*, Vol. 81, pp. 233–41.

MARS, G. (1987) 'Longshore Drinking, Economic Security and Union Politics in Newfoundland', pp. 91–101, in M. Douglas (ed.), *Constructive Drinking: Perspectives on Drink From Anthropology*. Cambridge: Cambridge University Press.

MARSH, A., DOBBS, J. and WHITE, A. (1986) *Adolescent Drinking: A Survey Carried Out on Behalf of the Department of Health and Social Security and the Scottish Home and Health Department*. London: HMSO.

MARSH, P. and CAMPBELL, A. (1979) *Final Report to Whitbread Ltd*. Oxford: CVRC.

MARSH, P. and PATON, R. (1986) 'Gender, Social Class and Conceptual Schemas of Aggression', pp. 59–85, in A. Campbell and J. J. Gibbs (eds), *Violent Transactions: The Limits of Personality*. Oxford: Basil Blackwell.

MARSHALL, M. (1981) ' "Four Hundred Rabbits": An Anthropological View of Ethanol as a Disinhibitor', pp. 186–204, in R. Room and G. Collins (eds), *Alcohol and Disinhibition: Nature and Meaning of the Link*. Rockville, Maryland: US Department of Health and Human Services.

MAYFIELD, D. (1976) 'Alcoholism, Alcohol Intoxication and Assaultive Behavior'. *Diseases of the Nervous System*, Vol. 37, pp. 228–91.

MAYHEW, P., CLARKE, R. V. G., STURMAN, A. and HOUGH, J. M. (1976) *Crime as Opportunity*. London: HMSO.

McBARNET, D. J. (1983) *Conviction: Law, the State and the Construction of Justice*. London: Macmillan.

McCAGHY, C. H. (1968) 'Drinking and Deviance Disavowal: The Case of Child Molesters'. *Social Problems*, Vol. 16, No. 1, pp. 43–9.

McCARTY, D. (1985) 'Environmental Factors in Substance Abuse: The Microsetting', pp. 247–81, in M. Galizio and S. A. Maisto (eds), *Determinants of Substance Abuse: Biological, Psychological and Environmental Factors*. New York: Plenum Press.

McCLEARY, R. (1978) *Dangerous Men: The Sociology of Parole*. Beverley Hills: Sage.

McCORD, W. and McCORD, J. (1962) 'A Longitudinal Study of the Personality of Alcoholics', pp. 413–30, in D. J. Pittman and C. R. Snyder (eds), *Society, Culture and Drinking Patterns*. New York: John Wiley and Sons.

MENDELSON, J. H. and MELLO, N. K. (1979) 'One Unanswered Question about Alcoholism'. *British Journal of Addiction*, Vol. 74, No. 1, pp. 11–14.

MILESKI, M. (1969) *Courtroom Encounters: An Observation Study of a Lower Criminal Court*. Yale: Yale Law School.

MILLER, B. A. and WELTE, J. W. (1986) 'Comparisons of Incarcerated Offenders According to Use of Alcohol and/or Drugs Prior to Offense'. *Criminal Justice and Behavior*, Vol. 13, No. 4, pp. 336–92.

MINOR, W. W. (1980) 'The Neutralization of Criminal Offense'. *Criminology*, Vol. 18, No. 1, pp. 103–20.

MINOR, W. W. (1981) 'Techniques of Neutralization: A Reconceptual and Empirical Examination'. *Journal of Research in Crime and Delinquency*, Vol. 18, No. 2, pp. 295–318.

MITCHELL, C. (1988) 'The Intoxicated Offender – Refuting the Legal and Medical Myths'. *International Journal of Law and Psychiatry*, Vol. 11, No. 1, pp. 77–103.

MITCHELL, C. (1990) 'Intoxication, Criminality, and Responsibility'. *International Journal of Law and Psychiatry*, Vol. 13, Nos 1–2, pp. 1–7.

MORAN, R. (1971) 'Criminal Homicide: External Restraint and Subculture of Violence'. *Criminology*, Vol. 8, No. 4, pp. 357–74.

MORGAN, P. (1981) 'Alcohol, Disinhibition, and Domination: A Conceptual Analysis', pp. 405–19, in R. Room and G. Collins (eds), *Alcohol and Disinhibition: Nature and Meaning of the Link*. Rockville, Maryland: US Department of Health and Human Services.

MORRIS, A. (1987) *Women, Crime and Criminal Justice*. Oxford: Basil Blackwell.

MOSHER, J. F. (1981) 'Alcohol: Both Blame and Excuse for Criminal Behavior', pp. 437–59, in R. Room and G. Collins (eds), *Alcohol and Disinhibition: Nature and Meaning of the Link*. Rockville, Maryland: US Department of Health and Human Services.

MULLER, D. J., BLACKMAN, D. E. and CHAPMAN, A. J. (eds) (1984) *Psychology and Law: Topics From an International Conference*. Chichester: John Wiley and Sons.

MUNGHAM, G. (1976) 'Youth in Pursuit of Itself', pp. 82–104, in G. Mungham and G. Pearson (eds), *Working Class Youth Culture*. London: Routledge and Kegan Paul.

MUNRO, A. K. (1972) *Autobiography of a Thief*. London: Michael Joseph.

MURPHY, D. J. I. (1986) *Customers and Thieves: An Ethnography of Shoplifting*. Aldershot: Gower.

NAPLEY, D. (1983) *The Technique of Persuasion*. 3rd edn. London: Sweet and Maxwell.

NISBETT, R.E and WILSON, T. D. (1977) 'Telling More Than We Can Know: Verbal Reports on Mental Processes'. *Psychological Review*, Vol. 84, No. 3, pp. 231–59.

NUSBAUMER, M. R. (1983) 'Responses to Labeling Attempts: Deviant Drinkers' Pathways of Label Manipulation'. *Deviant Behavior*, Vol. 4, Nos 3–4, pp. 225–39.

NUSBAUMER, M. R., MAUSS, A. L. and PEARSON, D. C. (1982) 'Draughts and Drunks: The Contributions of Taverns and Bars to Excessive Drinking in America'. *Deviant Behavior*, Vol. 3, No. 4, pp. 329–58.

ORFORD, J. (1980) 'Understanding Treatment: Controlled Trials and Other Strategies', pp. 143–61, in G. Edwards and M. Grant (eds), *Alcoholism Treatment in Transition*. London: Croom Helm.

PALEY, J. and LEEVES, R. (1982) 'Some Questions About the Reverse Tarrif'. *British Journal of Social Work*, Vol. 12, No. 4, pp. 363–80.

PALMERINO, M., LANGER, E. and McGILLIS, D. (1984) 'Attitudes and Attitude Change: Mindlessness – Mindfulness Perspective', pp. 179–95, in J. R. Eiser (ed), *Attitudinal Judgement*. New York: Springer–Verlag.

PARKER, H. (1974) *View From the Boys: A Sociology of Down-town Adolescents*. Newton Abbot: David and Charles.

PARKER, H, CASBURN, M. and TURNBULL, D. (1981) *Receiving Juvenile Justice: Adolescents and State Care and Control*. Oxford: Basil Blackwell.

PARKER, H., SUMNER, M. and JARVIS, G. (1989) *Unmasking the Magistrates: The 'Custody or Not' Decision in Sentencing Young Offenders*. Milton Keynes: Open University Press.

PATRICK, J. (1973) *A Glasgow Gang Observed*. London: Eyre Methuen.

PEELE, S. (1990) 'Does Addiction Excuse Thieves and Killers from Criminal Responsibility?' *International Journal of Law and Psychiatry*, Vol. 13, Nos 1–2, pp. 95–101.

PENNINGTON, D. C. and LLOYD-BOSTOCK, S. (1987) 'Introduction: Issues and Problems in the Psychology of Sentencing', pp. 1–9, in D. C. Pennington and S. Lloyd-Bostock (eds), *The Psychology of Sentencing: Approaches to Consistency and Disparity*. Oxford: Centre for Socio-legal Studies.

PERNANEN, K. (1976) 'Alcohol and Crimes of Violence', pp. 351–444, in B. Kissin and H. Begleiter (eds), *The Biology of Alcoholism*. Vol. 4: *Social Aspects of Alcoholism*. New York: Plenum.

PERNANEN, K. (1982) 'Theoretical Aspects of the Relationship Between Alcohol Use and Crime', pp. 1–69, in J. J. Collins (ed), *Drinking and Crime: Perspectives on the Relationships Between Alcohol Consumption and Criminal Behaviour*. London: Tavistock.

PERVIN, L. (1986) 'Persons, Situations, Interactions: Perspectives on a Recurrent Issue', pp. 15–26, in A. Campbell and J. J. Gibbs (eds), *Violent Transactions: The Limits of Personality*. Oxford: Basil Blackwell.

PETERSON, W. J. and MAXWELL, M. A. (1958) 'The Skid Road "Wino"'. *Social Problems*, Vol. 5, No. 4, pp. 308–16.

PFUHL, E. J. (1980) *The Deviance Process*. New York: D. Van Nostrand.

PHILLIMORE, P. (1979) 'Dossers and Jake Drinkers: The View from One End of Skid Row', pp. 29–48, in T. Cook (ed), *Vagrancy: Some New Perspectives*. London: Academic Press.

PITTMAN, D. J. and GORDON, C. W. (1958) 'Criminal Careers of the Chronic Drunkenness Offender', pp. 535–46, in D. J. Pittman and C. R. Snyder (eds), *Society, Culture and Drinking Patterns*. New York: John Wiley and Sons.

PITTMAN, D. J. and HANDY, W. (1964) 'Patterns in Aggravated Assault'. *Journal of Criminal Law, Criminology and Police Science*, Vol. 55, No. 4, pp. 462–70.

PITTMAN, D. J. and SNYDER, C. R. (eds) (1962) *Society, Culture and Drinking Patterns*. New York: John Wiley and Sons.

PLANT, M. A. (1976) 'Young Drug and Alcohol Casualties Compared: Review of 100 Patients at a Scottish Psychiatric Hospital'. *British Journal of Addiction*, Vol. 71, No. 1, pp. 31–43.

PLANT, M. A. (1981) 'Risk Factors in Employment', pp. 18–33, in B. D. Hore and M. A. Plant (eds), *Alcohol Problems in Employment*. London: Croom Helm.

222 *Bibliography*

POLICH, J. M. (1979) 'Alcohol Problems Among Civilian Youth and Military Personnel', pp. 59–86, in H. T. Blane and M. E. Chafetz (eds), *Youth, Alcohol, and Social Policy*. New York: Plenum Press.

POLICH, J. M. (1980) 'Patterns of Remission in Alcoholism', pp. 95–112, in G. Edwards and M. Grant (eds), *Alcoholism Treatment in Transition*. London: Croom Helm.

POTAS, I. (ed.) (1986) *Sentencing in Australia: Issues, Policy and Reform*. Canberra: Australian Institute of Criminology.

RADA, R. T. (1975) 'Alcoholism and Forcible Rape'. *American Journal of Psychiatry*, Vol. 132, No. 4, pp. 444–6.

RIX, K. J. B. (1981) 'Alcohol Problems in the Fishing Industry in North-East Scotland', pp. 77–104, in B. D. Hore and M. A. Plant (eds), *Alcohol Problems in Employment*. London: Croom Helm.

ROEBUCK, J. and JOHNSON, R. (1962) 'The Jack-of-all-Trades Offender: A Comparative Study'. *Crime and Delinquency*, Vol. 8, pp. 172–81.

ROIZEN, R. (1981) 'Loosening Up: General-Population Views of the Effects of Alcohol', pp. 236–55, in R. Room and G. Collins (eds), *Alcohol and Disinhibition: Nature and Meaning of the Link*. Rockville, Maryland: US Department of Health and Human Services.

ROLOFF, M. E. and BERGER, C. R. (eds) (1982) *Social Cognition and Communication*. Beverley Hills: Sage.

ROMAN, P. M. (1982) 'Situational Factors in the Relationship Between Alcohol and Crime', pp. 143–51, in J. J. Collins (ed), *Drinking and Crime: Perspectives on the Relationships Between Alcohol Consumption and Criminal Behaviour*. London: Tavistock.

ROMAN, P. M. and TRICE, H. M. (1968) 'The Sick Role, Labelling Theory, and the Deviant Drinker'. *The International Journal of Social Psychiatry*, Vol. 14, No. 4, pp. 245–51.

ROOM, R. and COLLINS, G. (eds) (1981) *Alcohol and Disinhibition: Nature and Meaning of the Link*. Rockville, Maryland: US Department of Health and Human Services.

ROWE, A. R. and TITTLE, C. R. (1977) 'Life Cycle Changes and Criminal Propensity'. *Sociological Quarterly*, Vol. 18, pp. 223–36.

ROYAL COLLEGE OF PHYSICIANS (1987) *A Great and Growing Evil: The Medical Consequences of Alcohol Abuse*. London: Tavistock.

RUBINGTON, E. (1958) 'The Chronic Drunkenness Offender', pp. 269–76, in M. B. Clinard and R. Quinney (eds) (1967) *Criminal Behavior Systems: A Typology*. New York: Holt, Rinehart and Winston.

RUMGAY, J. (1990) 'Taking Rehabilitation Out of After-care? The Post-release Supervision of Young Adult Offenders'. *British Journal of Criminology*, Vol. 30, No. 1, pp. 36–50.

RUMGAY, J. (1995) 'Custodial Decision Making in a Magistrates' Court: Court Culture and Immediate Situational Factors'. *British Journal of Criminology*, Vol. 35, No. 2, pp. 201–17.

SADAVA, S. W. (1987) 'Interactional Theory', pp. 90–130, in H. T. Blane and K. E. Leonard (eds), *Psychological Theories of Drinking and Alcoholism*. New York: Guilford Press.

SALES, B. D. (ed) (1977) *Perspectives in Law and Psychology*. Vol. 1: *The Criminal Justice System*. New York: Plenum Press.

SCHAFER, S. (1968) *The Victim and His Criminal: A Study in Functional Responsibility*. New York: Random House.

SCHEFF, T. J. (1966) 'Typification in the Diagnostic Practices of Rehabilitation Agencies', pp. 139–47, in M. B. Sussman (ed), *Sociology and Rehabilitation*. Cleveland: American Sociological Assocation.

SCOTT, M. B. and LYMAN, S. M. (1968) 'Accounts'. *American Sociological Review*, Vol. 33, No. 1, pp. 46–62.

SCOTT, R. A. (1970) 'The Construction of Conceptions of Stigma by Professional Experts', pp. 255–90, in J. D. Douglas (ed), *Deviance and Respectability: The Social Construction of Moral Meanings*. New York: Basic Books.

SCULLY, D. and MAROLLA, J. (1984) 'Convicted Rapists' Vocabulary of Motive: Excuses and Justifications'. *Social Problems*, Vol. 31, No. 5, pp. 530–44.

SCULLY, D. and MAROLLA, J. (1985) ' "Riding the Bull at Gilley's": Convicted Rapists Describe the Rewards of Rape'. *Social Problems*, Vol. 32, No. 3, pp. 251–63.

SEMIN, G. R. and MANSTEAD, A. S. R. (1983) *The Accountability of Conduct: A Social Psychological Analysis*. London: Academic Press.

SHAMBLIN, D. H. (1990) 'The Vocational Rehabilitation of Alcoholics: A Research Note on the Bureaucratization of Deviance'. *Deviant Behavior*, Vol. 11, No. 1, pp. 45–59.

SHAPLAND, J. (1979) 'The Construction of a Mitigation', pp. 152–64, in D. P. Farrington, K. Hawkins and S. M. Lloyd-Bostock (eds), *Psychology, Law and Legal Processes*. London: Macmillan.

SHAPLAND, J. (1981) *Between Conviction and Sentence: The Process of Mitigation*. London: Routledge and Kegan Paul.

SHAPLAND, J. (ed) (1983) *Decision Making in the Legal System: Issues in Criminological and Legal Psychology*. No. 5. Leicester: British Psychological Society.

SHAPLAND, J. (1987) 'Who Controls Sentencing? Influences on the Sentencer', pp. 77–87, in D. C. Pennington and S. Lloyd-Bostock (eds), *The Psychology of Sentencing: Approaches to Consistency and Disparity*. Oxford: Centre for Socio-legal Studies.

SHAPLAND, J., WILLMORE, J. and DUFF, P. (1985) *Victims in the Criminal Justice System*. Aldershot: Gower.

SHARP, D. and LOWE, G. (1989a) 'Asking Young People Why They Drink'. Paper Delivered to British Psychological Society, Scottish Branch Annual Conference, 1–3 September.

SHARP, D. and LOWE, G. (1989b) 'Teenage Alcohol Expectancies: How They Change with Age, Experience and Imagined Amount Drunk'. Paper Delivered to British Psychological Society, London Conference, 19–20 Deccember.

SHAVER, K. G. (1985) *The Attribution of Blame: Causality, Responsibility, and Blameworthiness*. New York: Springer–Verlag.

SHER, K. J. (1987) 'Stress Response Dampening', pp. 227–71, in H. T. Blane and K. E. Leonard (eds), *Psychological Theories of Drinking and Alcoholism*. New York: Guilford Press.

SHINER, R. A. (1990) 'Intoxication and Responsibility'. *International Journal of Law and Psychiatry*, Vol. 13, Nos 1–2, pp. 9–35.

SHOVER, N. (1983) 'The Later Stages of Ordinary Property Offender Careers'. *Social Problems*, Vol. 31, No. 2, pp. 208–18.

SHOVER, N. (1985) *Aging Criminals*. Beverley Hills: Sage Publications.

SILLARS, A. L. (1982) 'Attribution and Communication: Are People "Naive Scientists" or Just Naive?' pp. 73–106, in M. E. Roloff and C. R. Berger (eds), *Social Cognition and Communication*. Beverley Hills: Sage.

SMITH, D. I. and BURVILL, P. W. (1987) 'Effect on Juvenile Crime of Lowering the Drinking Age in Three Australian States'. *British Journal of Addiction*, Vol. 82, pp. 181–8.

SMITH, J. C. and HOGAN, B. (1982) *Criminal Law*. London: Butterworths.

SNYDER, M. L., STEPHAN, W. G. and ROSENFIELD, D. D. (1978) 'Attributional Egotism', pp. 91–117, in J. H. Harvey, W. Ickes and R. F. Kidd (eds), *New Directions in Attribution Research*. Vol. 2. Hillsdale, New Jersey: Lawrence Erlbaum Associates.

SOFTLEY, P. (1980) 'Sentencing Practice in Magistrates' Courts'. *The Criminal Law Review*, pp. 161–7.

SOKOLOW, L., WELTE, J., HYNES, G. and LYONS, J. (1981) 'Multiple Substance Use by Alcoholics'. *British Journal of Addiction*, Vol. 76, No. 2, pp. 147–58.

SOMMER, R., BURSTEIN, E. and HOLMAN, S. (1988) 'Tolerance of Deviance as Affected by Label, Act, and Actor'. *Deviant Behavior*, Vol. 9, No. 2, pp. 193–207.

STALANS, L. J. and DIAMOND, S. S. (1990) 'Formation and Change in Lay Evaluations of Criminal Sentencing: Misperception and Discontent'. *Law and Human Behavior*, Vol. 14, No. 3, pp. 199–214.

STEFFENSMEIER, D. J. and TERRY, R. M. (1973) 'Deviance and Respectability: An Observational Study of Reactions to Shoplifting'. *Social Forces*, Vol. 51, pp. 417–26.

STONE, G. P. (1962) 'Drinking Styles and Status Arrangements', pp. 121–40, in D. J. Pittman and C. R. Snyder (eds), *Society, Culture and Drinking Patterns*. New York: John Wiley and Sons.

SUDNOW, D. (1965) 'Normal Crimes: Sociological Features of the Penal Code in a Public Defender Office'. *Social Problems*, Vol. 12, No. 3, pp. 255–76.

SUSSMAN, M. B. (ed.) (1966) *Sociology and Rehabilitation*. Cleveland: American Sociological Association.

SUTTON, S. (1978) 'Social-psychological Approaches to Understanding Addictive Behaviours: Attitude – Behaviour and Decision-making Models'. *British Journal of Addiction*, Vol. 82, No. 4, pp. 355–70.

SYKES, G. M. and MATZA, D. (1957) 'Techniques of Neutralization: A Theory of Delinquency'. *American Sociological Review*, Vol. 22, No. 6, pp. 664–70.

TAJFEL, H. and FORGAS, J. P. (1981) 'Social Categorization: Cognitions, Values and Groups', pp. 113–40, in J. P. Forgas (ed.), *Social Cognition: Perspectives on Everyday Understanding*. London: Academic Press.

TAPP, J. L. and LEVINE, F. J. (eds) (1977) *Law, Justice and the Individual in Society: Psychological and Legal Issues*. New York: Holt, Rinehart and Winston.

TARLING, R. (1979) *Sentencing Practice in Magistrates' Courts*. London: HMSO.

TAYLOR, L. (1972) 'The Significance and Interpretation of Replies to Motivational Questions: The Case of Sex Offenders'. *Sociology*, Vol. 6, No. 1, pp. 23–40.

THOMAS, D. A. (1979) *Principles of Sentencing: The Sentencing Policy of the Court of Appeal Criminal Division*. 2nd edn. London: Heinemann.

TOCH, H. (1986) 'True to You, Darling, in My Fashion: The Notion of Contingent Consistency', pp. 27–39, in A. Campbell and J. J. Gibbs (eds), *Violent Transactions: The Limits of Personality*. Oxford: Basil Blackwell.

TONRY, M. and MORRIS, N. (eds) (1985) *Crime and Justice: An Annual Review of Research*. Vol. 6. Chicago: University of Chicago Press.

TURNER, R. H. (1972) 'Deviance Avowal as Neutralization of Commitment'. *Social Problems*, Vol. 19, No. 3, pp. 308–21.

TVERSKY, A. and KAHNEMAN, D. (1974) 'Judgement Under Uncertainty: Heuristics and Biases'. *Science*, Vol. 184, pp. 1124–31.

VAN DUYNE, P. (1987) 'Simple Decision Making', pp. 143–58, in D. C. Pennington and S. Lloyd-Bostock (eds), *The Psychology of Sentencing: Approaches to Consistency and Disparity*. Oxford: Centre for Socio-legal Studies.

VOLPICELLI, J. R. (1987) 'Uncontrollable Events and Alcohol Drinking'. *British Journal of Addiction*, Vol. 82, No. 4, pp. 381–92.

VON HIRSCH, A. (1976) *Doing Justice*. New York: Hill and Wang.

WADE, A. L. (1967) 'Social Processes in the Act of Juvenile Vandalism', pp. 94–109, in M. B. Clinard and R. Quinney (eds), *Criminal Behavior Systems: A Typology*. New York: Holt, Rinehart and Winston.

WALLACE, S. E. (1965) *Skid Row as a Way of Life*. Totawa, New Jersey: Bedminster Press.

WALSH, D. (1986) *Heavy Business: Commercial Burglary and Robbery*. London: Routledge and Kegan Paul.

WASHBROOK, R. A. H. (1977) 'Alcohol Versus Crime in Birmingham, England'. *International Journal of Offender Therapy and Comparative Criminology*, Vol. 21, No. 2, pp. 166–73.

WECHSLER, H. (1979) 'Patterns of Alcohol Consumption Among the Young: High School, College and General Population Studies', pp. 39–58, in H. T. Blane and M. E. Chaftez (eds), *Youth, Alcohol and Social Policy*. New York: Plenum Press.

WEST, D. J. and FARRINGTON, D. P. (1977) *The Delinquent Way of Life: Third Report of the Cambridge Study in Delinquent Development*. London: Heinemann Educational Books.

WIATROWSKI, M. D., GRISWOLD, D. B. and ROBERTS, M. K. (1981) 'Social Control Theory and Delinquency'. *American Sociological Review*, Vol. 46, No. 5, pp. 525–41.

WILLIAMS, G. (1983) *Textbook of Criminal Law*. 2nd edn. London: Stevens and Sons.

WILSNACK, S. C. and WILSNACK, R. W. (1979) 'Sex Roles and Adolescent Drinking', pp. 183–224, in H. T. Blane and M. E. Chafetz (eds), *Youth, Alcohol and Social Policy*. New York: Plenum Press.

WILSON, C. (1982) 'The Impact on Children', pp. 151–66, in J. Orford and J. Harwin (eds), *Alcohol and the Family*. London: Croom Helm.

WILSON, G. T. (1987) 'Cognitive Processes in Addiction'. *British Journal of Addiction*, Vol. 82, No. 4, pp. 343–53.

WILSON, J. Q. and LOURY, G. C. (eds) (1987) *From Children to Citizens*. Vol. 2: *Families, Schools and Delinquency Prevention*. New York: Springer–Verlag.

WISEMAN, J. P. (1970) *Stations of the Lost: The Treatment of Skid Row Alcoholics*. Englewood Cliffs, New Jersey: Prentice–Hall.

WOODS, S. C. and MANSFIELD, J. G. (1981) 'Ethanol and Disinhibition: Physiological and Behavioral Links', pp. 4–23, in R. Room and G. Collins (eds), *Alcohol and Disinhibition: Nature and Meaning of the Link*. Rockville, Maryland: US Department of Health and Human Services.

WRIGHT, R. T. and DECKER, S. H. (1994) *Burglars on the Job: Street Life and Residential Break-ins*. Boston: Northeastern University.

WRIGHT, R. T. and WEST, D. J. (1981) 'Rape – A Comparison of Group Offences and Lone Assaults'. *Medicine, Science and the Law*, Vol. 21, No. 1, pp. 25–30.

ZANNA, M. P. and COOPER, J. (1974) 'Dissonance and the Pill: An Attribution Approach to Studying the Arousal Properties of Dissonance'. *Journal of Personality and Social Psychology*, Vol. 29, pp. 703–9.

ZILLMAN, D. (1978) 'Attribution and Misattribution of Excitatory Reactions', pp. 335–68, in J. H. Harvey, W. Ickes and R. F. Kidd (eds), *New Directions in Attribution Research*. Vol. 2. Hillsdale, N.J.: Lawrence Erlbaum Associates.

ZIMRING, F. E. (1981) 'Kids, Groups and Crime: Some Implications of a Well-known Secret'. *Criminal Law*, Vol. 72, No. 3, pp. 867–85.

ZINBERG, N. E. (1984) *Drug, Set and Setting: The Basis for Controlled Intoxicant Use*. New Haven: Yale University Press.

ZUCKER, R. A. (1979) 'Developmental Aspects of Drinking Through the Young Adult Years,' pp. 91–146, in H. T. Blane and M. E. Chafetz (eds), *Youth, Alcohol and Social Policy*. New York: Plenum Press.

Author Index

Subject Index